8/97

AMERICAN CATHOLIC PACIFISM

Dorothy Day, circa 1940. Courtesy of the Adé Bethune Collection, College of
St. Catherine Library, St. Paul, MN 55105.

AMERICAN CATHOLIC PACIFISM

The Influence of Dorothy Day and the Catholic Worker Movement

Edited by

Anne Klejment
and Nancy L. Roberts

 PRAEGER

Westport, Connecticut
London

Library of Congress Cataloging-in-Publication Data

American Catholic pacifism : the influence of Dorothy Day and the
Catholic Worker movement / edited by Anne Klejment and Nancy L.
Roberts.
p.   cm.
Includes bibliographical references and index.
ISBN 0–275–94784–X (alk. paper)
1. Pacifism—Religious aspects—Catholic Church—History of
doctrines—20th century.   2. Catholic Church—United States—
History—20th century.   3. Day, Dorothy, 1897–1980.   4. Catholic
Worker Movement.   5. United States—Church history—20th century.
I. Klejment, Anne.   II. Roberts, Nancy L., 1954–
BX1407.P24A44   1996
261.8′73′08822—dc20   96–16264

British Library Cataloguing in Publication Data is available.

Library of Congress Catalog Card Number: 96–16264
ISBN: 0–275–94784–X

First published in 1996

Praeger Publishers, 88 Post Road West, Westport, CT 06881
An imprint of Greenwood Publishing Group, Inc.

Printed in the United States of America

The paper used in this book complies with the
Permanent Paper Standard issued by the National
Information Standards Organization (Z39.48–1984).

10 9 8 7 6 5 4 3 2 1

Royalties from the sale of this book will be donated to the Catholic Worker in New York City.

Copyright Acknowledgments

The editors and publisher gratefully acknowledge permission for use of the following material:

Selected letters from Dorothy Day to Thomas Merton, 1959 to 1968. Printed with permission.

"The Leaven," by James W. Douglass. From James W. Douglass, *The Nonviolent Coming of God.*
Maryknoll, NY: Orbis Books, 1991. Reprinted with permission.

Material from the Catholic Association for International Peace Collection. Reprinted with the
permission of the Marquette University Archives.

Every reasonable effort has been made to trace the owners of copyright materials in this book, but in
some instances this has proven impossible. The editors and publisher will be glad to receive information
leading to more complete acknowledgments in subsequent printings of the book and in the meantime
extend their apologies for any omissions.

Contents

Preface

In 1983 when the U.S. Catholic Bishops wrote their historic pastoral letter on war and peace, they singled out the pacifist witness of Dorothy Day, reinforcing what historians of pacifism already knew: that contemporary Catholic pacifism is rooted in the Catholic Worker movement.

Our aim is to provide a systematic and analytical study of the emergence and nature of pacifism in the largest single denomination in the United States, Roman Catholicism. This collection of primarily original essays by scholars and Catholic Worker activists underscores the pivotal role of Dorothy Day's Catholic Worker movement in challenging the Catholic Church, once linked to unquestioning American militarism, to assert its prophetic pacifist voice. *American Catholic Pacifism* also addresses the variety of religious and secular sources Day drew upon to develop modern Catholic pacifism.

Many of the articles use newly uncovered sources to update and critique existing studies. Previously unpublished letters of Dorothy Day to Thomas Merton are included, as is in-depth coverage of how the contemporary Plowshares movement emerged from the Catholic Worker. Among the activist contributors are Eileen Egan, who provides a participant account of the birth and early years of Pax, the Catholic Worker–inspired peace organization, and James Douglass, who shares personal reflections on how the Catholic Worker influenced the development of his pacifist commitment. Our intention in including chapters by both activists and scholars (and sometimes both) is to provide a balance of perspectives—much as the *Catholic Worker* has always aimed to reach both "workers and scholars."

American Catholic Pacifism explores three major themes:

— First, it removes the Catholic Worker movement, the mainspring of U.S. Catholic pacifism, from its denominational ghetto, placing the movement within the context of American peace activism, postwar religious thought and U.S. radical movements.
— Second, the book provides detailed analysis of the theological and spiritual roots of Catholic pacifism.
— Third, the book interprets Catholic pacifism during periods of crisis, including World War II and the Vietnam War.

We intend this work to complement the major histories of the peace movement in the United States (by Charles Chatfield, Charles DeBenedetti, and Lawrence Wittner), which devote only passing attention to our topic. *American Catholic Pacifism* is also intended to augment recent historical analyses of American Catholic peace thought (by William Au, Patricia McNeal, and George Weigel), which tend to focus on the development of nonpacifist theology and activism. Finally, we hope to enrich the several excellent studies of the Catholic Worker movement (by William D. Miller, Mel Piehl, Nancy L. Roberts, and Patrick Coy), none of which focuses primarily on key peace issues.

Acknowledgments

First, we would like to thank our contributors for their patience and willingness to undertake revisions. We believe readers will appreciate your scholarship.

Along the way, many people have eased our path to publication. When Joe and Mary Alice Zarrella put in an advance order for a copy of this book, they gave us an immeasurable boost of inspiration and confidence. For this and other acts of faith, we are deeply grateful. Nina Polcyn Moore and the late Thomas Eugene Moore likewise provided generous moral support over the years. Our thanks go to Andy Leet, indexer extraordinaire. Charles Chatfield of Wittenberg College graciously suggested improvements in the entire manuscript. We also thank our colleagues at the Universities of Minnesota and St. Thomas, especially Susan L. Alexander, Patricia C. Howe, and Scott K. Wright.

The University of St. Thomas provided unstinting material assistance at all stages of production. A grant-in-aid from Dean Noreen Carrocci paid for the indexing of the book. Secretaries from the Division of Social Sciences at UST prepared numerous drafts of the articles and the entire camera-ready manuscript. David M. Jones and Jan Amundson worked on the earlier stages. Most of the preparation was done with great care by Christine Igielski; we are especially grateful for her thoughtfulness and grace under pressure. The Computing Center at UST provided support for converting files and mopping up the mess from a computer virus; Lief Johnson, Marcy Vail, and Kim Kleinkauf performed magic.

Anne Klejment's research benefitted from a research assistance grant, a sabbatical year, a sabbatical assistance grant, and a National Endowment for the Humanities Travel to Collections Grant. An earlier version of the essay on Dorothy Day and World War I was presented at the 1993 spring meeting of the American Catholic Historical Association. Thanks go to Susan M. Weber for locating a union list of New Jersey newspapers. Frances Early of Mount Saint Vincent University, Halifax, Nova Scotia, shared her research on World War I pacifism. Judy Yaeger Jones of Herstory, Unlimited provided enthusiasm and probing questions. An earlier version of the Vietnam War essay was presented to the 1985 Organization of American Historians meeting by Anne Klejment. For their comments on one or both manuscripts, she wishes to thank Patrick G. Coy of Kent State University, David J. O'Brien of the College of the Holy Cross, Mary Alice Zarrella, and UST colleagues David W. Smith and Mary T. Swanson.

Finally, all Catholic Worker historians have been aided by Phil Runkel, archivist of the Dorothy Day–Catholic Worker Papers, who has speedily accommodated all requests and brought us up to date on CW activities.

AMERICAN
CATHOLIC
PACIFISM

The Catholic Worker in the United States Peace Tradition

Charles Chatfield

As most readers will understand, *pacifism* is used in this volume in the strict sense of altogether rejecting violence, particularly warfare.[1] Catholic pacifism has been a distinctive current within a larger stream of pacifism that, in turn, has flowed within the historic United States peace movement. In some respects, pacifism has been a current that connected the larger peace movement with other social reforms and also imbued it with a distinctive moral quality.

Dorothy Day (1897–1980) was the catalyst for the emergence, organization, and eventual recognition of Catholic pacifism in the United States. She interpreted conscientious objection to war as a personal commitment, and although she did not formalize it as a Catholic movement, she inspired and even occasioned its organization. She picked up pacifism along with other social ideas a full decade before she was baptized into the Catholic faith, following which her spiritual identity subsumed and enlightened all her social concerns. It is important to remember, therefore, that Catholic pacifism as it grew within the larger context of the Catholic Church and United States peace movement was but one dimension of the expansive spirituality of Dorothy Day and those whom she inspired.

Day brought to United States Catholicism a distinctive social conscience, rather than an ideology. It was largely *intuitive*: she identified with the victims of social misfortune, which she understood to be systemic—a matter of injustice rather than chance; and she was driven to redeem personhood from the abyss of impersonality, especially in the forms of poverty and war.

In some measure Dorothy Day sought redemption from her own self-conscious *Long Loneliness* (as she titled her 1952 autobiography). Aloneness characterized her youthful years, when she was part of socialist and antiwar movements in the Progressive Era; it was part of her experience with love, marriage, and motherhood; and it was carried even into the hospitality movement she created. She countered the feeling of aloneness with an all-encompassing Catholic faith and with a ministry to others who were outcast and alienated. Instructed and baptized after many years of meditation and reflection, she launched her lay ministry with the publication of the *Catholic Worker* paper and the formation of a Catholic Worker hospice in 1933. Her personal vision became a social movement. With the advent of World War II and the nuclear age, she became emblematic among Catholics of pacifism and the right of conscientious objection to war.

When Day embraced Catholicism she already had an active social conscience that was characterized by identification with the victims of social misfortune; understanding of social misfortune as systemic injustice; and concern to lift persons above impersonal forces such as ignorance, illness, racism, poverty, and war. She had sharpened those elements of social awareness as a fledgling journalist within the progressive left of World War I, and later introduced them into American Catholic pacifism as Anne Klejment effectively shows in "The Radical Origins of Catholic Pacifism," in this volume. During the war, Day found herself drawn into the vortex of socialist and antiwar activism that transformed pacifism in America. That development merits some explanation.

In one sense, pacifism is the expression of spirituality: a nonviolent *way of living*. The long heritage of this tradition drew directly upon the Christ of the scriptures. "The trumpet of Christ is his Gospel," wrote Clement of Alexandria in the second century. "He sounded his trumpet and we listened. Let us therefore learn to handle the arms of peace. Offering our breasts to justice, taking up the sword of faith and donning the helmet of salvation, let us take up as well the sword of the spirit, which is the word of God. These are our arms, and nowhere will they inflict wounds."[2] Two centuries later Gregory of Nyssa added, "Recognizing Christ as 'peace,' we shall exhibit the true title of Christian in ourselves through the peace in our life."[3] On that principle St. Francis of Assisi built a monastic order in the thirteenth century and the Mennonites created an alternative society in the sixteenth. About a hundred years later George Fox and the British Quakers proclaimed, "The spirit of Christ, which leads us into all Truth, will never move us to fight and war against any man with outward weapons, neither for the kingdom of Christ, nor for the kingdoms of this world."[4] On that ground United States Protestants like Noah Worcester organized peace societies early in the nineteenth century. Only the tradition's longevity is suggested by these few examples: its fullness came from the devotion of innumerable people and groups, even though it remained a distinctly minority tradition in the Christian West.

Before the nineteenth century, and with some exceptions, pacifists who opposed war altogether constituted *nonresistant* communities. In some respects the monastic order of St. Francis was such a community; but the more comprehensive models were the Protestant peace churches—the Mennonite,

Brethren, and Quaker bodies. They did not sanction violent resistance to force; nor did they challenge the right of secular society to use force. When in conflict with the larger society on this issue, they withdrew from it in order to maintain the principles of their communities.

This pattern broke down insofar as pacifists sought to influence public policy while also rejecting the use of violent force. William Lloyd Garrison and his friends attempted that with the abolition of slavery, but when the Civil War broke upon the nation, most of them succumbed to the militant crusade for justice.[5] Then and afterward, pacifists like Elihu Burritt and Alfred Lovejoy continued to reject social violence altogether while also promoting peaceful public policy, but for the most part the growing social activism of the century enhanced what may be called peace advocacy, or peace reform.

The tradition of peace advocacy began to acquire its modern character with the writings of persons like Erasmus, Sully, William Penn, and Immanuel Kant. It became a social movement in the nineteenth century as public associations were created to reform foreign policy. The result was organized, transnational effort to constrain war and to replace it with programs of international law, compulsory arbitration, and negotiated disarmament. By the time of Dorothy Day's youth, the goal of an international order had attracted members of the intellectual, professional, and business elite in the United States and abroad. It had also generated numerous societies (some of them were, like the Carnegie Endowment for International Peace, well funded and connected to the foreign policy establishment).

World War I moved a few peace advocates to support an international organization with collective sanctions, and it inclined many of them to be politically active. In the 1920s that translated into the promotion of the League of Nations, the world court, the outlawry of war, internationalization of the economy, and disarmament. In the critical years of 1916 and 1917, however, peace advocates' concern for international order often translated into support for World War I.

This volume opens with that period. Anne Klejment recounts the widespread opposition to U.S. involvement in the European phase of the war and the repression of wartime pacifism. United States intervention was challenged during the 1915-1917 period by several groups whose membership was comprised mainly of progressive reformers, social workers, socialists, and Protestant leaders imbued with the social gospel. A particularly vital role was taken by women who converted their suffrage associations into peace ones. These were all people accustomed to mobilizing public opinion for causes, and they brought their activism to bear on the issue of war. After the United States intervened, the antiwar remnants were indiscriminately lumped together with members of nonresistant communities and called "pacifists." Those who refused military service were known as conscientious objectors (COs).

What happened, then, is that a number of articulate, pragmatic, and activist progressives first promoted a European peace and then completely rejected U.S.

intervention. They refused to participate in war and organized to protect the civil rights of conscientious objectors. In their minds, war was associated with violence and injustice, and peace with justice and nonviolence. They identified with the victims of war on both sides—civilians, COs, and soldiers alike. They understood war as a destructive and counterproductive social process, a form of systemic injustice. They protected the civil rights of individuals while affirming the personhood of all in a shared community beyond national boundaries. And they created enduring organizations: The Fellowship of Reconciliation (FOR, 1915), the American Friends Service Committee (AFSC, 1917), and the United States Branch of the Women's International League for Peace and Freedom (WILPF, 1919; formerly Women's Peace Party, 1915).

Throughout the 1920s these activists effectively popularized their under-standing of war and the revisionist interpretation of World War I. They attracted considerable public influence, notably in mainline Protestant churches and the Young Men's Christian Association (YMCA). And they created strong political pressure groups, such as the National Council for Prevention of War (NCPW, 1922), through which they gave a positive and active connotation to pacifism. This was the generation of John Nevin Sayre and later A. J. Muste in the FOR, Mildred Scott Olmsted and Dorothy Detzer in the WILPF, Frederick Libby in the NCPW, the social evangelist Kirby Page, the socialist and journalist Devere Allen, the minister Harry Emerson Fosdick, and many others. In their hands pacifism in the classic sense of a total rejection of war was combined with peace advocacy in the sense of public, political pressure on foreign policy.

Dorothy Day did not follow the many progressive pacifists who became political peace activists, even though in most other respects she shared their motivating assumptions. She was still seeking a way of life. Although that search led her to cultivate the barren fields of economic and spiritual poverty instead of the shimmering hills of foreign policy in the 1920s, her pacifist understanding would carry her to the distant crags of war in the 1930s.

For several years after the war she was a wanderer—from New York to New Orleans and back, from one writing job to another, through love affairs, a brief marriage, and the birth of a daughter for whom she would be the single parent.   She wandered spiritually too, finding solace in meditation and inspiration in novels, the lives of the saints, and classic works on religious life. She found peace of soul most fully with the birth of her daughter, Tamar. The child's Catholic baptism took place in mid-1927, the mother's at the end of the year, after the father finally had left the household.

At that time Day was living in a Staten Island beach cottage, which she had purchased with a small windfall from a novel she had written several years before. Now, with a child and within the church, she sought some way to integrate her faith and her still troubled social conscience: could she find grace in service?

The answer did not come easily. She worked for social cause organizations such as the Anti-Imperialist League and the Fellowship of Reconciliation (of which she remained a lifelong member), and without giving up the beach house—it was ever a place for retreat and rejuvenation—she took short-term writing jobs in California and Mexico. The Great Depression generated fresh social activism, and Day joined hundreds of unemployed people in a Hunger March from New York to Washington. Afterward, she recalled, she went to her knees in "a prayer which came with tears and anguish, that some way would open up for [her] to use what talents [she] possessed for [her] fellow workers, for the poor."[6] Upon her return to New York, the way opened in the person of Peter Maurin.

A Frenchman who had been briefly a member of a Catholic teaching order, Maurin emigrated to Canada before World War I. He found enough manual labor to subsist there and in the United States in a Franciscan-like discipline of poverty. He also read widely and he taught—mainly the unemployed who gathered at Union Square, New York. In 1932 someone directed him to Dorothy Day, and Maurin found his most famous pupil.

"Pupil" may be too strong a word, for Day was a thoroughly independent thinker, if perhaps not an original one. It is likely that she let herself be guided by Maurin as she herself provided her fellow workers and the poor with voice and hands. The voice was that of the *Catholic Worker*, a radical newspaper that she put together and sold for a penny a copy. The hands were those of Catholic Worker houses that evolved from the hospitality of her New York flat. By 1936 her community occupied two buildings and extended its hands to thirty-three Catholic Worker houses elsewhere in the country. The houses provided lodging for some and meals for many (about 800 a day were fed at the New York house alone in 1937). No questions were asked, no forms filled out: open hands just welcomed the victims of social misfortune.

The New York house doubled as the office for the *Catholic Worker* paper, through which Day, Maurin, and others spoke to and for the poor. Instead of writing *about* them, the paper addressed them directly and personally, in a familial tone of respect and understanding. It was free from ideological cant but rich in religious faith, and it elevated the creation of community over abstract revolution. In these respects its goal was what a later generation would call "empowering the victims." The paper was very clear: the misfortune of poverty was systemic; it was injustice. Maurin's vision, which Day adapted from her own experience, was to respond to systemic injustice through small communities that might empower individuals.

The Catholic Worker houses were linked to one another and a broad base of supporters in the church by the *Catholic Worker* paper. In contrast to vocational orders of charity, this was a lay movement that imported a radical social conscience into the church while enveloping social concerns in religious faith. It was quite simply, as Dorothy Day wrote about pacifism, a realization of the Sermon on the Mount.

Other pacifists in the FOR and AFSC, overwhelmingly Protestant, might have described their own postwar journeys into social justice issues in similar terms. Some of them worked with schools for labor organizers such as Brookwood Labor College, some were active in the union movement or the Socialist party. A. J. Muste became the best known pacifist labor leader, but commitment to the workers' cause was pervasive among progressive pacifists. In fact, the question of whether the class struggle should be waged only with nonviolence became a serious voting issue in both the Socialist Party of America and the Fellowship of Reconciliation. In principle, nonviolence connected the pacifist way of life with an activist social strategy. That relationship was reflected in the FOR's attention to Mahatma Gandhi. It was integral to the Catholic Worker movement.

Day's explanation of pacifism in terms of the Sermon on the Mount indicated at least two things: she regarded pacifism as part of the larger social conscience on which the Catholic Worker movement was based; and her pacifism was a largely intuitive (which in a real sense is to say religious) response to war. She had opposed World War I as an unjust and imperialistic venture, but within the Catholic Worker movement she asserted the intrinsic immorality of war and the moral theology of pacifism. In that sense, as the authors in this book observe, she began a dialogue within the church about pacifism as a Catholic option, one which came to include civil disobedience. She also encouraged critical assessment of the just-war tradition. It was the combination of these two departures that was historically significant for the Catholic peace tradition.

The just-war tradition is the dominant ethical system regarding war in Western civilization. Actually the words *just war* are a bit misleading. It is not assumed that any war is in itself just. Rather, it is assumed that warfare may only be justified under certain conditions that became codified as nation states emerged. The merits of warfare are therefore relative to its cause, conduct, and consequences.

That view made it possible for socialists to reject World War I as a capitalist conflict and for many peace activists to challenge the war system even though they were not thoroughgoing pacifists. Among the mainline U.S. Christian churches in the 1920s, World War I was interpreted as having failed to meet just-war criteria. Pacifists themselves drove that point home, applying traditional criteria so as to preclude modern warfare. Thus Kirby Page, the most prolific pacifist writer and speaker of the period, insisted that in Christian terms "war is sin," while he also assessed foreign policy in terms of its presumed causes and consequences (characteristically just-war judgments).

On an organizational level too, pacifists were able to cooperate with peace advocates of just-war orientation until the mid-1930s. From then on the peace movement, like the country as a whole, became increasingly polarized by the alternatives of remaining politically neutral or risking collective warfare against Germany and Italy. Symbolic of the agony of the times, theologian Reinhold

Niebuhr broke from the pacifists with whom he had worked closely, arguing that a realistic assessment of power (which was his version of just-war criteria) could not preclude the use of military force.

Patricia McNeal, in "Catholic Peace Organizations and World War II," makes it clear that the dominant just-war tradition was assumed in the Catholic Association for International Peace (CAIP, 1927). That organization was designed to be the Catholic counterpart of other educational and pressure groups dealing with foreign policy in the interwar period. CAIP was part of the church establishment, and it interpreted just-war criteria to support Franco during the Spanish Civil War, an anti-Nazi alliance later, and eventually the United States war effort. Day dissented throughout that period, and "by World War II," as McNeal observes, "the Catholic Worker alone was proclaiming pacifism within the Catholic community."[7]

How did the Catholic Worker and Dorothy Day affect the dominant just-war tradition in the Catholic Church? First, Day used just-war criteria to challenge the conduct of World War II, notably the obliteration bombing of Germany and the atomic destruction of Hiroshima and Nagasaki. Protestant pacifists also objected to civilian bombing, appealing to the public on just-war grounds, and they protested the forced relocation of Japanese-Americans. Similarly, Catholic Worker pacifists argued that the technology of mass destruction inevitably violates the principles of proportionality and civilian sanctuary, rendering all modern war unjust. This position became the basis for so-called nuclear pacifism during the cold war.

The main wartime focus for the Catholic Worker, though, was the issue of conscription, and that too was challenged from within Catholic tradition. Thus, in "Conscription and the Catholic Conscience in World War II," Patrick G. Coy recounts the position of clerics George Barry O'Toole and the Reverend John J. Hugo, who interpreted the "primacy of the individual conscience," in Coy's words, as a "bedrock principle in Catholic moral theology" and, indeed, in the just-war tradition.[8] The corollary of the conditional justification of any war, they argued, always had been the moral responsibility of each Christian to evaluate its relative merit. On that basis, *Worker* articles honed the classic criteria into an argument sharply critical of modern war, one that was applied to nuclear warfare during Vatican II, as Eileen Egan explains in her dramatic chapter "The Struggle of the Small Vehicle, Pax." Meanwhile, Day also offered pacifism as a clear alternative to the just-war criteria on war, and as Egan shows, in Vatican II that approach contributed to the recognized legitimacy of individual pacifism.

Day introduced pacifism to the pages of the *Catholic Worker* in 1935. The context was the Spanish Civil War. Rejecting overwhelming Catholic support for Franco (and eventually suffering a two-thirds loss in subscriptions), she insisted on neutrality. Almost certainly, she empathized with the socialist republic; but she couched her position in spiritual terms—the pacifist ethic of the Sermon on the Mount. Increasingly through the succeeding neutrality debate and into World War II her approach shifted from an earlier class base to a spiritual one. It was to say that war is sin. It was to say that peace is an ethic of intrinsic, absolute, spiritual value.

Her allusion to the Sermon on the Mount implied that pacifism had the force of that Great Commandment. Given her spiritual personalism, she likely intended to present the ethical necessity that each individual choose for peace or war, hoping to elicit a pacifist response. In this regard, she posed pacifism as an ethical alternative to just-war criteria. That position was fully developed in the *Catholic Worker* during the war years, notably in the reflections of herself and John Hugo. In particular, they introduced what Coy describes as "the spiritual principle that penance and suffering freely and willingly undertaken by the individual, and prayerfully 'offered up' for the good of others . . . could effect change beyond the life of the individual doing the penance."[9] The invitation extended to individuals to "accept responsibility for the scourge of war" (as Coy puts it) came from the same personalist ethic that invited the faithful to take on themselves the social injustice of poverty. The penitential quality of their pacifism, which is noted by Mel Piehl in "The Catholic Worker and Peace in the Early Cold War Era," distinguished it from the religious pacifism of the FOR and AFSC, which was more rooted in the Social Gospel notion of corporate responsibility. In any case, the pacifism of Day and Hugo was grounded in Catholic spirituality.

On the other hand, Day's religious rhetoric may have obscured the fact that the Catholic Worker was challenging war on both just-war and strictly pacifist grounds, thus blurring the distinction between presenting an ethical choice and proselytizing for pacifism. The perception that the Catholic Worker was exclusively pacifist, whatever its merit, pushed the organization beyond the political pale during the Spanish Civil War and divided its offshoot houses during the Second World War. Francis J. Sicius, in "Prophecy Faces Tradition: The Pacifist Debate during World War II," provides a close view of the confusion and discord sown among wartime Catholic Workers in Chicago. As he shows, the very apprehension that Day intended to restrict the movement to religious pacifists hastened the departure of peace advocates who made an exception of that war on traditional just-war grounds. Consequently, the movement became the essentially pacifist organization to which Day's critics had objected, and the pacifist conscience acquired a formal locus within the church.

The profoundly spiritual and personalist quality of Catholic Worker pacifism is tenderly evoked in William Shannon's compilation of the correspondence between Dorothy Day and Thomas Merton from 1959 to 1968. James W. Douglass, in "The Leaven," recalls the combined power of intellectual rigor and (Day's) kingdom of God vision that motivated his own effort to recast the classic war tradition for the nuclear age. Applying just-war criteria critically to the nuclear age and interpreting pacifism as an ethical alternative to war: perhaps it was the combination of those two approaches—one rationalist and instrumental, the other pietist and intuitive—that in some significant measure transformed the Catholic peace tradition. In a general sense, that combination also transformed the U.S. peace movement in the twentieth century.

Civil disobedience makes moral witness an instrument of direct action. That is not to say only that moral witness has a political impact; it is, rather, that the form of moral witness is chosen in light of a particular objective. Nonviolent direct action is a social strategy. As noted above, progressive pacifists took that position between the world wars. Their fascination with Gandhi turned into a close study of his thought and social strategy. During World War II, pacifists connected with the FOR and A. J. Muste founded the Congress of Racial Equality (CORE), which applied nonviolent direct action against segregation. At the same time, some imprisoned COs experimented with it for other social changes. In the mid-fifties, nonviolent action, including civil disobedience, gained national attention when Martin Luther King, Jr., brought national attention to the nonviolent campaign in Montgomery, Alabama, and pacifists employed it against nuclear weaponry.

Each of the major pacifist bodies resisted the cold war, but all of them were affected by it, losing much of their access to the public. From about 1955 to 1963, however, an ever more effective national coalition challenged nuclear arms policy, specifically the atmospheric testing of weapons. The coalition employed strategies from public information and political lobbying to direct action and civil disobedience. It bridged the National Committee for a SANE Nuclear Policy and the Committee for Nonviolent Action. It linked constituencies of atomic scientists and students, churches and civic associations, liberal intellectuals and radical pacifists.

Radical in this case is used in the root sense of getting to the core of things (beyond nuclear testing to cold war, for example, or from atomic bombs to militarism). Direct nonviolent action against nuclear war policy included marches (from Quebec to Guantanamo, San Francisco to Moscow), vigils, and picketing. It also included civil disobedience, such as entering atomic testing zones in the United States or the Pacific, blockading nuclear submarines in port, and refusing to obey civil defense laws. And that recalls an image: the high-cheeked, weathered face of Dorothy Day, framed by white hair, looking up somewhat quizzically in a cell where she was under arrest for refusing to comply with civil defense regulations to take shelter. That was the import of radical pacifism: refusing to take shelter in conformity to law.

In the Workers' case, moreover, the core of things was spiritual, and that set them apart from pacifists who were radical in a more political sense, as Mel Piehl observes about Worker pacifism in the early cold war. Radical pacifism against nuclear arms was paralleled by nonviolent action in the civil rights movement as strategies of social change. Radical in the political sense of challenging authority, or radical in being grounded in the authority of spiritual principle: that distinction existed within the nonviolent action community of the late 1950s; but it became critically important a decade later in the opposition to the Vietnam War.

Anne Klejment and Nancy L. Roberts rightly observe in "The Catholic Worker and the Vietnam War" that in 1954 Dorothy Day extended her spiritual pacifism to condemn U.S. policy in Vietnam, and that in 1963 Catholic Workers Tom Cornell and Chris Kearns initiated the first public demonstration against the Diem regime's repression of Buddhist dissidents. There were at that time other voices of dissent, including those from established peace organizations. By 1965, many of the elements of the antiwar movement were in place, and they began to come together that spring as Lyndon Johnson launched the air war against North Vietnam and escalated the ground war in the south. For the following two years ever more constituencies of disillusioned citizens added vocal protest, while a growing number of Americans sullenly withdrew their support of the war. Amid the turmoil of 1968, opposition to the war was channeled through the presidential campaigns into mainstream politics, leaving the victor, Richard Nixon, struggling to salvage something—at any cost, it seemed—from an eastward tide of withdrawal.

The antiwar movement was a loose, shifting coalition of groups, many of which had little in common except opposition to the war. Its story is too complex to generalize in a few paragraphs, but in some real sense it encompassed two poles. One of them attracted the liberal orientation of groups and people who aligned on the specific issue of the war, challenged it within the political system, and sought to win the political center of the country from two administrations. The other pole attracted political radicals and radical pacifists for whom the war was the most serious of many problems of the political and social system itself, and who tried to align disaffected minorities in an antiwar coalition. Very few antiwar groups located themselves at one pole or the other, and major peace organizations like the FOR and AFSC encompassed both extremes. But there was a polar tension within the movement, and it was aggravated by the fact that the dominant image of antiwar protest was radical, confrontational, and countercultural, whereas the mass of it (especially after 1968) was politically and culturally in the mainstream.

The Catholic Worker movement was radical with regard to its societal goals, its ethical principles, and its historic civil disobedience. As the war continued, interminably it seemed, individual Workers fasted, engaged in picketing and sit-ins, withheld taxes, took CO status, and provided sanctuary to draft resisters. Roger LaPorte, a young man close to the New York house, even immolated himself, although that certainly was not encouraged by Day or the Catholic Worker movement. Meanwhile, the *Catholic Worker* itself included the war among its journalistic concerns. It was not so much the Catholic Worker movement, therefore, as the people it influenced that made distinctive contributions to the antiwar movement. There were at least three areas, and they are explained in this book by Klejment and Roberts, Douglass, and Egan.

Two of them predated the war, one being the work of Pax and its friends in Vatican II to secure the legitimacy of conscientious objection as an ethical option for Catholics. COs were not new in the Vietnam War; what was novel was the dramatic public rejection of conscription by eligible men and their ineligible supporters, together with a systematic network of draft resistance. A second contribution also came from the work at Vatican II: the application of just-war criteria selectively and critically (to condemn total nuclear war) was a precedent for selective objection to the Vietnam War. Both those contributions strengthened antiwar witness within the Catholic fold and aligned it with the orientation of Protestant and nonreligious war opposition. Indeed, Catholics had in some respects a stronger basis for selective conscientious objection to war and conscription because of the strength of the tradition they had adapted.

A third contribution was the escalation of civil disobedience to what some called "ultraresistance." The classic examples were the actions of priests Daniel and Philip Berrigan and others, in taking draft files and pouring blood on them in Baltimore, or burning them in Catonsville, Maryland. By the war's end those actions had been more or less replicated by some fifty others.

This innovation was difficult for Catholic Workers to deal with, the more so since the Berrigans, and especially Daniel, shared the Worker values, goals, and lifestyle. Some worried about making the burning of property into a protest symbol, given the turmoil of the era and the proclivity for violence of some elements on the edge of the antiwar movement: what the brothers saw as a symbol of napalm might appear to others as wanton destruction. Moreover, when they postponed serving their sentences and went underground, the priests broke the traditional boundary of nonviolent civil disobedience, with its distinction between illegitimate laws and the authority of law itself.

Finally, and probably of most concern to Dorothy Day, even the symbolic confrontation approach left demonstrators spiritually vulnerable to hate and a depersonalized sense of "enemy," or in the self-immolation of Roger LaPorte, emotion-driven sacrifice. Day's feelings are revealed in her correspondence with Thomas Merton, edited for this volume by William Shannon. Day did not quite criticize the Berrigans, but she did not trust their approach for the movement as a whole.

In fact, the Berrigans, and at least some of those who emulated them, were constrained by a spiritual sense of self-sacrifice and even repentance not unlike the feeling of some Catholic Workers in the 1950s whose resistance to civil defense was a redemptive form of penance for the sins of society. There were other feelings too, but the very discussion in the *Catholic Worker* and the larger Catholic community probably heightened concern for spiritual and political discipline in protests. In that respect, Catholics joined other radical pacifists to form the National Action Group in 1968.

Following the Vietnam War, the Berrigans built on their experience and applied it to the nuclear arms race, emerging in the 1980s as the Plowshares. Their actions were self-consciously grounded in the prophetic biblical tradition, penitential sacrifice, and spiritual discipline, as well as a close analysis of the potential consequences of symbolic acts. Those qualities were clearly characteristic of the ANZUS Plowshares action that is effectively narrated by Ciaron O'Reilly in "ANZUS Plowshares: A Nonviolent Campaign."

Within the historic U.S. peace movement there have been on the one hand an orientation to values such as harmony, human community, and justice, and on the other an emphasis on specific issues or programs, such as international law or organization, international exchange and friendship, and challenging specific wars. Few groups have reflected one emphasis to the exclusion of the other; but those that endured to the present were largely value-oriented: the Fellowship of Reconciliation, for example, the American Friends Service Committee, or the Women's International League for Peace and Freedom. Periodically, political issues have elicited coalitions with issue-oriented, political agendas: the campaign to keep America out of war in the 1930s, for example, the efforts to ban nuclear testing in the 1950s, the antiwar movement of the Vietnam War era, the nuclear freeze and campaign for solidarity with Central American people of the 1980s. Those associations gave outreach and latitude to the movement, just as the more value-based groups contributed depth and endurance.

Through the Catholic Worker movement, profoundly touched as it was by Dorothy Day, Catholics in the United States received peace ideals that were grounded in a prophetic view of peace as justice and in a spiritual sense of the individual as responsive to fellow human beings in need and to a redeeming God. In something like those terms, Dorothy Day and her friends established pacifism as a viable ethical option within the church. In some measure, Catholic spirituality constrained even the confrontational pacifism of ultraresistance and the Plowshares. That was the value orientation of Catholic pacifism. But there was a rigorous analytical and issue emphasis too. Through the Catholic Worker movement and the groups it spawned—Pax, and the Catholic Peace Fellowship and later Pax Christi USA—Catholic pacifists adapted just-war criteria to the critical assessment of nuclear warfare and the Vietnam War. Thus has the pacifism that Dorothy Day brought to the Catholic faith and nourished there enriched the larger U.S. peace tradition.

NOTES

1. The word *pacifism* was coined in Europe about the turn of the century as a positive identification for people who wanted to limit and ultimately eliminate war—those whom we might call peace advocates. During World War I the word was narrowed, especially in England and the United States, to connote those who rejected all wars altogether. There remains some ambiguity in usage.

2. From *Miscellanies and Cohortatio ad Gentes*, quoted in *The Idea of Peace in Antiquity*, by Gerardo Zampaglione, trans. Richard Dunn (Notre Dame, Ind., 1973), 251.

3. From Gregory of Nyssa, "On Perfection," in *Ascetical Works*, trans. Virginia Woods Callahan, vol. 58 of *The Fathers of the Church* (Washington, D.C., 1966), 102-3.

4. From "A Declaration from the harmless and innocent people of God called Quakers," in the *Journal of George Fox*, John L. Nickalls, ed. (Cambridge, England, 1952), 398-404.

5. See Valarie H. Ziegler, *The Advocates of Peace in Antebellum America* (Bloomington, Ind., 1992).

6. Quoted in Jim Forest, *Love Is the Measure: A Biography of Dorothy Day* (New York, rev. ed. 1994), 55.

7. McNeal, "Catholic Peace Organizations," 40.

8. Coy, "Conscription and Conscience," 47-48.

9. Ibid., 48.

2

The Radical Origins of Catholic Pacifism: Dorothy Day and the Lyrical Left During World War I

Anne Klejment

In the fall of 1916 as Europe plunged into the third year of the Great War, nineteen-year-old Dorothy Day was launching her career as a radical journalist in New York. Her work and social life centered on an eclectic radical circle later called the lyrical left.[1] Composed of Greenwich Village artists, writers, bohemians, and eccentrics, this fluid movement cultivated avant-garde arts, social rebellion, and left-leaning politics before and during World War I. Day, who was sociable, widely read, college educated, and a lifelong writer, enjoyed its free-spirited lifestyle.

Influenced by the experience of periodic familial poverty, voracious reading, and innate sensitivity toward the suffering of others, while still in her teens Day proclaimed herself a revolutionary socialist who favored the direct action of the masses over voting. The socialist creed of empowered workers overcoming capitalism captivated her, but she was slow to understand the convergence of socialism and pacifism.[2]

In the days before U.S. entry into World War I, one would have expected a socialist journalist to gravitate automatically to pacifism. The Socialist party taught that "capitalism . . . logically leads to war." And Dorothy Day worked for an official Socialist party newspaper, the *New York Call*, exposing the abuses of capitalism by writing vivid human interest features and stories of local protests, typically strikes and bread riots. A social realist and advocacy journalist, committed to living her beliefs and writing from experience, Day gathered facts while marching the picket line. But despite her obvious commitment to socialist revolution, she admitted to having paid "little attention" to the carnage overseas until days before Congress voted for war.[3]

Day's complacence about the impending military intervention of the nation ended by March 1917. As United States–German relations deteriorated and war fever swept through the country, her editor reassigned her to cover peace news. Geared to the interests of socialist stalwarts, intellectuals and workers alike, the *Call* mixed dull political reports with thoughtful opinion and lurid human interest tales, all in the interest of the party, and in the process, earned a reputation for stodginess.[4] As socialism crested in North America, the *Call* aimed to mold loyal partisans and shape public policy. How could it remain silent while young workers were slaughtering each other in the trenches? How could it ignore the conspiracy of the master class and the nation–state to profit from war? To promote socialism the *Call* decried militarism, nationalism, and imperialism for dividing the laboring class and lining the pockets of the rich.[5] Since the mainstream press usually promoted armed intervention, the *Call* presented an antidote to their views.

By January 1917, Dorothy Day had became one of the paper's agents in shaping antiwar opinion. Attending hours of meetings held by such groups as the Emergency Peace Federation (EPF) and the American Union Against Militarism (AUAM), she summarized the plans of local peacemakers in unsigned articles.[6] Eventually mastering antiwar thought through repeated exposure, Day began to see war's threat to human progress and the socialist revolution weeks before the government decided to go to war. The first stage of her pacifist conversion was underway.

Towards the end of March 1917, New York peace activists were desperately seeking a way to prevent U.S. military intervention in Europe. One campaign aimed to undercut the "militarists" by exposing the hidden costs of war. Peacemakers devised a controversial "conscription of wealth" gambit to remind all citizens, but especially the wealthy, that a sliding scale tax would require all to pay their fair share.[7] When the clever ploy failed to stop the interventionists, the peace groups resorted to the era's favorite trump: a call to democracy.

The peace coalition convened an immense anti-intervention rally in Washington hours before President Wilson's address to Congress on 2 April 1917. En route to their Armageddon, the peacemakers hoped to spark uprisings along the way, after propagandizing the masses. "Where two or three are gathered together," an Emergency Peace Federation directive declared, "let there be a peace meeting, and let that peace meeting be productive of delegates, letters or telegrams."[8] Thousands of peace proponents from throughout the country were expected in Washington. The swell of peace sentiment, they expected, would reach a crescendo at the rally in the District of Columbia, thus averting war at the last moment. "The President and Congress will decide that question [Shall the U.S. Go to War?] absolutely in accordance with the wishes of the people," the EPF claimed, confident that "the majority of the people [are] for peace."[9]

The New York groups that sent peace delegates to the nation's capital were familiar to Dorothy Day since she had covered their affairs for the *Call*. Of the four or five prominent local peace groups, she found the Collegiate Anti-

Militarism League (CAML) compatible and fraternized with several members of the Columbia University branch.

On 30 and 31 March two league members paid the Empire State Sightseeing & Trucking Company $370 to carry members of their peace pilgrimage from New York to Washington and back. The parties agreed to the rental of a forty-passenger open bus and an itinerary allowing stops at the direction of one of the organizers.[10] Besides the students, travelers included a chaperone, pacifist Professor Henry Wadsworth Longfellow Dana, and Dorothy Day, who was covering the peace tour and the Washington rally. Well-heeled New York peacemakers eschewed the novelty of a road trip for a more comfortable and convenient trip by Pullman coach.

Dorothy Day was delighted to have been assigned to the Washington peace rally. In addition to having the desirable companionship of the students, Day anticipated the adventure of her first interstate bus trip. Plus the ambitious reporter welcomed her initiation into covering national events, a boost to her career. Two hours late in departing from Union Square, the bus wended its dusty way through five states. Braving the elements, the light-hearted passengers were prepared to arouse the latent antiwar sentiments of folks along the way.[11]

Before being hounded from several New Jersey towns by police, the propagandists on wheels dispensed $10 worth of free peace literature and copies of a special antiwar edition of the *Call*. Despite their enthusiasm, the anticipated uprising of the antiwar masses did not ignite.

Dorothy Day's articles appear to be the only contemporary accounts of the New York-to-Washington leg of the peace tour.[12] Loyal to the *Call*'s party line, she optimistically asserted that workers opposed both the war and the "millionaire minority" that conspired "to force" the government into it. While Day's accounts honestly captured the student peacemakers' frivolity on the road, they overestimated the extent of active worker opposition to the war. Within a few years, and throughout her life, Day would disparage her newspaper journalism of this period, admitting to having invented facts to fit the wishes of her editors.[13]

When the peace tourists arrived in Philadelphia, they discovered that local reactionaries in the Department of Public Safety had without warning cancelled the evening's peace rally. Fuming New Yorkers from the Emergency Peace Federation, some of them future founders of the American Civil Liberties Union, wired a sizzling protest to President Wilson, but to no avail. With little time to lose, the peace procession sped to Baltimore for another major rally.[14]

Jammed into the Academy of Music, antiwar people, including Day and the Columbia students, heard David Starr Jordan, the distinguished academician and reformer, lecture on the pressure exerted by U.S. lenders to protect their loans to the Allies through armed intervention. Outside, an unruly crowd of prominent citizens, some fortified by alcohol, grew more and more intolerant of the "unpatriotic" talk of the pacifists, whom they considered "Jew radicals" from New York.[15] Barging past the police cordon, the mob marched into the theater and up the main aisle, until their leader literally waved the stars and stripes in Jordan's face, abruptly halting his address. The speedy arrival of a reinforcement of police, prepared to vindicate the earlier humiliation of their colleagues by the rowdy interventionists, added to the confusion. Cops began pummeling all within reach of their night sticks. Absorbed in gathering facts for her story, Dorothy Day was accidentally clubbed amidst the chaos. The blows were inflicted by a wounded police officer with impaired vision and they cracked two of Day's ribs.[16] Now Dorothy Day was a seasoned veteran of the peace cause, familiar with the indifference of the masses, the fanaticism of the superpatriots, and the inadequacy of government protection of dissenters. The inauspicious events of Philadelphia and Baltimore realistically depicted the polarized nation on the eve of war and forecast further domestic unrest.

A few days after the peace entourage returned home, the United States declared war and the antiwar movement diminished in size. Progressive peacemakers tended to abandon dissent during the national emergency. Some optimistically rationalized their change of heart by regarding war as a "plastic juncture," an opportunity to reengineer society along progressive lines.[17] A handful of radicals, however, continued to oppose the war in word and deed. All measures they considered hostile to individual rights and the common good, especially the draft, they opposed.[18]

Two key issues absorbed the energies of the protesters and resisters. Within six weeks conscription became law, a truly unprecedented development, since throughout its history the United States had relied on a volunteer army and resorted to the draft only in the most dire cases. Correctly noting that the draft law broke tradition, pacifists roundly condemned it as a coercive measure, destructive of personal liberty. An attorney for one of Day's anarchist acquaintances even tried to overturn the draft by attacking it as a violation of the thirteenth amendment, which prohibited involuntary servitude.[19] Both the conscription act and an espionage act passed in June muzzled freedom of expression for ordinary citizens and journalists alike. Openly voicing objections to mobilization was often enough to send an antiwar dissenter to prison.

Dorothy Day and her lyrical left friends protested against and refused to cooperate with war measures. The collective experience of wartime repression remained with Day throughout her life and was eventually absorbed into her religious pacifism. Watching some choose evasion, others confrontation, Day saw her closest friends arrested for violating various federal laws. No literate New Yorker could have avoided knowing about the trials of the pacifist lyrical left, which were extensively covered by the local dailies.

After returning from the peace tour and leaving the *Call*, Dorothy Day worked for the Collegiate Anti-Militarism League (CAML) at Columbia University, the group she consistently misnamed the Anti-Conscription League.[20] Her dedication to the cause of peace was probably only one of several reasons leading to the career change.[21]

Day managed the league office, working as receptionist, typist, and publicist.[22] At peace meetings she identified herself with the league. And a warm friendship developed between Day and three or four of her CAML colleagues. Charles Phillips, a league officer whom she had met during the peace tour, enjoyed Day's company at a saloon near campus where, over cigarettes, whiskey, and a free lunch, she entertained others with humorous stories.[23] For some time afterwards Day socialized with her new antiwar companions.[24]

In 1917 this national organization was one of the many peace groups that had sprouted up during World War I. A network with perhaps as many as eight thousand supporters on thirty-eight campuses, the league attracted a strong following in the greater New York area, with chapters at City College, New York University, Columbia, and Yale.[25]

Paying homage to progressivism, most leaguers were liberals hoping to improve society rather than radicals like Dorothy Day and Charles Phillips who hoped to create a new order. Members professed faith in the wholesome values of reform: an "enlightened and liberal education; . . . democracy, humanity, and world organization." They viewed militarism as "the father of Wars and the most damning social menace of the age" and condemned its tendency to undercut social and economic progress by competing for scarce public resources. A warless world was both a means and an end. They expected peace to safeguard national security and human welfare. The league's antimilitarist platform was promoted according to progressive custom: with mass protest meetings, petitions to the government, testimony before officials, and propaganda targeted at youth.[26]

Dorothy Day trusted in neither legislation nor education. At the time she thought that "nothing could be done except by the use of force."[27] Moderate in its tactics and goals, the league's program was at odds with Day's revolutionary sensibility. The CAML itself could not have sparked Day's pacifism in 1917. But she did find within the league a small group of students who attempted to push the organization from polite dissent to war resistance. These three activists and a few radical friends outside of the league remained steadfastly opposed to the war even after such a position became unpopular and illegal. Day would soon commit civil disobedience, but not as a peace activist.

Dorothy Day was probably working at the league while her friends Charles Phillips, his fiancée Eleanor Wilson Parker, and Owen Cattell formed a committee at a CAML meeting on 8 May to write an anticonscription pamphlet. "Will You Be Drafted?" was taken to a radical printer who lost his nerve and reported his customers to authorities. While court records show that the order of two thousand copies was never printed, New Yorkers learned of the pacifist ideas contained in the uncorrected proof from the *New York Times*. Parker was acquitted on a technicality, but the men were slapped with a $500 fine, a short jail sentence, and loss of citizenship, and Columbia University expelled them.

Even the official magazine of the league would later dissociate itself from the "illegal" pamphlet.[28]

Not a shred of evidence links Dorothy Day to the pamphlet project. Her name was never mentioned in the indictment or testimony; her accounts of the period slid over the incident.[29]   But Day knew the facts of the case and sympathized with the cause. She and her CAML friends attended the same anticonscription meetings during the end of May and in early June. Day continued to socialize with the defendants after their arrests and trial. Both Charlie Phillips and Owen Cattell attended an intimate meeting of dissenters at Day's communal apartment on MacDougal Street on the eve of draft registration. That summer Phillips was rooming with Day's friend Irwin Granich in a cramped basement. One of Eleanor Parker's poems was published in the *Masses* while Day was in charge.[30]

Besides the students, two of Dorothy Day's closest friends, both of them anarchists, challenged the draft. Artist Maurice Becker and writer Irwin Granich agonized over draft registration. Becker "had a [lifelong] horror of war" and opposed killing a person "under any circumstances." "This conscription business" worried him to the point of distraction.[31] Granich experienced suffering so profound over the draft that nearly a half-century later it still affected Day, who remembered: "It was a physical as well as a mental and spiritual anguish, and it undermined his health."[32] After registering on 5 June 1917, the two radical humanists, Becker, age twenty-eight, and Granich, age twenty-four, evaded induction by fleeing to Mexico.

Dorothy Day's antiwar activism dwindled after the deadline for draft registration just as her journalism career was skyrocketing. A fortunate meeting with Floyd Dell of the *Masses* led to his hiring the attractive young journalist for a new position as assistant managing editor. While the independent socialist monthly was a powerful vehicle at Day's disposal, she did not use it for expressing antiwar views. A lack of literary self-confidence in the company of writers like John Reed, Max Eastman, and Floyd Dell kept the neophyte assistant occupied with the technical aspects of producing a monthly magazine. When she did write an antiwar article, it was published in the Collegiate Anti-Militarism League's comparatively obscure magazine *War?* The amateurish opinion piece vigorously defended freedom of expression in wartime against the provincial tastes of the post office department.[33]

Day's fear about the sword of Damocles falling on the radical and pacifist press was justified. During her short tenure at the *Masses*, the government moved to ban the magazine from the mails for printing objectionable antiwar cartoons, poetry, and editorials. First, the local postmaster refused to send anything he considered to be treasonous through the mails. He stopped the *Masses*. Then, interruption of the *Masses*' mailing schedule triggered the denial of the magazine's special postal rate; the huge increase in mailing costs doomed the monthly. Its last issue was dated November-December 1917. Second, the senior editors, including Eastman and Dorothy Day's immediate superior, Dell, were charged with violating the Espionage Act, although they were later exonerated after ably defending themselves in two trials.[34]

The swift collapse of the *Masses* illustrated the destructive power of wartime censorship over dissenting publications.[35] By November 1917, with the prospect of unemployment looming ahead, Dorothy Day took whatever work came her way. Unwilling to bother to apply for positions with the moribund radical press, she decided to freelance. Day spontaneously accepted an offer from her artist friend Peggy Baird to join the National Women's Party's (NWP) suffrage campaign in Washington, but the jaunt had potential for furnishing the confirmed social realist with new material for freelance articles. At least one story, a mediocre and moralistic description of degrading jail conditions for women, resulted from the trip, but it said nothing about suffrage or wartime.[36]

Throughout the summer and the fall of 1917 the National Women's Party was campaigning to speed Washington's glacial pace in approving a women's suffrage amendment. Women of all ages, from all walks of life and from all areas of the country, banded together for their cause. These colorful protesters, wearing brilliant purple and gold sashes and carrying provocative banners, paraded before the White House, where Woodrow Wilson, who demanded that the world be made safe for democracy, stubbornly refused to sponsor the right to vote of female citizens of his country. Repeatedly submitting to arrest, the women exposed the hypocrisy of the antisuffragists who seemed to prefer "protecting" women by jailing them rather than allowing them a voice in government.

Educated, careerist, ambitious, independent minded, and emancipated from her family, Dorothy Day fit the "new woman" image in attitude and behavior. Although she picketed the White House and was arrested, Day had no interest in promoting women's suffrage. Very much a left-wing socialist, Day thought that voting, with its limited choices, and parliamentary politics rife with deal making, stifled genuine change. She trusted only in the direct action of the masses to result in social revolution and would *never* vote in an election.

For Dorothy Day the trip to Washington expressed her solidarity with all political prisoners: radicals, pacifists, and NWP suffragists. But it was through suffrage activities, rather than as a pacifist or radical, that Day earned her stripes as a political prisoner. When a drunken sailor took offense at her "unpatriotic" protest, Day forcefully repelled her attacker's violence. Her activism was based on knowledge of the suffrage movement from Peggy Baird and possibly Joy Young, wife of *Masses* colleague Merrill Rogers, both of whom were arrested that summer. With the NWP suffragists she engaged in the tactic of noncooperation with authorities to protest injustice. Together they refused to give their names, eat, work, or wear prison apparel.[37] In New York, Day's male radical pacifist comrades were the most likely candidates for political imprisonment. Thus, the suffrage protests ironically drew Day more completely into the largely male experience of political imprisonment.

The antiwar component of militant suffragism was obvious at the time. The press, the women's movement, ordinary citizens, and the Wilson administration all took aim at the allegedly unpatriotic activities of the suffrage protesters. Within the suffrage movement, conservatives urged women to win favor for suffrage by supporting the war effort. Liberal and radical suffragists decried the hypocrisy of "making the world safe for democracy" when women in the United States did not have the right to vote. The press covered the colorful militant protests and major dailies featured photographs of demonstrators lined up before the White House with signs likening the lack of women's suffrage to political conditions in imperial Germany. While not all militant suffragists espoused antiwar views publicly, many did. A few prominent radical suffragists like Crystal Eastman also held leadership positions in the antiwar movement. Official hysteria about the suffragists' ties to the enemy reached a ludicrous level after corrections officials misread an innocent letter received by Peggy Baird from her mother. When authorities imagined a German plot in a humorous remark that Mother Baird shared about the German government bankrolling Peggy's activism, even the prowar *New York Tribune* commented that officials are "taking no chances with jokesmiths these days."[38]

Released from jail during Thanksgiving week thanks to a presidential pardon for the suffragists, Dorothy Day contributed little to the faltering antiwar and radical movements in the following months. She briefly worked for the lackluster and "inconsistently Socialist"[39] successor of the *Masses*, the *Liberator*, and started a nurse training program in Brooklyn. In April 1918, Day was called to testify for the defense during the first *Masses* trial. The senior editors and some contributors were accused of providing or approving seditious material for the *Masses*. In at least one case, however, Day had "managed to slip the drawing [an allegedly seditious antiwar cartoon] into the issue without the knowledge of Eastman and Dell,"[40] who chivalrously shielded her from indictment. Although the trial presented Day with an opportunity to showcase her antiwar commitment, she volunteered no information about her role in choosing the offending Henrik Glintenkamp illustration.

Dorothy Day's opposition to World War I did not make headlines. At first she failed to grasp how domestic social reform and opposition to war were related; however, her exposure in the course of her work to individuals and organizations helped to educate her. As a revolutionary socialist, Day opposed an imperialist war without rejecting violence as an instrument of workers in a class war. She and her companions in the lyrical left shared an uncompromising opposition to the conflict based on their radical hopes for a more humane society. Together they experienced the vise-like grip of wartime laws that severely limited self-expression, and their memories of fettered freedom remained with them after Armistice Day.

During the early twenties, Dorothy Day, like many of her contemporaries, felt that the pacifism in wartime had accomplished little and repression had made survival problematic for radicals. Disillusioned by the national climate and also by the failure of a doomed relationship, Day briefly joined the postwar exodus to Europe along with more celebrated contemporaries, such as John Dos Passos and Ernest Hemingway. Returning, she clung to her social radicalism, but did not allow her principles to interfere with survival. Occasionally writing for the bourgeois press and clerking for capitalists, she worked wherever she could find a job. The wartime red scare, heightened by the success of the Bolsheviks in Russia, continued unabated into the twenties. Framed as a prostitute by police, Day was snared in an antiradical raid on a Wobbly dormitory in Chicago.

Gradually her restlessness and disappointment faded. Having achieved literary gratification and modest financial reward from *The Eleventh Virgin* (1924), she entered into a satisfying partnership with Forster Batterham and their daughter was born in 1926. About a year and a half after the happy birth, in December 1927, Day became a Catholic; her conversion resulted in a break with her lover, who scoffed at religious convention.

To support herself and her daughter, Dorothy Day turned to the All-America Anti-Imperialist League (AIL). Sharing quarters on Union Square with the *New Masses* magazine, the AIL office in New York was headed by a communist cadre, Manuel Gomez, formerly Charlie Phillips! The communist affiliate engaged in popular front politics, trying to craft a coalition of leftists and liberals to counter U.S. imperialism. Hired as a propagandist, Day conducted interviews and wrote appeals to raise funds and buy medical supplies for the Sandinista rebels in Nicaragua who were fighting U.S. Marines.[41]

Need, opportunity, and conviction drew Day to the work. "I am in agreement with it," she had said of the AIL's agenda. "We should not be sending our [U.S.] marines to Nicaragua."[42] Since World War I, Day consistently opposed imperialist wars. U.S. military presence in Nicaragua, not to speak of the longer-term occupation of the Philippines, validated her radical analysis of world politics: the capitalist government of the United States predictably sent troops abroad to prop up shaky reactionary regimes with ties to U.S. economic interests. Clearly in sympathy with the social aims of communism, Day still trusted in the direct action of the revolutionary masses.

Immediately after her baptism, Day hesitated about staying at the AIL. Troubled by communism's atheism and Catholicism's anticommunism, Day brought her spiritual discomfort to the attention of her confessor. "Father Zachary told me to keep my Communist job until I found another one," she noted, since she had a child to support.[43] After leaving the AIL, Day worked briefly for the Fellowship of Reconciliation and a few years later, before starting the Catholic Worker movement, she researched peace issues for an unnamed women's group. Unfortunately, we do not know if these activities hastened the Christianization of her pacifism.

In 1933 Dorothy Day founded the Catholic Worker movement, which advocated nonviolent social revolution, labor organization, civil rights, and peace. Responding to such situations as the Spanish Civil War and growing militarism in Italy and Germany, Dorothy Day became the spiritual leader of

American Catholic pacifism. The official policy of Catholic Worker by the late 1930s reflected a seismic shift in Day's understanding of peacemaking, since she grounded her activism in Christ's ethic of love.[44] To this ethic Day grafted some usable ideas from her radical past and traditional Catholic teaching, thus creating modern Catholic gospel pacifism.[45]

Long a reader of the Bible, Day frequently stated, "The Sermon on the Mount is our Christian manifesto."[46] Jesus' command to love God, neighbor, and self required the practicing of nonviolence according to Day. No lesser standard, she believed, should guide Christian behavior. Realizing that the public equated nonviolence with passivism and appeasement, Day distinguished between true and false pacifism, the former using traditional spiritual weapons like prayer and reception of the sacraments to actively resist evil. "If we are not going to use our spiritual weapons," she conceded, "let us by all means arm and prepare."[47]

From the *Baltimore Catechism*, Day remembered that all human beings who share in God's grace are "temples of the Holy Ghost." Christ's dual nature, divine and human, as understood in the mystery of the incarnation, further suggested the radical inclusivity of Christianity. Papal and episcopal pronouncements of the thirties, and later Pius XII's encyclical *Mystici Corporis* (1943), provided powerful reminders of the essential actual and potential community of humankind.[48] In contrast to her socialist opposition to war, and its condemnation of workers of one nation fighting workers of another, Catholic pacifism invoked the protection of the Christian law of love on everyone, "Jew, Gentile, black and white" and "our enemies as well as our friends." But at the same time that Day recognized the supremacy of the law of love, she had not forgotten the need for labor solidarity. "It is yours to say," she reminded workers, "whether the United States shall dip its hands in the blood of European workers. . . . You can proclaim to the world that at long last the workers are refusing to be the pawns of capitalist and imperialist gain."[49]

Dorothy Day's gospel pacifism was enriched by her early radicalism and experiences in World War I. The path she traveled toward Catholic pacifism was shorter for her than for most of her coreligionists. While as a Catholic Day considered war a sin, "a sin against Love [*sic*], against life," she specified that sin could take the form of imperialism, militarism, or nationalism.[50] Thus, modern Catholic pacifism spiritualized the familiar materialist analysis of the roots of war of the Progressive Era.

Day founded the Catholic Worker as a radical Catholic alternative to communism but refused to engage in baiting her old communist friends. As early as 1934 Day had insisted that communists had no monopoly on opposing imperialist wars; radical Catholics believed that imperialism violated the church's social justice teachings. "[I]t is not Christianity and freedom we [the United States during the cold war] are defending," she insisted in 1954, "but our possessions."[51] While the Left depended on the social sciences and Marxist theorists to clarify the intimacy between capitalism and imperialism, Day could refer to traditional Catholic teachings about the sinfulness of materialism to make the same point. Unlike the Left, the Catholic Worker condemned class warfare, since, as Dorothy Day had said on many occasions, employers were children of God, too.[52]

The antimilitarism and opposition to conscription of the lyrical left carried over into the Catholic Worker. Militarism violated the law of love by threatening harm on other nations. By the 1960s the Catholic Worker noted that reliance on arms expended resources that were better used to care for the poor, a point that Pope John XXIII made in *Pacem in Terris* (1963). Perhaps Day's most original contribution to modern Catholic pacifism was her insistence on resisting conscription by having men refuse to register for the draft. While she enlisted the help of philosopher G. Barry O'Toole to develop a challenge to military conscription rooted in scholastic theology, she took a practical approach: "[t]o fight war we must fight conscription." Noting modern warfare's dependence upon industry, Day suggested that workers refuse to make arms and that citizens oppose war taxation.[53]

The lyrical left's criticism of excessive nationalism was also incorporated into Catholic pacifism. World War I peacemakers had complained that nationalism resulted in policies based on emotionalism and artificial division of humanity into armed camps, defending their rights and seeking aggrandizement of power. Catholic pacifism emphasized that nationalism was yet another barrier to viewing humankind with the eyes of God. Day had little use for nationalism, since she believed in the primacy of God's laws over those of the State.[54] The kingdom of God, after all, was superior to human government, and Day believed that the law of love promoted the most inclusive vision of a genuinely Christian society. Day cautioned that "carping criticism" had no place at the Catholic Worker. Professing love for the "one country in the world where [folks] of all nations have taken refuge from oppression," she promoted community building that knew no national bounds.[55] Nationalism, like imperialism and militarism, symbolized false gods to be resisted, not worshipped.

The lessons of war as experienced by the lyrical left remained etched in Dorothy Day's religious pacifism. Just as wartime intensified public intolerance for dissenters and justified the passage of restrictive laws in 1917, Day expected that the outbreak of World War II would similarly pressure advocates of peace. In September 1939 Day pledged to oppose conscription as a way of opposing war, but added, "To this fight THE CATHOLIC WORKER PLEDGES ITSELF AS LONG AS WE ARE PERMITTED TO EXIST." Dissenting pamphlets, she prophesied, would be confiscated. When the United States did enter the war, Day continued to print the teachings of Christ, the Pope, and John Hugo, who was engaged in questioning the morality of modern warfare. Her experiences in World War I had taught her to expect government suppression of the press and speech. The *Catholic Worker*, she thought, was destined to follow the *Masses*, *War?*, and other dissenting periodicals into extinction.[56] But, as it happened, the entry of the United States into World War II did not stir up controversy in the same way as World War I had. Angered by the Japanese sneak attack at Pearl Harbor and horrified by Germany's atrocities against Jews, the public embraced World War II as the "good war," a just fight against fascism and Nazism. Government suppression and vigilante action were not needed to quell the few voices of dissent during the early 1940s.

Government agencies of World War II, like the Office of War Information (OWI), had learned lessons from 1917 as well. By sanitizing war information and creating propaganda, the OWI indirectly censored the press. The authorized vigilantes of World War I, whose "slacker raids" aided the Justice Department's enforcement of wartime measures, were gone by World War II, replaced by a well-oiled government agency. Beefed up to fight Reds during the twenties and thirties, the Federal Bureau of Investigation, under its legendary director J. Edgar Hoover, spent considerable energy monitoring the pacifist activities of Dorothy Day and her movement, especially in the forties and fifties. Zealous in their pursuit of Reds, FBI agents classified Dorothy Day as a communist in 1940 after she had opposed a peacetime conscription bill.[57] Before Pearl Harbor, Director Hoover himself recommended "custodial detention in the event of a national emergency," although the order was changed to restriction of her activities.[58] And the New York office promised to "conduct appropriate investigation in order to ascertain the present activities of subject."[59] For nearly thirty years, the FBI probed into Dorothy Day's pacifism.[60]

Both the lyrical left and the Catholic Worker looked to plain folks to share in the work of revolution and peacemaking. Dorothy Day long defended the right of workers and peacemakers to organize, but after her conversion, she urged them to depend upon spiritual tools combined with responsible collective action, such as boycotts and strikes. "[W]ith the help of God and by resorting to His sacraments and accepting the leadership of Christ," she wrote, "we can overcome revolution by a Christian revolution of our own, without the use of force."[61] Here was a Catholic alternative to communism and a radical renewal of conventional Catholicism.

Catholic pacifism called upon ordinary people "to keep our country aloof from the European war" by actively opposing "commercial, imperialist and sordid war." Advocating direct action over electoral process, Day counseled workers in the United States to "refuse to manufacture or transport articles of war." To underscore their noncooperation with war, workers "in organized fashion" were to threaten a strike before compromising their position.[62] She was encouraging a new generation of workers to take power into their own hands, the nonviolent power of the strike and the boycott. Dorothy Day was a journalist and activist, not a theologian. The task of developing a Catholic theology of pacifism she left to others.

Day's openness to peacemaking dates back to World War I and the war resistance she encountered in the lyrical left. From the peacemakers of this earlier time, Day absorbed an analysis of the causes of war. Because she understood that modern warfare mobilized citizens and soldiers, her Catholic pacifism emphasized the responsibility of ordinary people to refuse to cooperate with the draft, arms manufacturing, and the payment of war taxes. The World War I homefront prepared Day to face the rigors of public intolerance and government suppression of pacifists in wartime. Although Day carried with her portions of her lyrical left pacifism, her understanding of the means and ends of Christian revolution dominated Catholic pacifism. Day had become an absolute pacifist who rejected "the use of force as a means of settling personal, national, or international disputes."[63]

NOTES

1. Floyd Dell is credited for the use of "lyrical" to describe the rebellion of the teens. John Diggins appropriated it in *The American Left in the Twentieth Century* (New York, 1973), 73–106.

2. The meaning of pacifism was more inclusive during World War I than later. As popularly understood then, any opponent of war was a pacifist; the commitment to nonviolence was not necessarily implied. For a valuable history of the concept, see Charles Chatfield, "Pacifism," in Alexander DeConde, ed., *Encyclopedia of American Foreign Policy* (New York, 1978), 722–29.

3. "The Socialist Party of America, Position Against the War" (1915), in John Whiteclay Chambers II, ed., *The Eagle and the Dove: The American Peace Movement and United States Foreign Policy 1900-1922*, 2d ed. (Syracuse, N.Y., 1991), 63; Dorothy Day, *The Long Loneliness* (New York, 1952), 87.

4. Paul Buhle, *Marxism in the United States*, rev. ed. (London, 1990), 107.

5. An opinion piece that gives the flavor of the *Call*'s antiwar stand was reprinted from the *Masses*, John Reed, "'Whose War?'," *New York Call Sunday Magazine*, 18 March 1917.

6. Possibly as early as January 1917, but definitely by March, Day was covering the peace movement. Most of the *Call*'s peace reporting announced forthcoming events and described meetings; none of these were signed.

7. The Conscription of Wealth plan was mentioned in paid peace propaganda printed in the New York dailies. The best exposition of the campaign explained that it originated with interventionist and civic groups interested in financing the war without loans. Peace groups picked up the proposal for their own purposes: to remind the wealthy that those who would profit from the manufacture of armaments and loans to the Allies should return their profits to the war effort. "A 'Pay-As-You-Go' War," *War?* I (3) ca. April-May 1917.

8. Day, *Long Loneliness*, 57. Box 57, Folder: Speeches and Writings. Untitled—Pacifism. David Starr Jordan Collection. Hoover Institution Archives; and Jordan, *The Days of a Man* (New York, 1922), vol. 2, 716, 727. On the EPF, see Charles Chatfield, *For Peace and Justice: Pacifism in America, 1914-1941*, reprint (Boston, 1973), 26-27, and Barbara Steinson, *American Women's Activism in World War I* (New York, 1982), 247-48. The EPF instructions were quoted in "15,000 Peace Pilgrims Will Invade Capital," *Call*, 28 March 1917.

9. "ON TO WASHINGTON FOR PEACE!" [Emergency Peace Federation notice], *New York World,* 1 April 1917.

10. For documentation of the CAML's role, see the Henry Wadsworth Longfellow Dana Papers, Box 20, Swarthmore College Peace Collection, (SCPC).

11. Dorothy Day's account of the peace trip can be found in *The Eleventh Virgin* (New York, 1924), 144-47, *From Union Square to Rome* (Silver Spring, Md., 1938), 77-78, and *Long Loneliness*, 60-61. The peace trip was not mentioned in the memoirs of Charles Shipman (Charles Phillips), *It Had To Be Revolution: Memoirs of an American Radical* (Ithaca, N.Y., 1993).

12. It was not possible to obtain many of the small papers from the communities where the students held their spontaneous meetings. Those that were examined did not mention the peace tour. The spontaneity of the itinerary and the tour's weekend schedule minimized chances for local coverage.

13. Quote from Day, "Jersey Workers Not Urging War, Pacifists Find," *Call*, 1 April 1917. Day's other signed articles include "Peace Pilgrims Find Common People Don't Favor War's Madness," *Call*, 2 April 1917, and "Delaware Workers Emphatically Shout: 'We Don't Want War!'," *Call*, 3 April 1917. *Eleventh Virgin*, 147; cf. *Long Loneliness*, 65.

In the early twenties, disillusioned by the failure of radicals and pacifists to prevent U.S. intervention and by wartime repression, Day trivialized the antiwar commitment of the peace group in *The Eleventh Virgin* (1924). The fictionalized autobiography presented Day's most negative portrayal of her prewar peace activism. She and the students ultimately did not "care whether war was declared" (147). In contrast to a spectacular opening for the peace story, its ending was anticlimactic: "[T]hat was the end of the assignment," which falsely suggests that Day's interest in peace ended then (147).

In the book Day first corrected some of the erroneous material from the newspaper accounts. The "pacifist" chauffeur of the articles became two bus drivers who had no "conviction one way or the other" about the war; most of the crowds along the way were indifferent; and, "the country people were . . . too stolid . . . to care whether we were rabidly pacifists [*sic*] or not" (146-47).

Day's autobiographies differed from the "novel" in interpretation more than in fact. *From Union Square to Rome* (1938) challenged Day's assertion that her circle's antiwar activity had amounted to little. "A few days after war was declared," she remembered, "there was nothing for us to do but go back to New York and work with the [Collegiate Anti-Militarism League]" (78). She softened her harsh criticism of her reporting for the *Call*, commenting that all newspaper reporters worked under such pressure that they "lose all perspective" and have "no time at all for thought" (72). Readers are most familiar with *The Long Loneliness* (1952) in which Day downplayed the violent episodes of her young adulthood and neglected to verify details. The clubbing incident in Baltimore was omitted. Day mistakenly dated her assignment to the trip in April, when it started at the end of March. She spoke of the tour's opposing conscription, collapsing the anti-interventionism of the peace tour with the wartime pacifist anticonscription campaign. And, repeating an earlier error, Day misnamed the university peace group.

14. "Pacifist Meeting Barred by Police," *Philadelphia Inquirer*, 2 April 1917. For the missing link between feminist peace activism and the civil liberties campaign, see Frances Early, "Feminism, Peace, and Civil Liberties: Women's role in the Origins of the World War I Civil Liberties Movement," *Women's Studies* 18 (1990): 95-115.

15. Day, *Long Loneliness*, 61.

16. "Pacifists' Meeting Ends in Riot," *Baltimore Sun*, 2 April 1917. Day's accounts of the riot grew progressively milder over time. See her *Eleventh Virgin*, 144-47, *Union Square*, 77-78, and *Long Loneliness*, 61. Shortly after she returned from the Washington trip, Day left her position with the *Call*. Relating her decision to leave to her altercation with a new editor, this episode's contribution to the temporary end of her newspaper career remains unclear.

17. For development of the split in the peace movement, see Charles Chatfield, *The American Peace Movement: Ideals and Activism* (New York, 1992), 39-50. John Dewey's "plastic juncture" is covered in David M. Kennedy, *Over Here: The First World War and American Society* (New York, 1980), 50-53.

18. For an accessible survey of civil liberties issues during World War I, see Michael Linfield, *Freedom under Fire: U.S. Civil Liberties in Times of War* (Boston, 1990), 33-60. No satisfactory study of the World War I era resisters exists, but the best brief coverage is in John Whiteclay Chambers II, *To Raise an Army: The Draft Comes to Modern America* (New York, 1987), 205-37. See also Stephen M. Kohn, *Jailed for Peace: The History of American Draft Law Violators, 1658-1985* (Westport, Conn., 1986), 25-43.

19. "Draft Law Test," *New York Herald*, 12 June 1917 reported that defense attorney Harry Weinberger used the Thirteenth Amendment argument first in federal district court. Upon appeal to the U.S. Supreme Court, he used the same argument, again without success.

20. Day listed herself as a CAML member on attendance lists of at least two separate peace meetings. See "Meeting to Discuss Conscription—Tuesday, May 27th 1917," Dana Papers, Box 2, SCPC and "[Untitled List]," ca. April-May 1917, Margaret Rockwell Finch Papers (of Jessie Hughan). Day wrote of the "Anti-Conscription League" in *Union Square*, 78 and *Long Loneliness*, 60. Her description fits the Collegiate Anti-Militarism League. All of the students whose names she mentioned were members of the Columbia University CAML. Charles Phillips (alias Charles Shipman), one of Day's friends, confirmed her link with the group. See Charles Shipman to Dorothy Day, 22 December 1965, Dorothy Day and the Catholic Worker Archives, Series D-5, Box 2, Marquette University and *Revolution*, 30-31. Day wrote one article for the CAML magazine *War?* 1 (Summer 1917): 5-6. No evidence of an Anti-Conscription League exists in the scholarly histories of the World War I peace movement or in the memoirs of activists. Emma Goldman and her anarchist followers, who included Day's friend Irwin Granich, formed the No Conscription League (NCL) and Day might have jumbled the names of the CAML and NCL. Day's error has been widely perpetuated in scholarly works to date.

21. In the thinly fictionalized account of her life, Day told the story of a Washington peace trip and after her alter ego was clubbed, she concluded, "[N]ewspaper work was not a job for women." Other possible explanations include the deposing of her editor after his views on labor were denounced by his superiors; her dispute with the new editor of the *Call* whose politics were incompatible with hers; personal ambition to write "serious" literature; and a series of violent episodes in spring 1917. Devotion to the cause of peace probably played a role in her choice, too. *Eleventh Virgin*, 154-55. The violent episodes of Day's newspaper career include an attempted sexual assault, sexual harassment, and injury in the Baltimore riot, and are documented in Day, "Does Heaven Protect Working Girl? [sic] Taxi, Cop, Matron, Answer," *Call,* 28 January 1917; *Long Loneliness*, 58; *Union Square*, 77-78. After the peace trip, Day later wrote, "There was

nothing for us to do but go back to New York and work with the Anti-Conscription
League [Collegiate Anti-Militarism League]." *Union Square*, 78.

22. Day, *Union Square*, 76-78.

23. Shipman (Phillips), *Revolution*, 31.

24. Day's references to the trio are brief. Her friend Irwin Granich was Phillips's
roommate during the summer of 1917. Phillips and Day twice resumed their friendship
during the 1920s, after he joined the Communist party. *Union Square*, 78 and *Long
Loneliness*, 67, 68, 96, 149. Phillips, then known as Manuel Gomez, was secretary of
the Anti-Imperialism League in 1927. See Shipman (Phillips), *Revolution*, 30-31, 43,
143-44, 146, 165-66.

25. Unofficial figures cited by Charles Francis Phillips, *New York Times*, 20 June
1917. The best history of the CAML is "The Collegiate Anti-Militarism League," *War?*
1 (Summer 1917): 18-19.

26. "Statement of Principles and Organization of Collegiate Anti-Militarism League,"
War? 1 (February-May 1917): [2] and "The Collegiate Anti-Militarism League," 18.

27. Day, *Long Loneliness*, 66.

28. Some inaccuracies in Shipman's version of the trial are discussed in Anne
Klejment, "It Had To Be Revolution," *Catholic Worker,* May 1994, 7. For Phillips's
statement, see the *Call*, 7 June 1917. Cf. the disavowal of the pamphlet in "The
Collegiate Anti-Militarism League," 18 and Owen Cattell, Eleanor Parker, and Charles
Phillips, "Statement (Confidential until after the trial)," [n.d.] CAML papers, SCPC.

29. The dates of Day's employment with the CAML cannot be pinpointed from her
accounts, Phillips's memoirs, or the Dana Papers. However, Day's last signed article
in the *Call* appeared on 19 April 1917. By 4 June 1917, the eve of draft registration, she
had moved to the apartment shared by the editors of the *Masses*. Day was reticent about
the pamphlet incident, possibly because she wished to protect Eleanor Wilson Parker.
In Day's autobiographies she gave Parker the surname Carroll. The change was
deliberate rather than accidental. Day was aware of Parker's allegation that the press had
been rough with her. Parker claimed descent from one of the signers of the Declaration
of Independence; Carroll was the surname of a signer, with an added Catholic twist.
Long Loneliness, 68, mentions only a jail sentence and draft evasion in Mexico. The
pamphlet incident was not covered in *Union Square* and only a vague reference was made
to the aftermath: "A good many of my friends . . . evaded the draft by going to
Mexico." (79).

30. "Meeting to Discuss Conscription—Tuesday, May 27th 1917," Dana Papers,
SCPC, and "[Untitled List]," Finch Papers. The Christopher Street room is mentioned
in Shipman (Phillips), *Revolution*, 42. See E.[leanor] W.[ilson] P.[arker], "Red Cross,"
in the September 1917 issue.

31. *Call*, 10 November 1917. Maurice Becker to John Weichsel, 11 May 1917, John
Weichsel Papers, Archives of American Art.

32. Dorothy Day, *On Pilgrimage: The Sixties* (New York, 1972), 304.

33. Dorothy Day, "The Right to Criticize," *War?* 1 (Summer 1917): 5-6.

34. "7 On Masses Staff Indicted For Sedition," *New York Tribune,* 20 November
1917. For more thorough treatment of the topic, see John Sayer, "Art and Politics,
Dissent and Repression: The Masses Magazine Versus the Government, 1917-1918,"
American Journal of Legal History 32 (1988): 42-78.

35. For an overview of wartime censorship and repression, see Paul L. Murphy,
World War I and the Origin of Civil Liberties in the United States (New York, 1979).

36. Dorothy Day, "Lewd Sunday," [typed, signed ms. with annotation by Floyd Dell] [n.d.] Floyd Dell Papers, Newberry Library.

37. Day consistently discussed her participation in the suffrage protests in terms of support for political prisoners. See her *Eleventh Virgin*, 186-87; *Union Square*, 81-82, especially about the League for the Defense of Political Prisoners in Washington; and *Long Loneliness*, 72.

38. "Pacifism and Picketing Are Now Linked," *New York Tribune*, 22 November 1917.

39. The observation is Malcolm Cowley's in *Exile's Return* (New York, reprint, 1956), 71.

40. Day, *Union Square*, 89 or *Long Loneliness*, 87. Also, Floyd Dell, "The Story of the Trial," *Liberator* (June 1918): 7-18 and Sayer, "Art and Politics," 55-64, and especially n. 83 for evidence of Day's editorial independence. The quote is from Douglas Clayton, *Floyd Dell: The Life and Time of an American Rebel* (Chicago, 1994), 162.

41. Shipman (Phillips), *Revolution*, 165-66. The only source identifying Day with the Anti-Imperialist League is herself. See Day, *Long Loneliness*, 149; *Pilgrimage: Sixties*, 70. The small collection of All-America Anti-Imperialist League Papers at the SCPC did not name Day.

42. Dorothy Day, *Therese* (Notre Dame, Ind., 1960), ix-x.

43. Day, *Long Loneliness*, 152.

44. On the founding of the CW movement and its early history, see Mel Piehl, *Breaking Bread: The Catholic Worker and the Origin of Catholic Radicalism in America* (Philadelphia, 1982), 95-204.

45. From Peter Maurin, cofounder of the Catholic Worker, Day learned of papal teachings on peace. From clerical scholars John Hugo and G. Barry O'Toole, as Patrick Coy shows in "Conscription and the Catholic Conscience in World War II," American Catholic pacifism could be rooted in the rigorous application of traditional just-war theology.

46. Day, "Our Stand," *Catholic Worker* (June 1940).

47. [Dorothy Day], "Pacifism Is Dangerous So Is Christianity," *Catholic Worker*, January 1941.

48. Ibid. For Day on incarnation and human community, see [Dorothy Day], "Aims and Purposes," *Catholic Worker,* January 1939. Among the *Catholic Worker* articles on church statements on nationalism, see "Pope Pius XI on Nationalism," May 1934, "Root Nationalism Out to Assure Genuine Peace," March 1935, and "Holy Father Speaks Out on Nationalism," December 1938.

49. [Dorothy Day], "Aims"; "To the Workers," *Catholic Worker,* October 1939.

50. Day, *Pilgrimage: Sixties*, 237. On war and sin, see [Dorothy Day], "Truce of God Traditional in Europe," *Catholic Worker,* December 1939.

51. See "Not Pacifism," *Catholic Worker,* November 1934. Dorothy Day, "Theophane Venard and Ho Chi Minh," *Catholic Worker,* May 1954.

52. For example, Day, *Union Square*, 13.

53. Dorothy Day, "Fight Conscription!" *Catholic Worker,* September 1939. See also Day, *On Pilgrimage* (New York, 1948), 26, "Machinery Is All Ready for Next War," *Catholic Worker*, July-August 1939, and William D. Miller, comp., *All Is Grace: The Spirituality of Dorothy Day* (Garden City, N.Y., 1987), 148.

54. Anne Klejment, "War Resistance and Property Destruction," in Coy, ed., *Revolution of the Heart*, 278.

55. Dorothy Day, "Our Country Passes from Undeclared to Declared War," *Catholic Worker,* January 1942.

56. Day, "Fight Conscription," was also published in leaflet format.

57. Federal Bureau of Investigation, Freedom of Information Act files on Dorothy Day 62-61208-3, hereafter cited as FBI-FOIA.

58. JE Hoover to LMC Smith (3 April 1941) FBI-FOIA 62-61208-4; JE Hoover to Special Agent in Charge (3 February 1942) FBI-FOIA 62-61208-6.

59. FBI-FOIA 100-7885, (24 October 1941), 5.

60. Robert Ellsberg, "An Unusual History from the FBI," *Catholic Worker,* May 1979 and June 1979.

61. Day, *Union Square,* 145.

62. "To the Workers," *Catholic Worker,* October 1939 and "Truce," *Catholic Worker,* December 1939.

63. Dorothy Day, "Explains CW Stand on Use of Force," *Catholic Worker,* September 1938.

3

Catholic Peace Organizations and World War II

Patricia McNeal

In 1983 the National Conference of Catholic Bishops in the United States issued a historic document, *The Challenge of Peace*, which for the first time recognized both the just-war doctrine, long the official Catholic basis to oppose war, and pacifism as acceptable positions within the Catholic tradition. "We believe," wrote the bishops, "the two perspectives support and complement one another, each preserving the other from distortion."[1] The one person most responsible for this shift in Catholic thought was Dorothy Day.

Catholic pacifism—that is, opposition to war in any form—did not emerge in the United States until the 1930s when Dorothy Day proclaimed it. Since that time it has gained increasing support among Catholics. By the end of World War II, she had added to the Catholic theological agenda not only the concept of pacifism, but also conscientious objection and nuclear pacifism, opposition to the use of any form of nuclear weapons in warfare. Although she could not provide the theological rationale necessary for these positions, she did not hesitate to proclaim her pacifism as a moral response generated by the teaching of the Gospels.

Among Roman Catholics the pacifism of the primitive Christian church largely disappeared with the Age of Constantine. Augustine became the father of all modern Christian thought on war when he adapted the secular just-war criteria to Christianity. Since Thomas Aquinas then expounded the arguments for the just-war doctrine, it has developed into a refined theory that sets forth the principles both for going to war and for waging it. Though the just-war tradition admits a variety of interpretations, the core of its teaching lists the following conditions for going to war. First, war must be declared by a competent authority. Then there must be a just cause for engaging in war; that is, a grave wrong to be corrected or right to be defended. Pope Pius XII modified this further when he stated that, owing to the increasing destructiveness of nuclear weapons, war could not be waged morally except as an act of self-defense. Third, the likely beneficial results of a war must outweigh the evil results—the so-called principle of proportionality. Fourth, war must be waged only as a last resort, after all peaceful means have been exhausted. And, war must be waged with the right intention; that is, a war can be fought legitimately only if its purpose is to achieve a just end, not the uncharitable activities that usually accompany war. Since the fourth century, the Roman Catholic Church has used this just-war doctrine to address the morality of the State's public policy issues on war and peace.

Long before her conversion to Catholicism, Day was an ardent pacifist. During World War I, she reported on and often participated in strikes, picket lines, peace meetings, and antiwar demonstrations on New York's Lower East Side, where she lived. Reflecting later on this period, Day wrote, "I was pacifist in what I considered an imperialist war though not pacifist as a revolutionist."[2]

When she converted to Catholicism on 28 December 1927, Dorothy Day brought her pacifism with her. Its revolutionary dimension would not come until five years later when she met Peter Maurin, the French radical whose spirit and ideas dominated her life. He believed that "the most traditional Catholicism was of supreme social relevance to modern humanity, and that it was only necessary to blow the dynamite of that ancient church to set the whole world afire."[3] The radical ideal of Peter Maurin was rooted not in the material world but in the realm of the spiritual and his goals would be achieved at the end of time, with the second coming of Christ. Besides this eschatological view of history, the other distinctive feature that Maurin presented to Dorothy Day was personalism, an emphasis on direct, individual action—one on one—to help the poor.

While completely a man of peace, Maurin never made his pacifism a pronouncement. There is no clear explanation of why. In his writings he often pointed to the evil and futility of war. John C. Cort, a young Catholic Worker during the 1930s, wrote that "Dorothy says that Peter was a pacifist, but I don't recall seeing anything he ever wrote or hearing anything he ever said that supports that. The subject didn't seem to interest him, or else he didn't feel confident enough to challenge the traditional Catholic view that there are just wars and there are unjust wars."[4] When World War II began, Day recorded that Maurin said to her, "Perhaps silence would be better for a time than to continue our opposition to war. Men are not ready to listen."[5]

Nevertheless, Day herself never stopped proclaiming her Catholic pacifism and located it in Maurin's message of Christian personalism where the decision resided with the individual and was not dependent on historical circumstances. Victory also was assured because of a power beyond history—Christ. Thus, Day's commitment to pacifism was founded in "a matrix of personalism which called for a heightened sense of personal responsibility for one's neighbors and involvement in struggles for justice on their behalf."[6] She expressed her pacifism using the language of the gospels, not the language of governments. It was this spiritual vision that made Day's Catholic pacifism revolutionary. Her activism and her ability to give concrete expression to Maurin's vision gave birth not only to the Catholic Worker movement but also to Catholic pacifism.

Dorothy Day viewed pacifism as part of the total Catholic Worker vision that Peter Maurin presented to her. A total way of life, pacifism flowed naturally from the Worker ideal. As early as October 1933, Day's *Catholic Worker* stated that its "delegates" would "be among those present at the United States Congress Against War" and they would be representing "Catholic Pacifism." Since this was the first such collective statement in U.S. history of a group of Catholic pacifists, they well knew that they scarcely represented more than themselves.

By the late thirties, it became evident that the major crisis confronting Americans was not the depression, but war. The *Catholic Worker* stated that "during a time of war the nation state was invested with all the marks of power in the form of military might. At a time of war, the coercive power of the State reached its zenith."[7] A nation's decision to declare war was thus the ultimate question to be faced by the individual. Now Dorothy Day's Catholicism enhanced her pacifism of old and placed it within a revolutionary context. She placed her emphasis on the individual, not the State. During a time of war, she believed the individual had to supplant the power of the State with the gospel message of peace. She would not cooperate with the State in any way concerning the issue of war. Sarcastically, she began to refer to the government of the United States as "Holy Mother, the State."

Though the Catholic Worker was the first Roman Catholic group in the United States to proclaim pacifism, it was not the first Roman Catholic peace organization in the United States. The Catholic Association for International Peace (CAIP), founded in 1927, claimed that position. The individual most responsible for the CAIP was a priest, John A. Ryan, the architect of the "Bishops' Program of Social Reconstruction" in 1919.

In 1922 Ryan traveled to England, where he learned about England's Catholic Council for International Peace. Returning home, Ryan discussed with some of his friends the idea of founding a similar Catholic peace organization in the United States. He received support from a priest colleague, Robert McGowan, and from Carlton J. H. Hayes, a professor of history at Columbia University. Worth M. Tippy, Charles S. MacFarland, and especially Sidney L. Gulick, all of the Federal Council of Churches for Prevention of War, also urged him to organize a peace movement among Catholics,[8] as did Frederick J. Libby, executive secretary of the National Council for the Prevention of War (NCPW) on whose board Ryan then served. All of these men urged Ryan to enter a territory that Catholics had not previously entered. The popes had spoken vigorously for peace; the bishops had echoed them. But there it ended. Ryan did not exaggerate in 1925 when he said "he could tell the whole story of

American Catholic peace sentiment in a fraction of the sixteen hundred words that the *NCWC Bulletin* wanted him to write."⁹

Ryan did not want to start an American Catholic peace movement, but he did want to form a group of Catholics who could serve as a pressure group to lobby for significant legislation on issues of war and peace in Congress.¹⁰ His primary focus of attention was the issue of social justice. Yet Ryan did agree with the judgment of Peter J. Muldoon, episcopal chair of the Social Action Department, that "the department was not doing enough to educate Catholics on world affairs. It concentrated on domestic social justice alone."¹¹

An organizational meeting was finally scheduled for April 1927 at the Catholic University of America in Washington, D.C. For this meeting Ryan was to chair the subcommittee on international ethics and prepare a working paper for discussion. Ryan's report did not reach pacifist conclusions from applying the just-war doctrine. Instead, he rejected pacifism and accepted the use of force in international relations. Ryan's report based on the just-war doctrine became the manifesto of the new association when it was published in a pamphlet in 1927 under the title *International Ethics*. This April meeting realized the goal of establishing the first Catholic peace organization in American history. It adopted a constitution, elected officers, and chose a name for the society, the Catholic Association for International Peace. Its motto was that of Pope Pius XI's reign, "The Peace of Christ in the Kingdom of Christ." Its constitution declared its purpose as follows:

The Association did not look for mass support, but planned to seek to educate Catholics and non-Catholics on the Catholic point of view on international affairs, as drawn from what the Holy Fathers, the Bishops of the United States, and Catholic scholars had said on the principles of attaining world peace through justice and charity.¹²

Studies were to be made by experts and reports published on the principles of peace and their application to current issues. Also, the association would promote annual conferences, lectures, and study circles to present Catholic opinion on subjects relating to international morality. The CAIP was allotted office space in the National Catholic Welfare Conference headquarters in Washington, D.C. as an independent branch of the Social Action Department and was given the use of NCWC facilities, including the news service.

The structure of the CAIP was elitist from the beginning, though it intended to reach the general population of the laity. People invited to participate in the formation of the CAIP and later to serve on its committees were leaders from church, business, military, and university life. The key organizational components of the CAIP were its committees. All of them operated out of an internationalist vision that opposed interwar isolationism and sought to awaken in Catholics a sense of collective responsibility as well as support for a world organization. Since the CAIP, unlike the Catholic Worker, looked to the nation-state as the arbiter and authority on issues of war and peace, the just-war doctrine retained its normative position among CAIP members and provided the mediating language with which to address the government's public policy issues on war and peace in their lobbying efforts to gain support for its just-war principles.

With the build-up of war in Europe after 1935, the CAIP increased its support for the Roosevelt administration's move from neutrality legislation to collective security. The association grew increasingly critical of the pacifist position and sought to replace the pacifists' quest for strict neutrality with legislation favoring collective security. As early as 1937 the CAIP demonstrated its opposition to the Neutrality Act by contending that the act made no distinction between the aggressor nation and its victim.[13] In 1938 it reiterated its position by objecting to the "narrow conception of national interest upon which the Neutrality Act was based—[an] attitude of washing our hands of responsibility in present crime—[and it was] concerned primarily not with the prevention of war but with [the] avoidance of its consequences."[14] This paved the way for the CAIP to embrace wholeheartedly Roosevelt's move away from neutrality toward collective security.

By 1940 Ryan was firmly convinced of his position on war and his opposition to Nazism. In an article that appeared in *Commonweal* and was reprinted as a pamphlet, *The Right and Wrong of War*, he wrote:

The extreme pacifist position, that war as such is always wrong because it involves violence, does not deserve formal discussion. With the position of some recent Catholic authorities, that in our day war is practically never justified because of its awful consequences, I have considerable sympathy; if Hitler and his government intend to substitute paganism for Christianity not only in Germany but in foreign territories which they have annexed in the last two years and if they are aiming at world domination, then I have no hesitation in saying that a successful war against this immoral Nazi program would be the lesser evil. In other words, such a war would be justified, despite the enormous ensuing destruction of life and property.[15]

Thus, it was clear that by 1940 the CAIP was firmly committed to the just-war doctrine and supported the United States' entry into World War II.

The CAIP claimed to be the "official" organization seeking to present a unified program of peace within the Roman Catholic Church in the United States. By World War II its presupposition of the just-war doctrine demonstrated that it would support America's peace efforts during times of peace, but it would forego peace to support America's war efforts when a just war was declared. This pattern of response would remain constant until the demise of the organization in 1968.

The Catholic Worker movement, on the other hand, saw the incidents of aggression during the thirties and the world's response to them as the play of power politics. In its view, the League of Nations and the concept of collective security to prevent war seemed to fail each successive test. Rejecting the internationalist approach of the CAIP, the Catholic Worker endorsed a gospel pacifism that became more explicit at the time of the Spanish Civil War. Its newspaper condemned every aspect of Franco's revolt and would not be silenced, though this was contrary to the pro-Franco unanimity of the Catholic establishment. Rather than choose sides during the Spanish Civil War, the Catholic Worker adopted a position of strict neutrality. There was too much right and too much wrong on both sides, and, in words echoing the spirit of the earliest Christians, Catholic Workers preached this message of love and Catholic pacifism: "Love your enemies; do good to them that hate you, and pray for them that persecute and calumniate you."[16] Ironically, the issue of pacifism was overshadowed by anticommunism. American Catholics had found a rallying point for their anticommunism in the war. Thus, it was not the Catholic Worker's voicing of Dorothy Day's position of pacifism and refusal to take sides in the war that raised the ire of American Catholics. It was her refusal to support Franco against the communists that most angered American Catholics. Nevertheless, Day's pacifism remained constant, and in 1938 the *Catholic Worker* opposed the lifting of the arms embargo and declared that the United States "should not export arms to any country in peace or at war."[17]

Strict neutrality became for the Workers the only viable alternative to prevent U.S. entrance into World War II. This stance most clearly revealed the ideological differences of the Catholic Worker from the CAIP. After 1939 the CAIP supported the Roosevelt administration's policy of collective security. Once the United States entered the war, the pacifist manifesto of the Catholic Worker became the Sermon on the Mount. Dorothy Day again based her response to war on the gospel message found in Matthew 5 verses 1-12 where those who lack material goods and secular power stand in need of the spiritual blessings promised by God. As she put it, the members of the Catholic Worker movement "had been pacifists in class war, in race war, in the Ethiopian War, in the Spanish Civil War, all through World War II. . . . We had spoken in terms of the Sermon on the Mount and all of our readers were familiar enough with that."[18] By World War II the Catholic Worker alone was proclaiming pacifism within the Catholic community.

The cost of such witness to Dorothy Day and the Catholic Worker movement was great. Her pronouncement of pacifism as World War II approached caused dissension among members of the movement. Many held firmly to the just-war tradition. While some following this doctrine concluded that no modern war could be just and thus they reached the same pacifist conclusion, others believed that World War II was a just war. The Chicago House of Hospitality, with John Cogley as editor, had been publishing its own newspaper, the *Chicago Catholic Worker*, and it did not reflect the pacifist position of the New York paper. At the St. Francis House of Hospitality in Seattle, the Workers stopped distributing the New York *Catholic Worker* because it was filled almost entirely with pacifism; instead they distributed the *Chicago Catholic Worker*. In June, 1940 Dorothy Day sent a letter to all Workers concerning the issue of pacifism:

We know that there are those who are members of 'Catholic Worker' groups throughout the country who do not stand with us in this issue. We have not been able to change their views through what we have written in the paper, or by letters, or by personal conversation. They wish still to be associated with us, to perform the corporal works of mercy.

"And that," she said, "was all right. But there had been other cases when some associated with the movement had taken it on themselves to suppress the paper. In such instances she felt it would be necessary for those persons to disassociate themselves from the movement."[19]

Despite all of the debate and mounting tensions over the war, the Catholic Worker movement carried on, and Dorothy Day would not relinquish the pacifist position. Her adamant stance alienated some of her followers. By the end of 1942 sixteen of the houses or one half of the total number had been closed.[20] Day even admitted in the May 1942 issue of the *Catholic Worker* that she had been accused of splitting the movement from top to bottom by her pacifism.

The dominance of the just-war doctrine was also evident among Catholic Workers in the New York house. The issue was first raised by Bill Callahan, the managing editor of the *Catholic Worker* during much of the thirties. At every opportunity he raised the issue of pacifism, but unlike Dorothy Day, he used the just-war doctrine to reach pacifist conclusions. In October 1936 he announced through the *Catholic Worker* "the formation of a Catholic organization of conscientious objectors." Four months later the group was named Pax and Bill Callahan became its director. The group based many of its arguments against war on the just-war doctrine, contending that no modern war could be just because the means used to wage war violated the principle of proportionality and the rights of noncombatants. Thus before Catholic Workers were forced to clarify their stand by the approach of actual war, some in the movement who opposed the draft used the just-war doctrine to defend their position as conscientious objectors to war and to gain a hearing for their views within the church. Both a pacifism rooted in the gospel message and a just-war pacifism were being proclaimed by Workers.

Dorothy Day's pacifism, however, advocated total resistance to the draft. She believed the individual should not cooperate in any way with the United States government concerning the draft. This was the most extreme form of conscientious objection and the government did not recognize such a position as legal. Anyone who held such a position faced incarceration. A section outlined in heavy black type in the *Catholic Worker* urged men not to register for the draft. The government chose to ignore this legal offense; the Catholic ecclesiastical authorities did not. They thought Dorothy Day and the *Catholic Worker* "had gone too far" and Day was called to the New York Chancery and told, "Dorothy, you must stand corrected." She remarked:

I was not quite sure what that meant, but I did assent, because I realized that one should not tell another what to do in such circumstances. We had to follow our own consciences, which later took us to jail; but our work in getting out the paper was an attempt to arouse the consciences of others, not to advise action for which they were not prepared.[21]

Moreover, Day's respect for the individual, the heart of her Christian personalism, enabled her to reach out and assist all men who opposed the draft.[22]   Thus, it was the Catholic Worker movement alone, among all American Catholic groups, that offered assistance to individuals who conscientiously objected to World War II.

The Pax group was active until 1940 when military conscription became imminent. By that time, Bill Callahan had left the Catholic Worker and Arthur Sheehan, who had reached pacifist conclusions using the just-war ethic, was given the job of directing and reorganizing Pax. The name was changed to the Association of Catholic Conscientious Objectors (ACCO) in order to be self-explanatory. By not forbidding the name, church authorities tacitly recognized the association and with it the right of practicing Catholics to be conscientious objectors (COs). The group received many requests for information about conscientious objection and tried to keep informed about Catholics who were COs and those who had gone to jail for noncooperation with the draft. The ACCO also operated two camps for Catholic COs during World War II. After the war, the ACCO ceased to exist.

The dissension in the movement caused by the diverse just-war and pacifist positions of Catholic Workers led Dorothy Day to seek a close theological rationale for Catholic pacifism. She asked John Hugo, a young Pittsburgh priest on whom she relied for spiritual direction, to help her. In a note to her Hugo wrote: "No doubt [pacifism] is all clear to you; but then you have not tried to work it out doctrinally. If you knew no theology, it would probably be simpler to make a solution. Yet the decision must be based on doctrine. Pacifism must proceed from truth, or it cannot exist at all. And of course this attack on conscription is the most extreme form of pacifism."[23]   Day's inability to develop a rationale did not prevent her from continuing to proclaim Catholic pacifism. For her the gospel message was unequivocally peace.

While ideally resistance to the draft that consisted of total noncooperation with the State most clearly witnessed to the Catholic pacifist ideal, Day was willing to assist any individual who would not participate in war. Thus, she gave as much support as possible to COs who registered their dissent within the law and were granted CO status by the United States government. She also helped anyone regardless of whether they based their decision on the just-war doctrine or pacifism. The CAIP, however, supported the war effort and did not help any individual who objected to World War II whether they registered their dissent within the law or were resisters. The CAIP position was consistent with that of the Catholic hierarchy during World War II.

Very few Catholics refused to go to war during World War II. The highest estimate of the number of Catholic COs was 135—.001 percent—out of a membership then numbering 19,914,937. This was a substantial increase over World War I when, at most, four known Catholics had been COs, all of whom were sentenced to 25 years imprisonment.[24] During World War II, the National Service Board for Religious Objectors (NSBRO) compiled a list of 61 Catholics imprisoned in 16 of the 28 federal prisons for resistance to the draft. These 61 men were sentenced anywhere from 18 months to five years; the largest number, 30, were sentenced to three years' imprisonment. Though the number was small, the witness was significant. The Catholic hierarchy never assisted these men or expressed support for the right of conscientious objection. On the other hand, they also never denied an individual's right to become a CO.

Although Catholic COs did not stop the war nor succeed in impressing the world at large with their witness stands, they made a difference. Many of these men represented a self-reliance, as well as a dependence on God, that enabled them to hold themselves aloof from the dominating power of a state and a church that condoned war to achieve peace. Their witness has not been lost to history.

Other issues that separated the Catholic Worker from the CAIP and the "official" church during World War II were obliteration bombing and the nuclear bombing of Hiroshima and Nagasaki. During the course of the war, the obliteration bombing of European cities introduced a major challenge to the just-war doctrine. Pope Pius XII never criticized such bombing of European cities, except in the case of the bombing of Rome. The American Catholic hierarchy only privately questioned government officials concerning the morality of obliteration bombing when the Vatican pressured them to do so after the bombing of Rome. In this case, it appeared that "the American bishops had to balance their allegiances."[25] They wanted to support the Pope's concern over the bombing of Rome, but they would not publicly criticize the government's policies as the Holy See wanted. Not even the bombing of Rome or the urgings of the Pope could sway the American bishops from their loyalty to the United States government during World War II. Dorothy Day and the Catholic Worker did not hesitate to criticize obliteration bombing and they were joined by a few others in the Catholic community.

The person most responsible for developing a theological rationale for this moral protest against obliteration bombing was the theologian John C. Ford, S.J. In a scholarly article, "The Morality of Obliteration Bombing," published in 1944, he became the only American Catholic moral theologian during World War II to challenge the bombing of cities as a means of waging war. He maintained that such action was not admissible under the traditional just-war criteria. Obliteration bombing violated the just-war criteria set forth in the means used in waging war, particularly in relation to noncombatants and proportionality. He pointed out that the question of obliteration bombing led to the more general issue of the possibility of a just modern war: "obliteration bombing includes the bombing of civilians, and is a practice which can be called typical of 'total' war. If it is a necessary part of total war, and if all modern war must be total, then a condemnation of obliteration bombing would logically lead to a condemnation of all modern war."[26] A few other Catholics spoke out against obliteration bombing. The priest James M. Gillis in the "Editorial Comment" in *Catholic World* took such a stand. The editors of *Commonweal* flatly condemned obliteration bombing as murder. And the *Catholic Worker,* speaking from its pacifist position, condemned obliteration bombing and published the statement of Gerald Shaughnessy of Seattle, the only American bishop who spoke out during World War II on the immorality of obliteration bombing.[27] Though a few Catholics protested the United States' policy of obliteration bombing, most Catholics, including the CAIP, never addressed this issue.

If the protestations of American Catholics and others against the government's policy of obliteration bombing had been stronger, President Truman might have found it more difficult to drop atomic bombs on Hiroshima and Nagasaki. He did make the decision to drop the bombs and as one observer noted, "The general American reaction, is one of stunned disquiet. It is not jubilant, yet it contains no real feeling of guilt."[28]

Despite the "stunned disquiet" of most Americans, some did protest the bombing of Hiroshima and Nagasaki. Editors of Roman Catholic publications were spurred on by the Pope's criticism of the bombings. But Catholics who subjected the American decision to sharp attack were the same ones who had previously challenged the policy of obliteration bombing. Again, it was pacifists who stood in opposition. Dorothy Day in the *Catholic Worker* began her condemnation of the atomic bomb attack with extreme sarcasm as she talked of the president. "He went from table to table on the cruiser which was bringing him home from the Big Three conference," she noted, "telling the great news, 'jubilant,' the newspapers said. JUBILATE DEO. We have killed 318,000 Japanese." Quoting gospel, she asserted that "Christ had already given his judgment of the act: What you do unto the least of these my brethren, you do unto me."[29]

Catholic pacifists were dismayed at the U.S. use of atomic weapons, but the hierarchy, the CAIP, and most Catholics in the United States supported Truman's decision. This was also true of the clerical leadership and members of every denomination in the United States.[30] The same people who abstained from judgment on obliteration bombing reacted similarly when the atomic bombs were dropped on Hiroshima and Nagasaki.

In 1947, the CAIP finally spoke out on the issue of the atomic bomb. During the war the CAIP, like other peace groups that were advocates of collective security, supported the policies of the government during a time of war and focused its attention on planning for a postwar community of nations. When the United States helped to build the United Nations, the CAIP made many recommendations for a strong United Nations, offering the following recommendations on the use of the atomic bomb. The CAIP wanted a United Nations that would have "legislative powers . . . to make effective atomic control and inspection and general disarmament."[31] The CAIP stated that the use of atomic bombs was illegitimate or unjust when atomic bombing was used to break peoples' will to resist; atomic total war was pursued as an end in itself; and a war was started with a shower of atomic bombs. The use of atomic bombs was just, however, in the following situations: for counter-use by a nation in a defensive war when other means were insufficient, and if an aggressor nation's preparations and objective were clearly to enslave the world or a large part of it. The CAIP concluded its statement by declaring that "the United States was obliged to stop production of the A Bomb and publicly announce this due to suspicion aroused in Russia and by the armaments race."[32]

Thus, on the question of the use of the atomic bomb, U.S. Catholics evidenced a variety of positions. Most approved or, like the hierarchy, were silent. The CAIP, the official Catholic peace organization, applied the just-war doctrine to the new weapon and tried to bring it under the control of the United Nations and develop a rationale that would limit the use of nuclear weapons. For the CAIP, the just-war doctrine still provided an ethical rationale that permitted them to support their government in war, even "limited" nuclear war if it were necessary for the defense of their nation. The few pacifists at *Commonweal* and the *Catholic World*, and the *Catholic Worker* opposed the use of the atomic bomb under any condition. Some of these Catholics began calling themselves nuclear pacifists.

In the fifties the Catholic Worker movement continued to grow. It added nonviolence to its pacifist creed. Nonviolence offered more than pacifism's resistance to war, the draft, and obliteration and nuclear bombing. It offered a way of positing direct actions for peace that could directly influence public policy. In the succeeding decades Dorothy Day and the Catholic Worker movement served as the midwife for the birth of new peace groups in American Catholicism: Pax, the Catholic Peace Fellowship, and Pax Christi-USA. Even though their peace witness would not significantly change the public policies of the United States government on issues of war and peace, it did change the American Catholic church's teachings on pacifism, conscientious objection, and obliteration and nuclear bombing. The role of Dorothy Day in this transformation cannot be overestimated. Her proclamation of pacifism sparked a debate over the morality of war that still continues in the American Catholic community.

NOTES

1. National Conference of Catholic Bishops (NCCB), *The Challenge of Peace* (Washington, D.C., 1983), 37, par. 121.

2. Dorothy Day as quoted in Eileen Egan, "Dorothy Day: Pilgrim of Peace," in Patrick G. Coy, ed., *A Revolution of the Heart: Essays on the Catholic Worker* (Philadelphia, 1988), 71.

3. Mel Piehl, "Politics of Free Obedience," in *Revolution of the Heart*, 199.

4. John C. Cort, "Dorothy Day at 75," *Commonweal*, 97 (23 February 1973): 476.

5. Dorothy Day, *The Long Loneliness* (New York, 1952), 206.

6. Egan, "Dorothy Day: Pilgrim," 73.

7. As quoted in William D. Miller, *A Harsh and Dreadful Love: Dorothy Day and the Catholic Worker Movement* (New York, 1973), 3.

8. Francis L. Broderick, *Right Reverend New Dealer John A. Ryan* (New York, 1963), 136.

9. Ibid., 77.

10. Broderick, *Right Reverend*, 138.

11. Raymond McGowan, "Notes on CAIP," 4 August 1958, CAIP Collection, Marquette University Archives.

12. "CAIP Constitution," Section 2, CAIP Collection.

13. "Summary of CAIP Committee Work 1927 to 1952," 7, CAIP Collection.

14. Ibid.

15. John A. Ryan, *Social Doctrine in Action, A Personal History* (New York, 1941), 216-17. Broderick in his biography of Ryan, *Right Reverend*, states that Ryan resigned from the NCPW because it was too pacifist.

16. *Catholic Worker*, June 1940 and October, 1939.

17. *Catholic Worker*, October 1938.

18. Dorothy Day, *Long Loneliness*, 258.

19. As quoted in Miller, *Harsh and Dreadful*, 168.

20. Ibid., 174.

21. Dorothy Day, *Loaves and Fishes* (New York, 1963), 60.

22. Gordon Zahn, "Leaven of Love and Justice," *America*, 127 (11 November 1972): 383.

23. As quoted in Miller, *Harsh and Dreadful*, 166.

24. Paul Riley, a graduate student in the Department of Religion at Temple University, while doing research for Dr. Elwyn Smith on American Catholicism and conscientious objection from 1776 to 1924 found only four Catholics who were COs in World War I: John Dunn, Francis X. Henry, Christian Lellig, and Benjamin Salmon. Ammon Hennacy, a CO during World War I, later converted to Catholicism. Also see Torin Finney, *Unsung Hero of the Great War: The Life and Witness of Ben Salmon* (Boston, 1990).

25. Earl Boyea, "The National Catholic Welfare Conference: An Experience in Episcopal Leadership, 1935-1945," Ph.D. dissertation, Catholic University of America, 1987, 179. See 159-79 for his complete coverage of the "Bombing of Rome."

26. John Courtney Ford, S.J., "Morality of Obliteration Bombing," *Theological Studies* 5 (September 1944): 267.

27. Ibid., 271.

28. "Atomic Bomb," *Commonweal*, 43 (31 August 1945): 468.

29. *Catholic Worker*, September 1945.

30. Lawrence S. Wittner, *Rebels Against War: The American Peace Movement, 1941-1960* (New York, 1969), 126-28.

31. "Summary of CAIP Committee Work—End of War to 1952," 21, CAIP Collection.

32. Ibid.

4

Conscription and the Catholic Conscience in World War II

Patrick G. Coy

It was not always easy to be Catholic and American. Throughout the nineteenth century and part of the twentieth, U.S. Catholics faced nativist charges that their religion was inimical to a democratic way of political life. Their allegiance to Rome in doctrinal matters also called into question their allegiance to Washington in matters of war and peace. Catholics often went on the counterattack, seeking to prove their critics wrong with defensive explanations long on rhetoric but short on substance.[1] Catholics also went to war, accepting America's wars as just with little critical reflection. Of the nation's four thousand conscientious objectors to World War I, only four were Catholic.[2] Most Catholics apparently suspected that for many Americans the litmus test for patriotism lay in whether one answered an uncritical "yes" when the nation called its citizens to arms.[3] It was a well-founded suspicion, for the equation of military service during war with patriotism is prominent in the history of not only this nation-state, but most nation-states.[4]

The multifaceted response of the Catholic Worker movement to World War II revealed that Catholicism can nurture and affirm the independent thought and moral judgment that is the lifeblood of the democratic experiment. As war fever heated up and the nation carried on a debate over conscription, some Catholics, most notably those associated with the Catholic Worker movement, invoked a bedrock principle in Catholic moral theology in their opposition to conscription: the primacy of the individual conscience. This principle made it possible for Catholic Workers and Catholic conscientious objectors to step outside the current that swept the rest of the church and the nation into war.

Moreover, many of these Catholics later took the unusual step of using the church's just-war tradition—which empowers and requires the individual to make an independent moral assessment of the war, which is then translated into a particular political stance—as a basis for their unpopular stand against the war.[5] Although some no doubt refused to see it this way at the time, such moral reasoning, leading to concrete political options and behaviors, is a decidedly democratic activity.

Throughout the war years, articles in the *Catholic Worker* evinced a theme that was frequently found in Catholic moral theology manuals and preached to the faithful from the pulpit. This was the spiritual principle that penance and suffering freely and willingly undertaken by the individual, and prayerfully "offered up" for the good of others and the world, could effect change beyond the life of the individual doing the penance. The Worker took this to mean that the individual was invited to accept responsibility for the scourge of war.

The *Catholic Worker* regularly called on its readers to bear—in a very personal way—the spiritual burdens of war through prayer, fasting, and other penitential rites. A September 1939 editorial exhorted the faithful by noting that every night in Catholic Worker hospitality houses across the country the rosary was said, not for victory, but for peace. Moreover, Catholic Workers were making the stations of the cross in parishes, and taking daily communion. "We must prepare to suffer," the editorial said, "building up stores of endurance" through prayer and penitential rites.[6]

Acts of penance for the crime of war were seen as a conduit, or occasion of grace, uplifting and strengthening the little band of pacifists in time of war. Already the paper was gamely advising Catholics and other Christians to resign from war-related employment as unbefitting human dignity. When conscription came, Catholics would be encouraged to proclaim conscientious objector status, and to refuse to cooperate with the alternative service program. This was a minority tradition even within the peace movement.[7] True to form, registration day was proclaimed a day of fasting at the Catholic Worker, a day to contemplate the reach of the State into the confines of the human heart.[8]

But the Catholic Worker blueprint for avoiding war was more complex than spiritual admonishments and a call to popular piety. Many of the articles and editorials that called for resistance to the war invoked class analysis combined with a conviction that this war—much like the First World War—was being advocated by capitalists eager to turn a profit from the armaments business. Readers were consistently reminded that this war was the fruit of an unjust peace.

In a 1939 editorial entitled "We Are To Blame for New War in Europe," blame for the war was placed squarely on the shoulders of all, for "their materialism, their greed, their idolatrous nationalism . . . for their ruthless subjection of another country." As the entirely predictable fruit of capitalism, the *Catholic Worker* considered the war inevitable and imperialistic.[9] But here was no mere appeasement wrapped in Catholic theology. The *Catholic Worker* was in fact calling for a fundamental transformation of the world economic and social order, refusing to accept the notion that the brutalities then sweeping Europe were an aberration.

The Great Depression had hit the U.S. working class hard, such that the war clouds gathering on the European horizon sent mixed messages. While they indicated suffering and pestilence, they also spelled economic relief in the form of a reinvigorated economy geared up to support the war effort and, eventually, greater U.S. access to overseas markets.[10] In this climate, the paper made a series of desperate, and ultimately futile, pleas for U.S. laborers to unite in a refusal to work for "blood money."[11]

Playing off of the sacrifice theme, the paper reminded labor that it made its gains in the work-place and marketplace only because of the many overwhelming sacrifices of earlier workers willing to stand, and even die, for principles in the face of daunting odds. The appeal said, "Sacrifice has been labor's lot, it still is. Sacrifice is always the lot of the noble."[12] Not surprisingly given the long years of the depression, the appeal apparently generated little response as the nation's industrial work force continued to expand in number and output in response to the short-term economic benefits of a militarized economy.

The call to resign from war-related jobs was as ignored as it was unique. But that did not faze Dorothy Day and her Catholic Worker movement. On the contrary, as the war years continued, Day upped the ante. Initially her exhortations were based less on theology and more on the class analysis rhetoric she had been steeped in during her years in the radical, secular Left. But when she saw that her appeals fell on deaf ears, Day turned to the pietistic and penitential themes that were the mainstay of her retreat master, John Hugo.

Somewhat paradoxically, however, she then put forward increasingly radical invitations to a readership that was now dwindling. On the employment issue, for example, she raised the stakes considerably. She suggested that Catholics whose jobs did not contribute to the common good, or that did not directly have to do with the works of mercy, ought to consider giving them up. The basis for this astounding exhortation was the theological doctrine of the Mystical Body of Christ, where Christ is understood as the head of the Christian community and the faithful make up the rest of the body. Day interpreted this concretely: one could not go to war against others, for to do so was to tear at one's own body. Likewise, while it was possible to benefit materially from the exploitation of others, it was doomed to be short-lived material gain and would in the end result in grave spiritual danger. She eventually suggested, for example, that this meant jobs in advertising, insurance, and banking were all suspect, not just those in the armaments industry.[13]

During the late thirties until the end of the war, when the Catholic Worker joined with other organizations to resist peacetime conscription and then universal military training, no issue so galvanized the Worker as conscription. "Fight Conscription," yelled the heavy, block headline on the lead story in the September 1939 issue of the paper. The first sentence reveals how seriously the Worker took the conscription issue: "To fight war we must fight conscription . . . To this fight *The Catholic Worker pledges itself as long as we are permitted to exist.*"[14]

The sentence is telling. The Worker movement embraced a philosophy of personalism that situated the locus of social change and revolution not in institutions, but in the heart of the individual.[15] So it was with war. The way to stop the impending war was for individuals to refuse to fight in it. The way to arrest the steady march toward madness was to make it clear that large numbers of citizens would refuse to comply with conscription orders. "To fight war we must fight conscription," and this the Worker did with gusto.

As early as April 1938, the paper featured a pastoral statement by Cincinnati Archbishop James McNicholas, one of the most influential churchmen of his time. He called for Christians to form a "mighty league of conscientious objectors" that would help stem the rising tides of war.[16]

Over the next few years, the paper frequently referred to Archbishop McNicholas's call for a "mighty league" of objectors, just as it frequently highlighted passages from Pope Pius XII having to do with the rights of conscience vis-à-vis the modern nation-state.[17] The September 1940 issue was emblematic. An article entitled "Catholic Heads Point Out Tragic Consequences of Militarizing a Nation" consisted entirely of excerpts from the recent words of various priests, bishops, and cardinals critical of conscription and related issues. The battle for respect and legitimacy that the Worker and its sister organization, Pax, were fighting was so lopsided that it openly exploited the regard in which men like Archbishop McNicholas were held.[18] Referring to his call for conscientious objectors, one writer reminded readers, "This statement, remember, is not made by any wild-eyed street corner orator, but by a man whose thought carries weight and deserves our serious regard."[19]

The paper also retrieved the teachings and writings of the church fathers and medieval and Renaissance theologians and philosophers on the question of military service. And the *Catholic Worker* featured the words and actions of saints both famous and obscure on issues of military service and the Christian's civic rights and duties. Readers were introduced to saints of whom they knew little, such as Telemachus, who interposed himself between two gladiators in Rome's arena in 404. Telemachus was killed in the process, but the outrage over his death was credited with helping to bring that barbaric spectacle to an end in Rome.[20] Readers were also reminded of some of the obscure actions against war by more familiar saints, like Francis of Assisi and Martin of Tours. What the stories about these and other saints had in common was a principled refusal to take up arms or to do the bidding of the state.[21] This clever bit of revisionist history was an attempt to ground the Catholic Worker's unpopular objection to military service and war in the popular and hallowed traditions of the church.

Influential church leaders were doing all they could to undercut the legitimacy of the Catholic Worker and the conscientious objection claims of Catholics. John A. Ryan, chairman of the ethics committee of the Catholic Association for International Peace (CAIP), and a leading churchman throughout the first half of the century, stated in the *Washington Post* that he had examined the published statements of a number of conscientious objectors and found "it difficult to reconcile their position with the . . . Church's traditional doctrine on war and on the relation of the individual to the state."[22]

There was no better source for legitimacy than the pope himself, and to him the editors of the *Catholic Worker* turned. The September 1942 issue pointed out that the words of the pope on war and peace would be featured in succeeding issues "by placing them as in this issue on the front page with pictures, begging our readers to use them for meditation."[23] The search for respect took other forms, too. Dorothy Day invited G. Barry O'Toole, a philosophy professor at Catholic University, a pronounced anticommunist, and a vocal opponent of conscription, to write for the paper. O'Toole responded in earnest. In 1940 he contributed a series of eight lengthy articles exploring conscription and the conditions of a just war. The editorial stands of the paper, and its attempt to grant conscientious objection theological legitimacy, made it a magnet for Catholics concerned with the morality of conscription and the war. According to Arthur Sheehan, over nine hundred letters flowed into the Worker offices during a two-month period in late 1940, requesting information on Catholic pacifism.[24] To meet the demand, the *Catholic Worker* collected O'Toole's pieces and published them in pamphlet form (90 pages).[25]

Day also asked John Hugo to write on these matters. Hugo was a controversial retreat master who was popular with Dorothy Day and a few others in the Worker movement for his rigorous, uncompromising approach to the spiritual life.[26] Between O'Toole and Hugo, the foundations for a theology of peace for the U.S. Catholic church in the last half of the twentieth century were about to be laid in the pages of the *Catholic Worker*.

The series of long articles in the paper mapping the intersection of conscription and the Christian calling were heavy on philosophical speculation and relatively weak on biblical exegesis. Unlike their Protestant counterparts who opposed war and conscription largely on scriptural grounds, Catholics grounded their opposition as much in the philosophical categories of neo-scholasticism as they did in the Gospels.[27] It was a juridical and at times somewhat mechanistic approach. Much of the Thomistic language and categories in the many articles by Hugo and O'Toole probably seemed foreign to the paper's relatively few non-Catholic readers. For educated Catholics, however, Thomism was more than familiar as it was the main school of philosophical thought taught in Catholic seminaries, colleges, and universities. It was the main school of thought because it was mandated so by the magisterium. Pope Leo XIII stipulated Thomism as the official philosophy of the Catholic church in his 1878 encyclical, *Aeterni Patris*. It took some time for Thomism to take hold, however, especially in the United States, where many Catholic scholars joined their colleagues in exploring modern systems of thought.[28] A number of factors eventually coalesced in the early twentieth century to insure that Thomism would soon achieve a near-hegemonic presence in most American Catholic institutions of higher learning.[29]

O'Toole and Hugo rigorously applied the Thomistic system to the thorny issues of conscription and just-war ethics. The Thomistic penchant for highlighting the primacy of individual conscience, and for placing the freedom and dignity of the human person at the center of ethical issues, was well represented in their *Catholic Worker* articles.

The conscription issue was viewed through the Thomist lens of individual freedom. Hugo and O'Toole did not, of course, mean freedom to do as one pleased. Far from it. They meant freedom to follow the natural law as revealed by God and to answer one's vocational call unrestricted by the demands of the State.[30] The issue was not simply whether one's vocational call precluded military service. That one's vocation might actually be disrupted by military service was also at issue. It was seen as no mere inconvenience. A disruption of one's vocation that entailed the waging of war and the concomitant grave moral dangers associated with war and killing invoked serious spiritual consequences for the individual Catholic.

For O'Toole and Hugo—as for most Catholic moralists of the time—the individual must be free to respond to her or his vocational call. The individual's right to voluntarily choose his or her state of life must be jealously guarded, especially from the long reach of the State.[31]

O'Toole's argument against conscription rested on the presumption that it was impossible, given the state of modern weaponry, for an aggressive war to meet all the conditions of a just war.[32] Moreover, when modern weapons were combined with the propensity of modern nation-states to conscript and field huge armies, the negative effects of war were seen to far outweigh any possible positive effects.[33] He further argued that in the case of defensive wars, the populace of the nation would freely rally to the defense of their homeland; therefore, no conscription would be needed in such cases. Since conscription had to do with aggressive wars, and since aggressive wars waged with the indiscriminate weapons and conscripted armies of the modern age could not fulfill all of the criteria of a just war, O'Toole argued that Catholics—and, indeed, all citizens—ought to oppose conscription as a violation of the conscript's human freedom. He further suggested that such an initial violation was likely to lead to even greater violations on the battlefield given the methods employed in modern war.[34]

O'Toole's opposition to conscription was spirited. He characterized it as nothing less than "military slavery" since the conscience of the conscript—like that of the slave—was not recognized, much less honored.[35] But he also cloaked his vigorous opposition to conscription in the rationalistic rhetoric of Thomism, where reason was understood as the highest and most distinctive attribute of human nature.

In his article exploring the just-war tradition's criteria of "no alternative" (last resort), O'Toole summed up his argument on behalf of mutual discussion, third-party mediation, and arbitration by saying that these are rational means of resolving conflicts and are, therefore, befitting human beings. War, on the other hand, he saw as irrational because it does not establish on which side right and reason stand, only which side is more powerful militarily. War is consequently not a means of resolving conflict that is befitting those endowed by God with the supreme moral faculty of reason. In O'Toole's Thomistic framework, war involves rejection of the greatest gift God granted to humankind.[36]

The just-war theory lends itself, by its very nature, to a casuistic approach to morality. One takes the theory, comprehensively designed and stipulated in an attempt to account for all the exigencies of human experience, and applies it to the situation in question. Moral casuistry was, of course, long at the center of Catholic moral theology, especially with respect to the issue of warfare and the participation of Catholics in it. So it is not surprising that O'Toole, when constructing his case against modern war and conscription, supplemented the just-war theory with material from the various manuals on moral theology.

The manuals were used by priests in the confessional and in the training of seminarians. Unique about O'Toole's use of the manuals was that he quoted so directly and so heavily from them with reference to issues of contemporary social import while writing for a lay publication.[37] As in so much of the material in the *Catholic Worker* on conscription and the just-war tradition, O'Toole endeavored to ground and legitimate the movement's controversial stand on war in the safe and secure traditions of the church.

The stated goal of O'Toole's series of articles was to "convince the American citizen of his imperative duty to strive for the abolition of the abuse of governmental power involved in conscripting civilians for presumably unjustified wars on foreign soil."[38] But like the good casuist he was, his analysis extended beyond the conscription issue.

He included a series of judgments on particular aspects of the war already raging in Europe and China, and on tactics common to modern war. For example, on the basis of the proportionate means criteria of the just-war theory, O'Toole argued that the British blockade of Germany was unjust because of the damage done to neutral commerce. He judged the German tactical response of floating mines in shipping lines immoral for the same reason.[39] Moreover, he determined that the modern practice of subjecting civilian populations to air raids and bombing with poison gas was proscribed by the church's mandate against using evil means to obtain just ends, as well as by the "right way" criterion of the just-war tradition.[40]

O'Toole's case against conscription and for conscience was supplemented by the editors of the paper. In late 1941 they ran a four-part series on conscience, excerpted from Bede Jarrett's *Meditations for Layfolk*. When originally published in 1915, the book marked a departure in spiritual literature as it was designed for the daily meditation of the laity on the whole range of Catholic teaching. Jarrett was a well-known English Dominican friar, for many years the provincial of his order, and the founder of the Dominicans' Blackfriars Hall at Oxford. A historian whose expertise lay in the social and political theories of the Middle Ages, Jarrett was working on the contributions of the Catholic Church and the great Catholic thinkers to the cause of international peace when he died. Jarrett turned a good phrase and wrote in a descriptive, accessible manner.[41]

In the excerpts the *Catholic Worker* ran, Jarrett distinguished conscience from mere moral principles, the former being dynamic and changing, the latter static and unchanging. Conscience thus conceived is always more than a collection of principles to be predictably applied. Jarrett compared conscience to a faculty, like "a musical faculty, which must first of all be inherent before it can be cultivated, but which assuredly requires cultivation."[42] That conscience was in need of training, of being nurtured and developed in order to be able to make informed applications of such moral principles as those contained in the just-war theory, for example, was the central motif of the series.[43] Judging by the sheer amount of material in the paper during this time on the issues of conscription and a justified war, the paper apparently took the challenge to help inform the consciences of the U.S. Catholic laity quite seriously.

The significance of this attempt must not be understated. In the pre–Vatican II church, initiatives that empowered the laity to come to independent judgments on social issues of grave moral import were relatively rare. Moreover, lay initiatives like the Worker's that sought to help the laity inform their conscience, and that honored the wisdom of lived experience as well as the wisdom of the moral manuals, were also not common. This was especially so when it came to issues like conscription and war, which touched at least peripherally on the sensitive and thorny question of church-state relations and the responsibilities of the individual to the State. What is important here is that Dorothy Day chose to stake the future of her Catholic Worker movement on a position that ran absolutely contrary to this historical pattern.

The important role the paper played in the formation of individual consciences is demonstrated by the many letters the paper carried from Catholic young men struggling with conscription and just-war questions. Not surprisingly, the influence and role of the *Catholic Worker* and its many articles on conscription are cited frequently in the U.S. Catholic conscientious objectors' applications for CO status.[44]

The movement was honoring what Dorothy Day saw as one of the central points of the Catholic Worker: "That you don't need permission to perform the works of mercy. You don't need permission to form your conscience. . . . We must have the courage to form our conscience and follow it regardless of the point of view of cardinal or bishop. I mean we go ahead. That's all."[45] It was a good thing, too, that the movement went ahead, for if the Catholic Worker had not devoted itself to the conscience formation of the laity on the issue of conscription, there would have been precious little information available to most Catholics. As we shall see shortly, the hierarchy did not do it. It was certainly not done from the pulpit. Indeed, most parish priests were unsupportive of the conscientious objector claims of their parishioners, and many priests actually testified against them.[46] Even the Catholic press, with the notable exception of the *Catholic Worker*, did not take up the challenge.[47]

During World War II, the U.S. Catholic bishops issued five official statements on issues of war and peace. Using the just-war framework, they nevertheless managed not to condemn any aspect of the Allied obliteration and fire bombing campaigns. Likewise, the five statements were strangely, yet tellingly silent on the one issue most relevant for the laity: conscientious objection. It simply received no mention whatsoever.[48] To the extent that the bishops were concerned at all about the role of Catholics in the military, it was only for their clerical family: priests, brothers, and seminarians. Even though congressional draft legislation was discussed at the bishops' annual meetings, it was only in reference to how the draft would affect clergy and seminarians.[49] Into this void stepped the *Catholic Worker* with its focus on conscience formation of the laity on war and peace.

Still, the paper never stopped holding out hope that the church's clerics would rise to the pastoral occasion. The September 1944 issue contained no less than three front-page articles detailing the antiwar stand of three different clerics. Each headline took note of the fact that a priest had gone on record against some aspect of the war. One told the story of Pittsburgh priest Joseph Meenan, who handed in his registration card to his local draft board in protest of conscription. At the close of the Meenan article, the lay editors offered a simple but pointed invitation to other clerics: "We believe that many priests are coming to see that silence means consent. . . . We invite further letters from our spiritual leaders."[50]

During the height of the war and with most of the nation mobilized and militarized in one form or fashion, the *Catholic Worker* ran yet another series on conscription, John Hugo's "Immorality of Conscription."[51] This one took the form of an extended, seven-page supplement to the November 1944 issue. But it was so popular and the demand for it ran so high, that less than six months later the paper included it again, this time as a supplement to the April 1945 issue.

Letters printed in the December issue extolled the significance and the educational usefulness of Hugo's writing. Orders for extra copies poured in. The paper explained that they had intended to reprint it as a pamphlet but due to the urgency of immediate bulk orders they printed more supplements instead. To spur distribution, the supplements sold for one cent each. Ten thousand copies were distributed beyond the initial mailing, and ten thousand extra copies of the April 1945 issue of the paper—with Hugo's article in it—were printed as well. Rev. Felix O'Neill in Newark asked for one thousand, while Rev. John Wright in Pittsburgh ordered four hundred. Others suggested that every bishop in the country ought to read it. George Lloyd of New York wrote to say that he thought the supplement and the accompanying editorial made the November issue the "finest issue ever published."[52] Hugo's article apparently wore well, too. In April 1948 it was reprinted in the paper a third time, along with seventy-five thousand extra copies for handout distribution.[53]

Hugo's "Immorality of Conscription" arrived at a time when the nation was confronted with the possibility of universal military service becoming a permanent reality in the United States, in peace as well as in war. Lobbying to that effect was already strong in Washington, D.C., even though no bill had yet been submitted to Congress.[54] Into this highly charged political marketplace, Hugo inserted a conception of the human person, and the rights and duties of the State that were both firmly grounded in Thomistic philosophy.

Hugo granted the proponents of conscription their argument that the State was within its rights to conscript the wealth and services of its citizens, but only within certain, important limits. If its conscription of wealth amounted to a denial of the right to private property, or an absorption of the total wealth of the nation, then Hugo maintained the State had crossed over the boundary of its rights. Similarly, if the conscription of human services were so broad that it resulted in the subordination of persons in their essential being to the wishes of the State, this, too, must be rejected.[55]

Following Thomas Aquinas, Hugo maintained that the person was both a part of the State and at the same time above the State, since the human person contained within himself or herself the image of God, a reflection of the whole. In the highly ordered world of Thomism, human personality was understood as spiritual, and therefore above the solely material interests of the State. Moreover, Hugo reminded his readers that the person has a supernatural end, while the State has merely a temporal end. The State thus conceived also has duties toward the person; State and society are bound to help the person obtain his or her supernatural destiny, not violate it.[56]

Once Hugo established the primacy of the person's spiritual nature over the State's material nature, he went on to argue that while the State may require that which is material of the person—including the body and life itself—the person may never be forced to relinquish to the State his or her spiritual and supernatural rights. And Hugo insisted that that is precisely what conscription requires.

Like O'Toole before him, Hugo centered his argument on the notion that conscription violates the spiritual rights and destiny of the person since it infringes on the right to vocation. He denied that fundamental rights emanate from the State to the person, claiming instead that human rights are ineradicably located in human personality itself. The State, therefore, cannot revoke these rights; they have to do with the final end of the human person and are, in that sense, supernatural.[57] Military training, moreover, suppresses that which is good in the human personality while arousing that which is bad, thereby corrupting the soul of the conscript. Hugo argued that the nature of war requires hate and the celebration of death, not the affirmation of love that he saw as the end of the person.[58]

While the foregoing tries to render the heart of Hugo's argument plainly, his entire argument against conscription included the following planks: it forces people to postpone marriage, which creates an increased occasion of sin; it corrupts youth at an impressionable age; it destroys spiritual values and impulses; it has deleterious effects on the family; it is inimical to democracy; and it is not supported in either the Bible or in the teachings of the church.[59]

Hugo's critique of conscription was so thoroughgoing, he posited so much evil in it, that he even argued that conscription alone was enough to make a war unjust. Since the criteria of the just-war tradition and Catholic moral theology forbids the use of evil means to achieve good ends, Hugo claimed that it did not matter how just the cause was. If the war was waged with conscription, it could not be justified given the evils of conscription. And since he argued that modern war was always waged with conscripts, he essentially disallowed the possibility of a just war in the modern age.[60]

This line of reasoning—where the sanctity and dignity of the human person is placed at the center of ethical discourse, becoming the ledger against which to measure proposals such as conscription—dovetailed nicely with the larger philosophy of the Catholic Worker movement.[61] The critique that Dorothy Day and Peter Maurin offered of modern industrial society included a conviction that the spiritual and the human were subordinated to the material. They believed that the forces of industrial capitalism had violently and tragically restricted people's vocational choices, making it difficult, as Maurin so often said, "for people to be good." Unable to respond to the "still, small voice" of conscience within themselves, people could easily deny their own calling.[62] Indeed, when it came to war and conscription, they could be forced to deny their very being.

This is why the work of hospitality, and resistance to war and conscription, were of a piece for the Catholic Worker. They were cut from the same bolt of cloth. The works of war were seen as antithetical to the works of mercy, that formed the backbone of Catholic Worker spirituality. Moreover, conscription and industrial capitalism (and state socialism, for that matter) were understood to violate fundamentally the integrity of the human person. So Day could stake the future of her movement on the issues of war and conscription because those issues cut to the heart of the movement's fundamental values.

In their introduction to Hugo's study on conscription published in 1944, the *Catholic Worker* editors reminded their readers of the pledge the paper took in 1940 to fight conscription for as long as the Catholic Worker movement was permitted to exist. The editors renewed that pledge in their introduction to Hugo's piece, once again inviting their readers to join them in the upcoming fight against universal military training.

In his study of Camp Simon, one of the Civilian Public Service camps housing primarily Catholic conscientious objectors, Gordon Zahn has shown that if it were not for the Catholic Worker movement, there "would have been no viable Catholic witness against American participation in World War II."[63] By nurturing Catholic consciences during the war years, the Worker movement and its paper fulfilled a gaping hole in the mission of the church.

In their 1983 pastoral letter on war and peace, the U.S. Catholic bishops argued that one of the roles of the church in society is to help "create a community of conscience in the wider civil community."[64]   The bishops suggested in the pastoral letter that the church creates this "community of conscience" in two ways. First, by teaching clearly *within* the church the moral principles that inform a Catholic conscience. But they also insist that the church has a role to play in the larger society, which includes sharing the moral wisdom of the Catholic moral tradition with the larger culture.[65]

Based on the public process the U.S. bishops used to formulate and disseminate their pastoral letters on peace and the economy in the eighties, a credible argument could be made that the bishops are living up to the standards they set for themselves. Perhaps they have learned from past mistakes and failures, like the one outlined in this chapter. In any event, the bishops largely failed to accomplish either task during the World War II period: They neither nurtured Catholic consciences in a manner befitting their clear pastoral responsibilities within the church, nor did they use whatever "moral wisdom" there is in the just-war tradition to help the whole nation examine the ethics of the war it was waging. They even ignored opportunities created by the Catholic Worker to influence policy makers, including the following one.

The material covered and the positions occupied by the *Catholic Worker* during World War II were upsetting to many Catholics. Letters complaining about the positions of the Worker movement were common at the chancery office of the New York archdiocese. Some said the paper was anti-American; others thought that Day and the movement were sacrilegious, even enemies of the church.[66]

J. Francis McIntyre was a bishop in New York during the war period. He would later become cardinal archbishop of Los Angeles and make a name for himself as an ardent conservative voice at the Second Vatican Council. One of his tasks in New York included answering letters from disgruntled Catholics regarding the radical politics of the Worker.[67]   When the Hugo and O'Toole articles began to appear in the paper, Bishop McIntyre called in Dorothy Day. She recounted the meeting, "He spread the *Worker* out in front of him and looked at me and said, 'We never studied these things in the seminary.' But he made no objections to our bringing them out in the paper."[68]

In 1943 the U.S. Justice Department asked the bishop's National Catholic Welfare Conference to clarify the church's position on pacifism. Bishop McIntyre had a ready response. Since he had not "studied these things in the seminary," and since the *Catholic Worker*'s positions had resulted in numerous complaints, a year earlier he had asked the Jesuit theologian Joseph O'Connor for an evaluation of the theological worthiness of Day's pacifism and the critiques of the war regularly appearing in the *Catholic Worker*. O'Connor had nothing but praise for Day and the paper, arguing that they stood on solid theological grounds. He also noted that the clergy ought to go slowly in criticizing the pacifism or conscientious objection of the laity since the Catholic clergy received exemption from military service.[69]

The message that went back to the Justice Department through the National Catholic Welfare Conference focused on the fact that the *Catholic Worker* paper did not speak for the church, nor was it approved by the diocese.[70] This is unfortunate because McIntyre and the bishop's conference ignored an unusual opportunity—created by the criticisms published in the paper—to pass judgment on the way the U.S. government was conducting the war.

The conference might have echoed at least some of the just-war-based critiques of Allied methods like obliteration bombing and the bombing of the Ruhr dam that appeared in the *Catholic Worker*. In doing so, the bishops' conference would have privately engaged the government in discussion of the morality of its battlefield choices, and they could have opened up a broader public dialogue as well.

There is evidence that the Roosevelt administration was especially concerned with the positions taken by individual Catholic clerical leaders and with their collective attitudes toward government policy as reflected by the National Catholic Welfare Conference.[71] A critical word from the bishops at this time would likely have been taken differently than the stream of criticisms that appeared in the *Catholic Worker* over the years. One can also wonder whether the absence of any criticism from the bishops of the war effort in general, and of the obliteration bombing policies in particular, made it easier for Truman to drop the atom bombs at the close of the war.[72]

The task of Catholic moral judgment and dissent in a time of great ethical import for the nation was left to a lay movement—not just any lay movement—but one that embraced an ethic of voluntary poverty and depended on individual donations for its precarious existence. To the extent that any "community of conscience" was created—and the public mission of the church therefore served—was largely due to the untiring efforts of Dorothy Day and her *Catholic Worker* newspaper.

NOTES

1. William M. Halsey, *The Survival of American Innocence: Catholicism in an Era of Disillusionment, 1920-1940* (Notre Dame, Ind., 1980), 70.

2. James Hennesey, S. J., *American Catholics: A History of the American Catholic Community in the United States* (New York, 1981), 225. A notable exception to this pattern were Irish-American Catholics, many of whom protested the Mexican War, and even the Civil War.

3. Dorothy Dohen, *Nationalism and American Catholicism* (New York, 1967). Budde has recently argued that, contrary to some conservative fears and radical hopes, U.S. Catholic nationalism remains a potent ideological force to this day, and one that is largely subservient to the capitalist agenda and ethos. See Michael L. Budde, "The Changing Face of American Catholic Nationalism," *Sociological Analysis* 53 (1992): 145-255.

4. Brian Martin, *Uprooting War* (London, 1984), 112-34; and Richard J. Barnet, *Roots of War* (Baltimore, 1973).

5. It was unusual because although the just-war tradition and criteria were centuries old, they were seldom used as a basis to critique public policy, even by Catholics. See John Courtney Murray, "Theology and Modern War," *Theological Studies* 20 (1959): 40-61, cited in John H. Yoder, "The Credibility and Political Uses of the Just War Tradition," Joan B. Kroc Institute for International Peace Studies, Conference Paper Series, University of Notre Dame, October 1990, 1.

6. "Fight Conscription," *Catholic Worker*, September 1939, 1.

7. Lawrence Wittner, *Rebels Against War: The American Peace Movement, 1933-1983* (Philadelphia, 1984), 62-96.

8. "The Draft Reaches Us on Mott Street," *Catholic Worker*, February 1941, 5.

9. "We Are To Blame for New War in Europe," *Catholic Worker*, September 1939, 1, 4.

10. William Appleman Williams, *The Contours of American History* (Chicago, 1966), 451-69.

11. See for example, "To the Workers: An Appeal to Workers to Sacrifice for Peace," *Catholic Worker*, October 1939, 1, 3.

12. Ibid.

13. See for example, Dorothy Day, "Poverty and Pacifism," *Catholic Worker*, December 1944, 1, 7. On the importance of the Mystical Body of Christ doctrine for Dorothy Day, see Patrick G. Coy, "The Incarnational Spirituality of Dorothy Day," *Spirituality Today*, 39 (1987); 114-25. For a popular and influential early work on the doctrine, see Fulton Sheen, *The Mystical Body of Christ* (New York, 1935).

14. "Fight Conscription," *Catholic Worker*, September 1939, 1, emphasis in original.

15. For a thorough treatment of personalism, see John Hellman, *Emmanuel Mounier and the New Catholic Left, 1930-1950* (Toronto, 1981). For an interpretation of personalist politics at work in the United States during the 1980s, see Robert D. Holsworth, *Let Your Life Speak: A Study of Politics, Religion, and Antinuclear Weapons Activism* (Madison, Wis., 1989).

16. "A Mighty League," *Catholic Worker*, April 1938, 1.

17. See for example, "Lay Apostolate," *Catholic Worker*, November 1939, 2.

18. Pax was a Catholic peace organization, originally founded in England by Eric Gill and others. An American chapter of Pax was formed within the Catholic Worker by William Callahan and Joseph Zarrella in February 1937. Members pledged not to carry weapons or to assist in war, and the organization supported the right of Catholics to pursue conscientious objection. See Eileen Egan, "Dorothy Day: Pilgrim of Peace," in Patrick G. Coy, ed., *Revolution of the Heart: Essays on the Catholic Worker*, (Philadelphia, 1992), 76.

19. Raymond W. Friem, "Lauds 'Pax' at Pittsburgh Rally," *Catholic Worker*, May 1938, 2, 4.

20. G. Barry O'Toole, *St. Telemachus—Martyr, Catholic Worker*, March 1940, 7.

21. See for example, "Conscientious Objectors in St. Francis' Time," *Catholic Worker*, July-August 1941, 1; and "On the Use of Force by St. John Chrysostom," *Catholic Worker*, July-August 1941, 1. See also "Patristics and Peace," *Catholic Worker*, June 1943, 2, 3, cited in Eileen Egan, "Dorothy Day: Pilgrim of Peace," in Coy, ed., *Revolution of the Heart*, 83-84.

22. Quoted in Francis Sicius, "Catholic Conscientious Objectors During World War II," M.A. thesis, Florida State University, 1973, 43.

23. "Our Dear Sweet Christ on Earth," *Catholic Worker*, September 1942, 1.

24. Sicius, "Catholic Conscientious Objectors," 45.

25. George Barry O'Toole, *War and Conscription at the Bar of Christian Morals* (New York: Catholic Worker Press, 1941).

26. For Hugo's own account of the retreat material, see John J. Hugo, *Your Ways Are Not My Ways: The Radical Christianity of the Gospel, 2 vols.* (Pittsburgh, 1986). See also a collection of his articles from the *Catholic Worker* under the same title: *Weapons of the Spirit* (New York, 1943). Secondary sources on Hugo include William Miller, *All Is Grace: The Spirituality of Dorothy Day* (New York, 1987), which includes excerpts from Day's notes on the retreat, and Brigid O'Shea Merriman, O.S.F., *Searching for Christ: The Spirituality of Dorothy Day* (Notre Dame, Ind., 1994). For a critical interpretation of Hugo and the effects of his retreats on Day's spirituality, see James Terence Fisher, *The Catholic Counterculture in America, 1933-1962* (Chapel Hill, N.C., 1989).

27. The best overall treatment of conscientious objection during World War II is probably Mulford Sibley and Philip Jacob, *Conscription of Conscience: The American State and the Conscientious Objector, 1940-1947* (Ithaca, N.Y., 1952). For a survey of the Catholic perspective on war and conscription, see Ronald G. Musto, *The Catholic Peace Tradition* (Maryknoll, N.Y., 1986), especially 168-86. For the Protestant peace church perspective, see Albert N. Keim and Grant M. Stoltzfus, *The Politics of Conscience: The Historic Peace Churches and America at War, 1917-1955* (Scottdale, Pa., 1988). For the wider Protestant perspective, see Leyton Richards, *Christian Pacifism After Two World Wars* (London, 1948). An oral history with valuable analysis of the moral reasoning of World War II conscientious objectors can be found in Cynthia Eller, *Conscientious Objectors and the Second World War* (New York, 1991). And for a comparative listing of official statements from a variety of religious traditions, see Beth Ellen Boyle, *Words of Conscience: Religious Statements on Conscientious Objection* (Washington, D.C., 1983).

28. Three useful surveys of the role of Thomistic thought in American Catholicism are Philip Gleason, *Keeping the Faith: American Catholicism Past and Present* (Notre Dame, Ind., 1987), 166-77; Patrick W. Carey, ed., *American Catholic Religious Thought* (New York, 1987), 36-57; and Halsey, *The Survival of American Innocence*, 138-69. For an especially influential expression of Thomism from an American Catholic, see John Courtney Murray, S.J., *We Hold These Truths: Catholic Reflections on the American Proposition* (New York, 1960). On the general lack of knowledge and acceptance of Neo-Thomism outside Catholic circles, Gleason cites Charles A. Hart, "Twenty-five Years of Thomism," *New Scholasticism* 25 (1951): 41-44. There were exceptions to this pattern, including at the University of Chicago in the thirties.

29. Gleason, *Keeping Faith*, 168.

30. John J. Hugo, "The Immorality of Conscription," *Catholic Worker*, November 1944, 6.

31. G. Barry O'Toole, "Against Conscription," *Catholic Worker*, December 1939, 1, 3; and G. Barry O'Toole, "A Council—Not a Commandment," *Catholic Worker*, November 1940, 1, 3, 4. See also Hugo, "The Immorality of Conscription," *Catholic Worker*, November 1944, 4, 5. On the role of vocation in Catholic moral theology, see Josef Fuchs, S.J., *Human Values and Christian Morality* (Dublin, 1970), especially 8-25.

32. For O'Toole's position on the immorality of aggressive war, see especially his "Further Conditions of Just War," *Catholic Worker*, May 1940, 6. See also O'Toole, "St. Thomas and Aggressive War," *Catholic Worker*, February 1940, 1, 3, 6, where he addresses issues of lawful authority, just cause, and right intention. Beyond the aforementioned Thomistic conditions for a just war, O'Toole also addressed the three conditions added to the theory after Aquinas: right way, due proportion, and no alternative. Unlike some other theorists, O'Toole maintained that unless *all* of the criteria were met, a war could not be considered just. See O'Toole, "Further Conditions of Just Wars," *Catholic Worker*, June 1940, 2, 6. For a different and more recent perspective on the criteria and modern war, see James Turner Johnson, *Can Modern War Be Just?* (New Haven, Conn.), 1984.

33. O'Toole, "Against Conscription," *Catholic Worker*, November 1939, 1, 3.

34. G. Barry O'Toole, "Conscription," *Catholic Worker*, October 1939, 1, 3.

35. O'Toole, "Against Conscription," *Catholic Worker*, December 1939, 1, 3.

36. O'Toole, "Further Conditions," *Catholic Worker*, June 1940, 2, 6.

37. Ibid. Although material from the moral manuals is sprinkled through most of O'Toole's writing for the *Catholic Worker*, this article is especially illustrative of the practice.

38. G. Barry O'Toole, "Thou Shalt Not Kill," *Catholic Worker*, January 1940, 3.

39. O'Toole, "Further Conditions of Just War," *Catholic Worker*, May 1940, 4.

40. O'Toole, "Further Conditions of Just War," *Catholic Worker*, March 1940, 6.

41. See for example Bede Jarrett, O.P., *The Emperor Charles IV* (New York, 1935), and *Social Theories of the Middle Ages* (London, 1926).

42. Bede Jarrett, "Conscience," *Catholic Worker*, October 1940, 4.

43. See Bede Jarrett, "Infallibility of Conscience," *Catholic Worker*, November 1941, 4.

44. Some examples include: "Letters from Conscientious Objectors Strive to Give Their Basis of Belief," *Catholic Worker*, January 1941, 2, 3; "Catholic Inductee States His Indictment of Force," *Catholic Worker*, April 1941, 4; X. Y., "We Are Not Alone," *Catholic Worker*, February 1941, 1, 6; Mary A. Dougherty, "Rochester Letter Discusses C.O.'s in War and Peace," *Catholic Worker*, May 1942, 3; and "English Court Tests Conscience," *Catholic Worker*, March 1940, 1, 2.

45. Dorothy Day, "Fear In Our Time," in *Peace Through Reconciliation*, Proceedings of Pax Conference at Spoede House, Rugeley, England, 18 October 1963, p. 14 (mimeo).

46. For examples of this sort of clerical behavior, see Gordon C. Zahn, *War, Conscience and Dissent* (New York, 1967), 147-48; and Gordon C. Zahn, *Another Part of the War: The Camp Simon Story* (Amherst, Mass., 1979), 26-27.

47. Charles E. Curran, *American Catholic Social Ethics: Twentieth-Century Approaches* (Notre Dame, Ind., 1982), 157.

48. McNeal, *Harder Than War*, 51-52.

49. Earl Boyea, "The National Catholic Welfare Conference: An Experience in Episcopal Leadership, 1935-1945, Ph.D. diss., Catholic University of America, 1987, 179, as quoted in McNeal, *Harder Than War*, 53.

50. "Pittsburgh Priest Repudiates Draft," *Catholic Worker*, September 1944, 1. The two accompanying articles on the front page were entitled "Catholic U. Priest on Bombings" and "St. Paul Priest Goes on Record." In the former, a talk in Boston by Paul Hanly Furfey was reported, in which he denounced the obiliteration bombing of

Hamburg and the bombing of the Ruhr dam. In the latter article, Harvey Egan called the war unjust and in violation of the ethical demands of the gospels, and he encouraged the Catholic Worker in its stand.

51. John J. Hugo, "The Immorality of Conscription," *Catholic Worker*, November 1944, 3-10.

52. "About the Special Supplement," *Catholic Worker*, December 1944, 3.

53. McNeal, *Harder Than War*, 78.

54. The real battle on universal military training took place after the war, from 1946 to 1947, when the Truman administration proposed a bill to that effect to replace the Selective Service Act, which was to expire in March 1947. An uncommon coalition of pacifist and non-pacifist organizations defeated it, led by John Swomley. For an account of the campaign, see John M. Swomley, Jr., *The Military Establishment* (Boston, 1964).

55. Hugo, "Conscription," 4, 5.

56. Ibid., 5.

57. Ibid., 7.

58. Ibid., 6, 7.

59. Ibid., 4-10.

60. Ibid., 6; and John J. Hugo, "Catholics Can be Conscientious Objectors," *Catholic Worker*, May 1943, 6.

61. For Maurin's thought see Marc H. Ellis, *Peter Maurin: Prophet in the Twentieth Century* (New York, 1981), especially 45-72, and Geoffrey B. Gnuehs, "Peter Maurin's Personalist Democracy," in Coy, ed., *A Revolution of the Heart*, 47-68.

62. This characterization of conscience is from the Vatican II document *Gaudium et Spes*.

63. Zahn, *Another Part of the War*, 33.

64. *The Challenge of Peace: God's Promise and Our Response*, Pastoral Statement of the U.S. Conference of Catholic Bishops, para. 328.

65. For a useful discussion of this two-track approach to the church's role in society, see Garry Wills, *Under God: Religion and American Politics* (New York, 1990), 305-17.

66. Thomas A. Lynch, "Dorothy Day and Cardinal McIntyre: Not Poles Apart," *Church* (Summer 1992): 10-15.

67. Ibid.

68. Interview with Dorothy Day in James Finn, *Protest: Pacifism and Politics* (New York, 1967), 376.

69. Lynch, "Dorothy Day and Cardinal McIntyre," 13-14.

70. Ibid, 14.

71. Leo V. Kanawada, Jr., *Franklin Roosevelt's Diplomacy on American Catholics, Italians, and Jews* (Ann Arbor, Mich., 1980).

72. McNeal, *Harder Than War*, 67.

5

Prophecy Faces Tradition: The Pacifist Debate During World War II

Francis J. Sicius

"Damn war! Damn Pacifism and Stands! I think I miss the peace—the tranquility of order within the CW [Catholic Worker] more than the peace that went with Munich."[1] In the fall of 1941, a disheartened John Cogley left the Catholic Worker movement. He had lived and worked with the movement on Mott Street in New York, and he took the dream with him to Chicago where he helped start a Catholic Worker house and a newspaper that, Dorothy Day admitted "far outshines our own poor effort."[2] But in 1941, Cogley could no longer call the Catholic Worker his spiritual and intellectual home. He wrote to Day telling her that he had to "disassociate [himself] from the movement."[3]

World War II marked an important watershed in the history of the Catholic Worker and historians have documented Day's personal commitment, which brought pacifism into the sphere of American Catholic thought.[4] This act precipitated a debate between the Chicago and New York Catholic Worker houses, a debate that reflected the intellectual and spiritual chasm created throughout the entire Catholic Worker when Dorothy Day presented pacifism as the cornerstone of the movement.

As a socialist, Day had opposed World War I before her conversion to Catholicism, and it was easy for her to transform this very personal conviction into a Catholic one.[5] As early as the first year of publication of the *Catholic Worker* in 1933, Day announced that its delegates would attend the United States Congress Against The War and they would represent "Catholic pacifism."[6] In the early years, from time to time the paper published articles against conscription, reviews of books written by European Catholic pacifists, and articles calling for the formation of a Catholic organization of conscientious objectors.[7] In the fall of 1936, with the majority of influential Catholic voices calling for a Franco victory in Spain, Dorothy Day strongly reiterated her pacifist position in the *Catholic Worker*. "When nobody thinks any longer of fraternity or their duties of charity and one seeks his brother to kill him, it is then," she declared, "that as Catholics and among Catholics we have to condemn the wrong sense of those of our co-religionists who deliver themselves up to violence, to insult, and to reprisals for the sake of pagan principles."[8] Throughout the isolationist thirties, followers and members of the Catholic Worker had accepted Dorothy Day's pacifism.

Until the end of 1940, the Chicago Catholic Worker also appeared to follow the banner of peace unfurled by Dorothy Day. In May 1939, as the Spanish Civil War was ending, the Chicago paper published an article by Lawrence Heaney entitled "The Spirit of Peace." In it, Heaney wrote that the only way to obtain "tranquility of order in society" is to follow Christ's counsel to "love your enemies." "We have not loved our enemies," he concluded, "and the result [is] universal distrust and hatred." Later that same year, as the United States began to debate the issue of peacetime conscription, John Cogley voiced the Chicago Catholic Workers' opposition. "We oppose conscription of men and money during war time," he editorialized. "If rights of conscience are inalienable, war . . . cannot nullify that right." He also supported the New York Catholic Worker's national effort to have all readers register their "opposition [to the draft] to Congress now."[9] The *Chicago Catholic Worker* also called for a rewriting of the neutrality statutes to end the exportation of all war material to foreign nations. "With 11 million men unemployed [in 1939]," Cogley warned that it would be "no easy matter for the government to steer clear of the shoals of war profiteering."[10]

When it became obvious that President Roosevelt was preparing the country for entry into the war, the *Chicago Catholic Worker* joined its New York counterparts in denouncing the country's "mad scramble . . . forward into an armament program." Cogley seemed to have been influenced and certainly agreed with Peter Maurin's "Easy Essay" published the year before in the *Catholic Worker*. "They are increasing armaments," Maurin wrote, "in the fallacious hope that they will preserve peace by preparing for war." But, he warned, "before 1914 they prepared for war and got it."[11] Similarly, Cogley remarked, that arms buildup would not provide for security but only "serve as an occasion for furthering the rapidly increasing war hysteria."[12] Through 1940, opposition to a national draft and to military preparedness unified the peace movement within the Catholic Worker. However, during the early months of 1940, Dorothy Day's search for a deeper basis for her pacifism placed the Catholic Worker on an intellectual and spiritual path that would eventually separate it from many of its followers.

It had become clear to Day that slogans and pious expressions of peace were meaningless in the face of the horrors of Nazi Germany. Others noted this shortcoming in her early pacifism. John Hugo, a priest who had a tremendous intellectual and spiritual influence on Day in the early forties, wrote to her, "No doubt pacifism is clear to you, but you have not tried to work it out doctrinally

. . . [pacifism] must proceed from truth or it cannot exist at all." Historians have also pointed out that at the beginning of World War II, Catholic pacifism occupied a "weak intellectual position."[13] However, William Miller notes that faced with the tremendous challenge that World War II presented to her pacifism, Day turned to the very spiritual position that "nothing—neither political forms, economic forms, nor even . . . life—was equal to that act . . . that looked only to God's love as an example."[14] Increasingly, articles concerning the Catholic Worker's spiritual basis for pacifism began to dominate the paper.

Day emphasized a tradition of Catholic nonviolence once maintained by Francis Assisi, Isadore Pelusiate, and other, more obscure saints. During the same year she also published Franziskus Stratmann's call for Catholic pacifism and G. Barry O'Toole's explanation of the connection between pacifism and the counsels of Christ.[15] But as the New York Catholic Worker became clearly and absolutely pacifist, the rest of Catholic America, including many Catholic Workers, were moving in the opposite direction. As historian George Flynn noted, "[W]ithout Vatican guidance, American Catholic leaders had concluded that World War II satisfied the criteria for a just war in accordance with the definition of that concept in Catholic theology."[16] Even Jacques Maritain, who had lectured at both the New York and Chicago Catholic Worker Houses and wrote for the New York *Catholic Worker* in the thirties, separated himself from it on the issue of the war. Although he opposed intervention in the Spanish Civil War, Maritain saw the Second World War differently.[17] Calling it a just war, the French philosopher said that the "Allies could count on the help of God" in their struggle against the Nazis.[18]

In the spring of 1940, challenges to pacifism exploded throughout the Catholic Worker. One reader complained, "The pacifism you preach is false, unpatriotic and dangerous." Jerome Drolet, a labor priest associated with a Catholic Worker house in Louisiana, also urged Day to change her stand, since the war demanded every means necessary "to preserve our civilization, or what's left of it, so it will not be set back a couple of centuries by the Nazi Iron Heel."[19] Charles Owen Rice, leader of the Catholic Radical Alliance in Pittsburgh, also broke with the Catholic Worker on the issue of pacifism.[20] And from the Catholic Worker house in Seattle, H. A. Reinhold asked Day, "I wonder if you can take the name of the whole movement which stands for more things than conscription and tag it on this one issue, throwing out all those who do not agree with you." Complaining that the pacifist articles in the *Catholic Worker* had caused disruptions in the Seattle house that "were far from pacific," Reinhold informed Day that they had suppressed the New York paper but continued to distribute the *Chicago Catholic Worker*.[21]

Although there were no strict pacifists in the Chicago Worker house, there were a number of conscientious objectors. In Chicago, the issue remained one of individual conscience worked out within the tradition of just-war theology. Thus, dialogue on war at the Chicago house did not take on a bitter tone. Ed

Marciniak, a noninterventionist, and John Cogley, an interventionist, remained close friends sympathetic to each other's point of view. Jim O'Gara, a Chicago Catholic Worker at the time, recalled that there were many discussions but little animosity. "Cogley and Marciniak both thought as Thomists," he said. They both scrutinized the war in the context of the just-war theory. One concluded the war was just, the other that it was not. It was ultimately a matter of conscience, which each respected."[22]   John Hayes, a Chicago priest who frequented the house in the thirties, had similar recollections. He remembered "a great deal of discussion around the house" [on the pacifist issue]. He felt that "Dorothy Day could arouse enthusiasm, but her position did not promote reasonable argument. Simply by force of her personality and goodness she could make pacifists out of people. Dorothy was overzealous as a pacifist," he recalled, "and perhaps in the long run she was right. But at the time pacifism was not such an open and shut case—given the reality of Hitler."[23]   Hayes surmised from conversations at the Chicago Catholic Worker that those opposed to the war agreed that Hitler was wrong and should be stopped; they just personally could not put themselves in a position where they would submit themselves to what they viewed as the demands of an amoral war machine. Ed Marciniak's letter to his draft board seemed to support Hayes's observation: "If the means Hitler uses have been judged immoral," he wrote, "then those actions would be immoral no matter who utilized them."[24]

But even many of the conscientious objectors in Chicago had difficulty accepting Day's theology of pacifism, which was based on her interpretation of the counsels of the gospel and not on Thomistic philosophy. As the controversy unfolded, three positions eventually became clear: the absolute pacifist (Day) who followed the counsels of Christ to determine that all war was evil, the noninterventionist (Marciniak) who followed the church teachings on war to determine that World War II was not a just war, and the interventionist (Cogley) who determined from the same church teachings that World War II fulfilled the requirements for a just war. The guiding principle among the Chicagoans remained the right and responsibility of individuals to develop their own conscience on the issue of war and peace. It troubled them that Day and others in New York had become, at least for a while, "dictatorially" pacifist.[25]

Cogley questioned Day's adoption of pacifism as a "Catholic Worker stand." He had assumed that "the approved teachings of the Church were . . . the only charter the movement had." Until there was a definitive statement by the bishops, Cogley reasoned that intervention should remain an issue of individual conscience. Without any discussion, he felt, Day had made pacifism the position of the movement, and all of a sudden he was in opposition to the Catholic Worker movement. Having read in the New York paper, "We [Catholic Workers] believe in pacifism," Cogley complained, "nobody asked me [if I was a pacifist]." He reminded Day "that bishops receive special help from the Holy Ghost to lead their people. We don't. We had a lot of nerve," he wrote, "offering theological and philosophical advice to the mass of

Catholics." Years later Cogley wrote, "I am astonished now at the high ideals we had . . . , ideals that grew out of the tradition of Roman Catholicism. The Church laid down the guidelines, whatever the subject." But Day's devotion was different, Cogley suggested. Her "piety was nurtured by the ideals found in the lives of the saints, somehow marvelously integrated with the noble Marxism she had been exposed to earlier."[26] Day was closer to the eschatological theology of the early Christians than most traditional Catholics. Although she had the devotion of a primitive Christian, Cogley observed that she also had a spiritual need for the sacramental element of the church. "She took pleasure," he later wrote, "in genuflecting, holy water, sacred signs and bodily movements in worship."[27]

In the thirties, the Catholic Worker had embodied much more than pacifism. The movement had applied Church teachings to current social problems. Catholic Workers helped the poor, supported labor, and advocated Catholic rural life. The radicals within the movement accepted Peter Maurin's view that it was time to "build the new within the shell of the old" by using the "dynamite" of Catholic social teaching.[28] But with the concentration on pacifism and the division it caused, Cogley feared that the broader meaning of the CW movement would be lost. Furthermore, he believed that Day's pacifism was "heresy" and to agree with her would mean "cutting off from a much larger world."[29]

Despite these philosophic differences between the Chicago and the New York groups, few readers or casual volunteers were cognizant of the conflict. Jim O'Gara recalled that he came to the house relatively late (1940) and he was there "quite a few months" before he was aware of the "pacifist controversy."[30] Editorially, throughout 1940 the *Chicago Catholic Worker* supported the New York position. In January 1940 the *Chicago Catholic Worker* noted: "Today when international questions are being settled by force of arms we need another St. Francis Assisi who would outlaw wars by forbidding his followers to carry arms."[31]

In September 1940, in an attempt to help people resolve their consciences on the issue of war and peace, the *Chicago Catholic Worker* published Jesuit Daniel Lord's advocacy of Catholic pacifism. "A Christlike pacifist is not antiwar, but pro Christlike peace," Lord wrote. "He [Christian pacifist] knows it is harder to be a saint than a soldier. . . . He believes that Christ the peacemaker is far stronger than Caesar the conqueror." In the same issue the paper denounced the Burke-Wadsworth Conscription Bill. "When President Roosevelt signed the bill on September 16 [1940] . . . , the princes of darkness and despair had prevailed against the princes of light and liberty . . . . the totalitarian forces of oppression and contempt for human personality had triumphed over the Christian standards of freedom and justice and of an appreciation of men's worth as temples of the Holy Ghost." In this same issue the *Chicago Catholic Worker* pledged "by prayer and example and by the use of every constitutional means possible to fight for the repeal of conscription."[32] The September 1940 issue, the strongest that the Chicago movement ever published against intervention, brought them into conflict with the official church hierarchy. This did not happen often since the Chicago Catholic Worker normally fell comfortably under the mantle of the local Catholic hierarchy. It was even included, Jim O'Gara recalled, in the official Catholic directory of the city.[33]

In the 1930s, Cardinal George Mundelein and Auxiliary Bishop Bernard Sheil made the Catholic church in Chicago one of the most socially progressive in the country. The archdiocese sponsored the foundation of the CYO (Catholic Youth Organization), Cisca (Catholic Intra Student Catholic Action), Catholic labor schools, a Catholic theater, and other groups that supported Catholic social action. In this environment, the Catholic Worker in Chicago received a great deal of support from the official church. The seminarians of the diocese took up regular collections for the Catholic Worker, the Poor Clare nuns made monthly food deliveries, and Cecilia Himbaugh frequently sent members of the archdiocesan youth group Cisca to the Catholic Worker house to help out.[34] Cogley even remembered receiving visits and donations from one of the bishops.[35]

But when the Chicago Catholic Worker attempted to publish an antiwar edition of its paper, the archdiocese suppressed it. Cardinal Mundelein and his successor Samuel Stritch (after May 1940) were both staunch supporters of the New Deal. Mundelein was one of the first of the hierarchy to support Roosevelt in his push for preparedness. As early as 1938, Mundelein sent ripples through the diplomatic world with his speech against Hitler in which he called him an "Austrian paperhanger and a bad one at that." And in 1939 after he made his important and controversial "Quarantine the Enemy" speech, Roosevelt dined with Mundelein. According to his biographer, Mundelein's pro-Roosevelt speeches and activities certified for Catholic voters that Roosevelt was a safe, noncommunist political leader. In return for Mundelein's support, Roosevelt had put the unofficial American seal of approval on Catholicism.[36] The alliance established by Mundelein marked an important watershed in the history of American Catholicism, and the hierarchy clearly did not want to threaten it or betray the president's preparedness campaign with Catholic antiwar propaganda. Perhaps this helps to explain the Machiavellian tactics adopted by the chancery office against the Chicago Catholic Worker on this occasion.

The same month that the *Chicago Catholic Worker* peace issue appeared, the archdiocese staged a youth conference that in essence became a prowar rally.[37] A few days before the event was scheduled to begin, the archdiocese called the Chicago Catholic Worker asking if they had any more issues containing Fr. Lord's article on pacifism for distribution. Although Marciniak and Jay Morgan filled the request, no one ever saw the papers at the meeting. Marciniak and Cogley attended, and the latter described it as "steam roller military machine," which offended him, "a non-pacifist just as [much as] Marciniak the fervent pacifist." Shocked and dismayed, Cogley described the event as a "farce." Amid continuous shouts of 'God Bless America,' Bishop

Robert Lucey told listeners that anyone who said that modern war couldn't be justified was "as stupid as he was morally haywire." Those who held opposing views were silenced. "I feel certain, Cogley wrote, "if at that moment the Archbishop had put his fatherly approval on immediate entrance into the war they would have immediately left the hall and unquestioningly moved right on into the nearest battle-field." The whole technique, he observed "was Nazi."[38]

Later, Cogley and Marciniak learned that the pacifist issues of their paper had been destroyed specifically to prevent their distribution at the rally.[39] Ironically, the same month that the Chicago Catholic Workers prepared their strongest stand against the war, Dorothy Day decided to send out to all the Catholic Worker Houses a letter, which Tom Sullivan later referred to as "Dorothy's Encyclical."

"We know that there are those who are members of the Catholic Worker groups throughout the country who do not stand with us on this issue," she wrote. "We have not been able to change their views through what we have written in the paper, by letters, or by personal conversation." Groups could continue to disagree with pacifism, but they must continue to distribute the *Catholic Worker*.[40] In Chicago, they must have taken the last comment very personally because they knew that some houses had decided to distribute the *Chicago Catholic Worker* only and that the Chicago House was becoming the focal point for those opposed to Day's pacifism. At one point Cogley complained to Marjorie Crowe at the New York house that all he ever heard about was "the CW war position and our being in disagreement [with it]." In this letter Cogley tried to clarify that he was not in opposition to people following the counsels of perfection; he just did not think people should be compelled to accept that position.[41]

In *Loaves and Fishes* Dorothy Day stated, "Our work in getting out the paper was an attempt to arouse the conscience of others, not to advise action for which they were not prepared."[42] But her letter was not perceived that way. Day was accused of "adopt[ing] dictator's methods, lay[ing] down party lines, [and] purg[ing] dissenters."[43] In Chicago, John Cogley received Day's letter as an ultimatum and prepared to leave the movement. "It was a shock to get your letter," he wrote to Day. "You know I cannot agree with the editorial policy of the CW regarding war."[44] In a few days, however, his initial bitterness dissipated and he accepted Day's invitation to all Catholic Workers to come to Maryfarm, the Catholic Worker farm in Easton, Pennsylvania, to join her in a spiritual retreat. There, they could step back from the controversies that were pulling the Catholic Worker apart.

Following a model established by Onesimus Lacouture, these retreats consisted of a week of absolute silence, meditation, and spiritual exercises. In the late thirties Father John Hugo began conducting Lacouturian retreats at his parish in Pittsburgh and after attending one, Day wrote, "This is what I was looking for. This is what I expected when I became a Catholic." Day saw in Hugo's radical gospel of perfectionism, a spiritual model for the Catholic

Worker, and the priest became a lifelong and influential friend to Day and the Worker movement.[45]

In August of 1940, about seventy-five Catholic Workers joined the retreat at Maryfarm, and when it ended, Day rejoiced in the sense of "comradeship . . . of Christian solidarity" that came out of the meeting.[46] But not all in attendance shared her enthusiasm. After the retreat, Cogley and fellow Catholic Worker Tom Sullivan returned home to Chicago even more distressed than when they had left. The retreat made it clear to them that they had to leave the movement that had played such an important part in their lives. Cogley wanted to discuss intervention, but every time he brought up the question, he was told that pacifism had been the position of the Catholic Worker all along. "That is supposed to answer everything," he complained. "But that doesn't answer anything; all that does is point to the consistency of the Worker. And consistency," he pointed out, "can be a virtue of fools."[47]

The lack of debate on the war troubled Cogley. He considered the implications of a retreat conducted by pacifist priests and dominated by pacifists. Although Day insisted that her letter did not mean he had to accept her pacifism to be a Catholic Worker, Cogley resented the very clear attitude at the New York Worker that he was now, because of his views on the war, simply "tolerated" as a member.[48] He had always felt that the Catholic Worker had supported a spirit of intellectual and spiritual freedom. The only "charter" the movement had was the teachings of the Church.[49]

The *Chicago Catholic Worker*, Cogley felt, had attempted to stimulate debate on the issue. After publishing Daniel Lord's pacifist article, they received a letter from Edgar Smothers, S.J. which contradicted Lord's position. "If the Jesuits can disagree on the issue," he asked Day, "why can't we?" He complained that the spirit of debate and intellectual curiosity typical of the Worker was stifled on the issue of pacifism. This atmosphere was, he complained, "foreign to the Catholic Worker."[50]

But he also blamed himself. "I had a fine chance to start a controversy at the retreat," he confessed, "but I failed. I felt too hopelessly outnumbered [by the pacifists] and a little self-conscious with the [pacifist] priests present."[51] Day convened an even greater retreat the following year, the first one conducted by Hugo, but Cogley, Sullivan, and the other interventionists at the Chicago house did not attend.[52]

The Chicago Catholic Worker continued under Cogley until the end of 1941. There was even enthusiastic talk of opening another house, but with the war upon them, the Catholic Workers soon became caught up in the sweep of events. Jim O'Gara had been drafted along with Tom Sullivan, while Marty Paul, John Doebele, and other members applied for conscientious objector status, and were sent to the Catholic CO camp in New Hampshire. Ed Marciniak received a deferment and immersed himself in the labor movement while earning a living teaching sociology part time at Loyola University. Sullivan passed by the Catholic Worker house in New York before he went to boot camp and recalled that Day tried one last time to influence his decision. Finally, in frustration Sullivan told her, "Hitler won't be persuaded by pietistic phrases, Dorothy, the only thing he understands is a gun put to his head."[53]

Ironically, Cogley had a hard time trying to enlist in the army. Reynold Hillenbrand, the director of the Chicago seminary and a well-known social activist in the city, had taken it upon himself to explain to Cogley's draft board the significance of the young man's work on Blue Island Avenue. He urged that Cogley be allowed to continue there. This letter from the distinguished priest so impressed the draft board, dominated (in Cogley's words) by "Italian-American Catholics," that they decided Cogley should be exempted from the draft.[54]

Cogley could not accept the deferment. He persuaded the draft board to induct him, but only after he had found a home for each of the men living at the Catholic Worker house. The Little Sisters of the Poor volunteered to take all of his charges and, early in 1942, the Chicago Catholic Worker house closed. Cogley married Theodora Schmidt and shortly thereafter he entered the army.[55] The Catholic Worker movement in Chicago did not remain defunct for long. In the summer of 1942, a group of Catholic conscientious objectors working at the Alexian Brothers hospital opened a house at 1208 Webster Street. In the ensuing decades there would be other Catholic Workers and houses.[56]

The economic collapse of the thirties had provided the common cause around which the Catholic Workers of that decade rallied. The movement had attracted all those who shared a sense of social justice, but the pacifist debate diminished this bond. Day's stand on war alienated many, but those who remained in the movement believed that the Catholic Worker was more than an instrument of liberal social reform. They embraced Christ's counsels of perfection as the basis for a radical community that stood as a protest to the bourgeois world and all its instruments, especially modern warfare.

Some historians have noted that it was the pacifist issue that separated the liberals from the radicals within the movement.[57] But the controversy's more important contribution was that it marked the beginning of an evolution of U.S. Catholic thought on war that led to an eventual acceptance of pacifism within the Catholic tradition. The demonic nature of World War II, or rather the demonic characteristics attributed to Hitler, led Catholic thinkers to scrutinize their church's position on war and peace. Catholic leaders perceived the war as a crusade against evil. Historian George Flynn pointed out that "Catholic periodical literature repeatedly explained Hitler in terms of his alliance with the devil. . . . Equally persuasive was the assumption that a special providential hand guided the United States."[58]

Within the Catholic Worker, both the pacifists and the interventionists saw Hitler as a manifestation of evil which they had to oppose. The pacifists, following the wisdom of the counsels of perfection, believed that the only way to defeat hate was through love. The interventionists saw the need to destroy this manifestation of evil with armed force in alliance with Divine Providence. There was no room for compromise.

The division inside the Worker movement between conventional just-war advocates and absolute pacifists can be seen as a manifestation of the tension between tradition and prophecy, which is a characteristic of the church. On one side Cogley and the interventionists, and even some noninterventionists, arrived at their position by applying the just-war theory and so represented the traditional temper of the church. On the other hand, Day and the pacifists followed the counsels of perfection to the point of opposing all war and so represented its prophetic dimension.

Theologian Franziskus Stratmann called the Catholic pacifists prophets, and he reminded them that, although the traditional church was opposed to "pacifism and did not support the movement toward the condemnation of all war," the traditional church at one time had opposed many positions that it now embraced, for example, slavery and serfdom. He maintained great faith in the evolutionary power of the church, however, and wrote that only the person "who does not realize the wonder of the Church and her life in Christ can be disturbed that her process is impeded." Stratmann affirmed that those who believe "in Christ and his Church know that the Church will eventually accept non-violence."[59]

History has proven Stratmann correct. As early as 1944 *Commonweal*, which supported the war, condemned the unrestricted bombing of Germany as being against the principles of a just war. And in the early sixties, the Vatican Council, continuing the political debate on pacifism that had begun within the Catholic Worker during the Second World War, concluded that within the context of the just war theory, modern nuclear war was immoral. Although this statement did not satisfy the pacifists, it did move the church in their direction.[60] Finally, in their 1983 pastoral letter, the bishops of the United States formalized the trend toward a theology and practice of peace. This document combined the counsel of the gospels with the just-war teaching of the church and represented for the first time an attempt by theologians to reconcile the just-war tradition with pacifism.[61] With this historic letter, the pacifist dispute begun by the Catholic Worker came to a point of accommodation, if not reconciliation within the American Catholic Church.

NOTES

1. John Cogley to Dorothy Day, n.d., Catholic Worker Papers, W-4 Box 1, Marquette University Archives, Milwaukee, Wisconsin (hereafter referred to as CW Papers).

2. *Catholic Worker*, September 1938.

3. Cogley to Day, September, 1940, CW Papers, W-4, Box 1.

4. Mel Piehl, *Breaking Bread: The Catholic Worker and the Origin of Catholic Radicalism in America* (Philadelphia, 1982), 158-59, 198; Patricia McNeal, *Harder Than War: Catholic Peacemaking in Twentieth-Century America* (New Brunswick, N.J., 1992), 36, 46-48; William D. Miller, *A Harsh and Dreadful Love* (New York, 1973), 13, 182-84.

5. Miller, *Harsh and Dreadful*, 161; McNeal, *Harder Than War*, 36-38.

6. Miller, *Harsh and Dreadful*, 159; *Harder Than War*, McNeal, 37.

7. McNeal, *Harder Than War*, 37-38; Piehl, *Breaking Bread*, 192-193.

8. *Catholic Worker*, December 1936; Piehl, *Breaking Bread*, 122-23, 192-193; McNeal, *Harder Than War*, 23-24; Miller, *Harsh and Dreadful*, 138-39.

9. *Chicago Catholic Worker*, May 1939; September-October 1939.

10. *Chicago Catholic Worker*, September-October 1939.

11. Marc Ellis, *Peter Maurin: Prophet in the Twentieth Century* (New York, 1981), 144; *Catholic Worker*, April 1938. Maurin's own position on the war is not explicit. His most recent biographer hints that he was against conscription and modern war, yet he never embraced Day's pacifism. See Ellis, 144-46. On the other hand, Tom Sullivan, who managed the Catholic Worker in New York in the late forties and early fifties asserts that Maurin was not a pacifist and that he hoped for a strong United Nations–type force to maintain peace among nations. Tom Sullivan, interview by author, tape recording, Rockville Center, New York, 24 June 1976, Marquette University Archives.

12. *Chicago Catholic Worker*, June 1940.

13. Piehl, *Breaking Bread*, 193.

14. Miller, *Harsh and Dreadful*, 167. McNeal also points out Day's spiritual commitment to pacifism after 1940. McNeal, *Harder Than War*, 41-42.

15. *Catholic Worker*, June 1940; November 1940.

16. George Q. Flynn, *Roosevelt and Romanism: Catholics and American Diplomacy, 1937-1945* (Westport, Conn., 1976), 189.

17. Miller, *Harsh and Dreadful*, 139.

18. Jacques Maritain, "Just War," *Commonweal*, 22 December 1939, 199.

19. Quoted in Miller, *Harsh and Dreadful*, 169.

20. Ibid., 119, 174.

21. Ibid.

22. Jim O'Gara, interview by author, tape recording, New York City, 22 June 1976, Marquette University Archives.

23. John Hayes, interview by author, tape recording, Chicago, Illinois, 14 June 1976, Marquette University Archives.

24. Marciniak's written statement to the draft board (n.d.): Marciniak's personal papers.

25. John Cogley, *A Canterbury Tale, Experiences and Reflections: 1916-1976* (New York, 1976), 31; John Cogley to Dorothy Day, 26 September 1940, CW Papers, W-4, Box 1.

26. Cogley, *Canterbury Tale*, 34.

27. McDonald quoted in Cogley, *Canterbury Tale*, 34.

28. Miller, *Harsh and Dreadful*, 158; Peter Maurin, *Easy Essays* (Chicago, 1976), 3, 109.

29. John Cogley to Dorothy Day, n.d., CW Papers, W-4, Box 1.

30. O'Gara interview.

31. *Chicago Catholic Worker*, January 1940.

32. *Chicago Catholic Worker*, September 1940.

33. O'Gara interview.

34. Francis J. Sicius, "The Chicago Catholic Worker 1936 to the Present," Ph.D. diss., Loyola University of Chicago, 1979, 121.

35. Cogley, *Canterbury Tales*, 29.

36. Edward Kantowicz, *Corporation Sole: Cardinal Mundelein and Chicago Catholicism* (Notre Dame, Ind., 1983), 224-28, 235-36.

37. Flynn, *Roosevelt and Romanism*, 116.

38. John Cogley to Nina Polcyn, 8 October 1940, CW Papers, W-17, Box 1.

39. *Chicago Catholic Worker*, December 1940.

40. Miller, *Harsh and Dreadful*, 168.

41. John Cogley to Marjorie Crowe, June 1941, CW Papers, W-4, Box 1.

42. Dorothy Day, *Loaves and Fishes* (New York: Harper, 1963), 60.

43. The objections of other Catholic Workers appear in Miller, *Harsh and Dreadful*, 169.

44. John Cogley to Dorothy Day, 15 August 1940, CW Papers, W-4, Box 1.

45. Piehl, *Breaking Bread*, 87; Miller, *Harsh and Dreadful*, 185-200.

46. Miller, *Harsh and Dreadful*, 187-88.

47. John Cogley to Dorothy Day, 10 October 1940, CW Papers, W-4, Box 1.

48. Cogley to Polcyn, 8 October 1940, CW Papers, W-4, Box 1.

49. John Cogley to Dorothy Day, 26 September 1940, CW Papers, W-4, Box 1.

50. Ibid.

51. Ibid.

52. O'Gara Interview.

53. Sullivan interview.

54. Cogley, *Canterbury Tale*, 58.

55. Ibid.

56. Francis J. Sicius, *The Word Made Flesh: The Chicago Catholic Worker and the Emergence of Lay Activism in the Church* (Lanham, Md., 1990), 181-82.

57. Miller, *Harsh and Dreadful*, 158; Piehl, *Breaking Bread*, 154-55; Sicius, *Word Made Flesh,* 120-24.

58. Flynn, *Roosevelt and Romanism*, 186.

59. *Catholic Worker*, June 1940.

60. Ronald G. Musto, *The Catholic Peace Tradition* (Maryknoll, N.Y., 1986), 252.

61. Ibid., 255-56, 262.

6

The Catholic Worker and Peace in the Early Cold War Era

Mel Piehl

In 1917, writer and critic Randolph Bourne wrote that "the penalty the realist pays for accepting war is to see disappear one by one the justifications for accepting it. . . . The utopian knows that he is ineffective . . . while the realist, evading disillusionment, moves in a twilight zone of half-hearted criticism and hopings for the best."[1] Though less fervently justified than the "war to end war" that Bourne criticized, World War II was also widely presented to Americans as a means to erect a new postwar world order based on democracy and international peace. But compared to the millennial hopes generated by the Wilsonian appeals that Bourne so scathingly attacked, the general American mood at the end of World War II soon turned more anxious and fatalistic than hopeful. While some Rooseveltian liberals still looked to the new United Nations as an idealistic instrument to prevent future wars, other Americans and their leaders began to envision essentially a *Pax Americana* "backed by force if necessary," as President Harry Truman stated on 27 October 1945.[2] But within two years after the end of the war the notion that there could be even a unilateral American-sponsored world order had faded, as conflict with the Soviet Union over Eastern Europe generated the beginnings of the bitter cold war that was to last for decades. The military victory of 1945 thus yielded not peace but the near-constant threat of war with the Soviet Union and other communist states—a danger made far more threatening by the advent of nuclear weapons.

In this context of developing cold war, nuclear weapons, and an increasingly hegemonic national security state, the small groups of Americans like the Catholic Worker movement who rejected all war seemed even more "irrelevant" to realists than Bourne could have imagined. As Charles DeBenedetti, a historian, has observed, radical pacifism in the immediate postwar era "seemed frankly anomalous in a society that had gained so much from war. Neither sympathetic Protestants nor political liberals could comprehend the second failure within a generation to bring peace through war."[3]   With their tiny numbers and weak organization—and facing the near-universal hostility of American society and government to any form of dissent on "National Security" matters—the surprise is not that radical pacifists were relatively ineffective in the years from 1945 to 1960, but that they survived at all.   Even though their activities were small and mostly unnoticed at the time, their very persistence in maintaining their peace witness under duress became perhaps their most effective argument for their cause.   In the case of the Catholic Worker, however, it is not only the intensity and persistence of the peace commitment that deserves notice, but also its particular ideology and means of promoting peace.   The Catholic Worker shared many of these perspectives with other pacifists of the time; but some of its most valuable contributions represented more distinctive products of its own peculiar history and outlook.

When two atomic bombs were dropped on Japan as the last military acts of World War II, the Catholic Worker's reaction to the unprecedented event established one primary theme of its entire postwar peace witness: an attack on all nuclear weapons as an especially heinous means of war.   As pacifists the Workers held that all war was wrong, but Hiroshima and Nagasaki revealed a new dimension to the horror.   Dorothy Day's column in the September 1945 *Catholic Worker*, "We Go on Record," ranks as perhaps the most impassioned and eloquent public protest by any American writer in immediate response to the bomb.   Day inveighed vehemently against the "jubilant" President Truman and the "scientists, army officers, great universities (Notre Dame included), and captains of industry" who had produced this new "slaughter of innocents."   She juxtaposed newspaper accounts of the nuclear laboratories and plants at Oak Ridge, Tennessee ("a large, comfortable-looking chapel benignly settled beside the plant") with back-page headlines about starving Europe ("Germany is Told of Hard Winter by Eisenhower"; "Pall of Apathy Surrounds Bitter, Hungry Vienna").   She sarcastically contrasted the public relations projection of a slick, nuclear-powered postwar prosperity with the daily realities at the Catholic Worker: "And as I write Pigsie . . . sleeps on our doorstep in this best and most advanced and most progressive of all possible worlds . . . here in this greatest of cities which covered the cavern where this stupendous discovery was made, which institutes an era of unbelievable richness and power and glory for man."   And she brought home to her readers the humanity they shared with the hundreds of thousands of anonymous Japanese people who had disappeared in a flash of light: "It is to be hoped they are vaporized, our Japanese brothers, scattered men, women, and babies, to the four winds, over the seven seas. Perhaps we will breathe their dust into our nostrils, feel them in the fog of New York on our faces, feel them in the rain on the hills of Easton [the Catholic Worker farm in Easton, Pennsylvania]."[4]

In the same issue, the pacifist priest John Hugo stressed that it was the peculiar conviction of democratic righteousness with which America had perpetrated the act, even more than its sheer physical destructiveness, that made the bomb so terrible: "This was done, not by Nazis or barbarian militarists," he said, "but by a nation that claimed to be acting in the very name of freedom, of moral justice, of civilization itself."[5]

These instantaneous reactions to Hiroshima and Nagasaki set the tone and agenda for the Catholic Worker's antinuclear propaganda and activism in the following years. The Workers' focus on nuclear issues was especially strong from 1945 to 1949, as it was in the peace movement generally. The issue faded somewhat from the center of Catholic Worker attention in the early fifties but was revived again with new fervor later in that decade. In this latter period the Catholic Worker's particular emphasis became especially identified with the old-time American radical Ammon Hennacy's arrival and with the movement's civil disobedience against nuclear civil defense drills in the late fifties.

Although it advocated immediate and unilateral renunciation of all atomic weapons as a general policy, the Catholic Worker initially focused its antinuclear concern on two immediate issues: atomic testing and the arms race with the Soviet Union. In February 1946, the Catholic Workers protested impending nuclear tests in the South Pacific, although they "held no fatuous hope that . . . [their] small voice raised in protest . . . [could] bring about abandonment of the plans." At the same time their paper also published criticisms of nuclear testing by Dr. Andre Bethune, a Columbia University physical chemist who had worked on the Manhattan Project.[6]

Repeatedly in the immediate postwar years, the Workers contrasted the expense and effort devoted to the nuclear buildup with the widespread hunger and poverty abroad. "Protest Bomb Tests, Feed Europe and Asia" read one *Catholic Worker* headline. As they did with other issues, the Workers diligently sought out and publicized those rare occasions when Roman Catholic leaders—bishops, religious, theologians, or lay groups—made statements that could in any way be interpreted as critical of nuclear weapons or nuclear warfare. The advent of the hydrogen bomb in 1950 brought another round of criticism and protest against what Dorothy Day called "the Satan bomb." Day drew parallels between the H-Bomb and the extraordinarily powerful demons that confronted the disciples in the Gospel of Mark: "People are beginning to say, 'This kind can only be cast out by prayer and fasting.'"[7]

While the Workers considered nuclear weapons to be intrinsically evil, it quickly proved impossible for them and other American peace activists to separate the nuclear buildup from its political justification in the United States, the cold war with Soviet communism. Although more strictly personal conscientious objectors to war could largely dismiss such political contexts as irrelevant to their stance, the more politically engaged Catholic Workers could not ignore the reasons that many people—and especially their fellow Catholics—gave for endorsing the postwar nuclear buildup. As veteran independent radicals since the early thirties, the Worker movement had long experience with the issue of communism, and their perspectives could now be employed to argue the folly of the cold war. Unlike many leftist peace activists, especially some "progressives" drawn to the Henry Wallace campaign of 1948, the Catholic Worker's peace positions were not compromised by implicit or explicit defenses of Soviet foreign policy or communist expansion in Eastern Europe. The Catholic Workers were aware of the character of the communist dictatorship and periodically criticized such things as the suppression of labor organizations and religious liberty in the Soviet Union.

Despite this awareness, the Workers steadfastly refused to join the cold war anticommunist crusade, or accept the idea that military preparation was the only way to defend human freedoms. As they had contended since the thirties, the Workers held that communism was essentially a response to Christian failures to promote social justice, and they maintained that it could only be countered by a deeper Catholic commitment to the welfare of workers and the poor, not by political or military confrontation. The Catholic Workers could not support America's conflict with the Soviet Union, however lofty its justifications, because, they said, they belonged to "the other International," the Catholic Church. "We are Un-American; We are Catholics," they proclaimed in 1948, as patriotic sentiment soared.[8] Quotations from European Catholic writers and newspapers, including the official *Osservatore Romano*, were frequently used to suggest that the universal Catholic Church and even the pope, however anticommunist, did not favor war with the Soviets. The Catholic Worker movement also tried to establish contacts with European Catholic pacifists as a means of demonstrating the international character of their church's witness. In 1952, for instance, the *Catholic Worker* reported on a gathering of European Catholics whose goal was "unifying Catholic opposition to war."[9] Furthermore, the Workers consistently attempted to humanize the Russian people, who were increasingly demonized as an abstract and mindlessly monolithic enemy of the United States.[10]

While the atomic bomb and the cold war were thus the foundational concerns for Catholic pacifists in the late forties, they proved difficult to sustain as public issues because they were at once so overwhelming and so abstract. The brief postwar flowering of American peace activism faded in part because such matters came to seem so remote and intractable, and also because the momentarily influential groups like the United World Federalists and the Federation of Atomic Scientists had trouble maintaining their commitments once the tide of events and American public opinion so plainly turned against them.[11] American pacifists, however, held a rather different outlook, perhaps because so many of them had had intimate experience with draft opposition and the Civilian Public Service system during World War II. Generally more pessimistic about public opinion and international events, and more oriented to immediate experience than many liberal peace advocates, they were able to sustain their opposition to war in general by resisting its impact on the individual in particular.[12] For the Catholic Worker this meant especially a focus on the issue of conscription.

Throughout the postwar period the Catholic Worker upheld the right of conscientious objection, especially for Catholics who were widely believed to be ineligible for such a position. They also opposed conscription in general and promoted draft resistance as an effective and practical means to oppose war. The World War II Catholic objectors, especially Gordon Zahn and Robert Ludlow, formed the core promoters of Catholic pacifism during the postwar years, and their writings in the *Catholic Worker* and elsewhere kept the conscription issue alive in the Catholic community. Until 1948, for instance, the *Catholic Worker* still printed occasional "Pax" columns reporting on Catholic conscientous objectors, some of whom were still being held in civilian camps, work sites, and prisons after the end of World War II. The draft did end for a time, but the cold war quickly brought its return, as well as new proposals for universal military training of all citizens. The CW movement from the beginning viewed with alarm this threat of a permanent, universal draft, especially considering its profound consequences for both civilian society and individual consciences. "If military control of atomic energy is morally wrong," the *Catholic Worker* argued, "is not the same control of human life a far greater evil? We believe that the authority to cut a young man off from his normal life and vocation, to separate him from his family and community, is of far greater importance."[13] When the draft was reinstituted in 1948, the Workers reprinted and distributed seventy-eight thousand copies of John Hugo's pamphlet, "The Immorality of Conscription," publicized the work of pacifist priest Father Marion Casey, and urged young Catholics to refuse to register for the draft. (One published statement urging draft resistance brought Dorothy Day one of her occasional invitations to visit the New York Archdiocesan Chancery.)[14]

The draft remained a primary focus of CW peace concern during the early fifties. Workers criticized conscription as "peacetime militarism," but they felt no differently about it when actual war broke out in Korea in 1950. News of Catholics, Quakers, and other Selective Service nonregistrants received attention, and young people who came to the Catholic Worker frequently found themselves confronting the intensely personal issue of their own service. One dramatic instance of how contact with the Catholic Worker could affect individuals involved Michael Harrington, who first came to St. Joseph's House while still serving in the military reserves. "On drill nights . . . I would wait until everyone was at dinner and then sneak out of the House in my uniform, the livery of my compromise," Harrington later recalled. "There was constant discussion of how I could be so unprincipled. One gentle CW pacifist, Hector Black, was particularly persuasive."[15] Before long Harrington became a committed pacifist, writing articles and speaking on behalf of Catholic pacifism. While such Catholic Worker activity directly affected only a few young men within the movement's orbit, and had almost no public impact beyond periodically rousing the Federal Bureau of Investigation to investigate and harass the Workers, the focus on conscription effectively kept the movement's pacifism from becoming purely abstract and moralistic. Even if the world pursued conflict, and Catholic pacifism had no political impact on American society or the American church, it still demonstrated the power to affect deeply the real lives and destinies of a few people—a more convincing form of witness than many causes could muster.

The fourth focus of Catholic Worker peace activity in the forties and fifties involved the movement's increasing engagement with self-consciously Gandhian forms of nonviolence. This development was not, of course, entirely new or unique to the Catholic Worker. Pacifists of many stripes had long known of Gandhi's nonviolent struggle for Indian independence, and other activist groups—particularly the radical Peacemakers and the Congress of Racial Equality (CORE)—had pioneered efforts to apply Gandhian ideas in the United States after World War II. And all the small, earnest efforts by tiny bands of pacifist and racial activists eventually came to seem to be mere preludes to the spectacularly successful use of nonviolent methods by a young Baptist minister in Montgomery, Alabama, in 1955. Like Gandhi himself, Martin Luther King, Jr. was able to draw into his nonviolent struggle not only a few morally sensitive activists, but the great masses of an oppressed people.[16]

In its own unique way, however, the Catholic Worker was also thinking through and experimenting with Gandhian theories of nonviolence. The Catholic Worker movement grasped more readily than many American pacifists the essentially spiritual underpinnings of Gandhi's principles. Dorothy Day and her followers, along with A. J. Muste and Martin Luther King, Jr. deserve credit for making Gandhianism in America not only a form of morally high-minded politics, but an essentially religious approach to the major social problem of violence. The Catholic Workers underscored the key Gandhian insight that "the means are the ends in becoming" with their own strong emphasis that all ethical means and ends would find their surest foundation in faith.

The Workers' association with other pacifists in the late forties served both to introduce them to more politically active forms of nonviolence and to point out some differences between their outlook and that of some other nonviolent revolutionaries. In August 1947 the Committee For Non-Violent Revolution, a new coalition of antiwar activists, met for a conference at the Catholic Worker farm at Newburgh, New York. While the Workers discovered many points of agreement between themselves and the CNVR activists, especially regarding active nonviolence and distrust of the state, they also noticed some differences in premises. Some of these American radicals' opposition to the state stemmed, some Workers felt, "from an individualism that may err in positing complete liberty as an end in iself." Such self-contained libertarianism was contrary to a properly Catholic understanding of both objective morality and the purpose of human freedom: "The instincts for justice, the divine governance of the world, the realization of truth—all these go on independently of our successes or failures, aside from the 'Revolution,' aside from personalities."[17] Implicit in such commentary was criticism of some of the tendencies in CNVR, for example, the proposals in the journal *Direct Action* for "radical banditry" whereby anarchist activists were urged to "take rather than buy what we want" from illegitimate capitalists, and housewives with hungry families were encouraged to stage a "mass invasion of A&P supermarkets" for the "express purpose of emptying the shelves" and "keeping down the profits of the masters."[18]

As such examples showed, it was not automatically clear what was meant by nonviolent revolution, or how compatible various forms of nonviolent action would be with the Catholic Worker movement's ethical and religious outlook. Throughout the late forties and early fifties, *Catholic Worker* writers like David Mason, Irene Mary Naughton, Robert Ludlow, Michael Harrington, and Eileen Fantino promoted and critically analyzed Gandhian *satyagraha*, gradually refining their own understandings and trying to apply such ideas and methods to a movement based on Catholic principles. The achievement of Indian independence in 1947 and Gandhi's assassination the following year sparked greater interest in the Indian leader's ideas. At first some Catholic Workers worried that Gandhi's outlook might be partially tainted by Indian nationalism. But even national independence was, for Gandhi, not primarily a nationalistic political goal, but a means of restoring human relations between Indians and their British masters on a new, ethical basis. Soon, Robert Ludlow was arguing that *satyagraha* was not simply another useful political technique, but actually "a Christian way" of bringing peace and justice to the world. Furthermore, following scholastic principles, he contended that humanity's growing awareness of the viability of such methods laid new burdens on advocates of just-war theory. "One of the conditions [of a just war] was that every other means must first have been tried and failed. Today that means we are obliged to try the method of Gandhi, that we must try *satyagraha*, and if we refused to do so, then even under natural ethics we are wrong, as we are always wrong when we used violence from a supernatural standpoint."[19]

Gandhianism was especially attractive to the Catholic Worker movement for three reasons: it was spiritually based; it justified and explained the value of morally based social action by individuals or small minorities; and most appealing, it suggested that pacifism could actually be effective in the world. Catholic pacifists, like others, had long faced the charge that their stance was a form of individualistic and self-righteous escape from evil, since they could witness to the evil of war but could not really show how war could be stopped. Gandhianism provided at least a potentially plausible response. "In the event of invasion, direct, nonviolent action by the people, refusal to cooperate with the government on any level, would be its downfall," asserted Eileen Fantino. "Jails would be filled, as in India, but there would come a time when the jails would not be big enough."[20] Whether or not nonpacifists found such arguments persuasive—and mostly they did not—they performed an important function in bolstering Catholic pacifists' morale and gradually altering their self-understanding from that of "moral witness" to a theoretically more practical and politically engaged activism. This was especially important for Catholic pacifists whose religious tradition, unlike that of the historic peace churches and some other traditional war objectors, insisted very strongly on the Christian's responsibility for public and political life.

The Gandhian outlook suggested that nonviolence need not be politically irrelevant. And even more appealing was the idea that if there were, in fact, a morally better way to maintain international peace, order, and justice, the Catholic Church itself might be led to change its mind about just war and declare pacifism a universal Christian norm. This line of argument was developed by Robert Ludlow and others. He pointed out that prior Catholic teaching on war and peace had not been based on the full doctrinal authority of the church, and that therefore prior pronouncements were not necessarily permanently binding. Drawing on Cardinal Newman's argument that Catholic doctrine is never static but rather evolutionary, as the church's tradition develops under the guidance of the Holy Spirit, Ludlow contended that there were good reasons to believe that Catholicism's deepest instincts were to oppose all organized violence. He cited, for example, the strong, ancient tradition in Eastern Orthodoxy of imitating Christ's own self-surrender: "Let us also remember that the Christian East has, more than the West, honored evangelical non-resistance to violence. This is an aspect of Communion with the Lamb."[21]

All of these elements of the Catholic Worker's peace concern, antinuclear activism, rejection of the cold war, hostility to personal conscription, and the practice of Gandhian nonviolence figured directly in the movement's most dramatic and well-known public demonstrations during this period, the civil disobedience against compulsory civil defense drills. The resistance to these drills by Catholic Workers and members of other pacifist groups took place in New York City every year between 1955 and 1960. In 1955 the New York State Defense Emergency Act made the failure to take shelter during the drills a crime subject to one-year imprisonment and a $500 fine. Ammon Hennacy, Dorothy Day, and other Catholic Workers initiated the resistance to the drill in June 1955, and they were joined in what became annual summer demonstrations and arrests by numbers of people from other pacifist groups, primarily the War Resisters League. The details of the events surrounding these demonstrations have been recounted by several historians and need not be repeated here.[22] What will be emphasized instead are the ways in which the actions of Dorothy Day and other Catholic Workers involved in these demonstrations were derived from the broad perspective on effective peace witness and civil disobedience that they had been developing since 1945, and before.

First, the civil disobedience campaign was directly linked to the issue of nuclear war in general, and specifically to the 1945 American atomic devastation of Hiroshima in particular. It was evident to most people of the time, demonstrators, government officials, and the public at large, that the pacifists who refused to take shelter when the air-raid sirens sounded were aiming their protesting specifically against nuclear weapons. The compulsory civil defense drill was known to be part of Operation Alert, a nationwide "war game" conducted by the federal establishment to test the capacity of the American government and society to withstand nuclear attack.[23] To the Catholic Workers, the very idea of a "game" that provided practice for potential nuclear holocaust was revolting. Dorothy Day declared that reliance on the hydrogen bomb for "defense" was "utter atheism," perhaps the strongest epithet in her vocabulary.[24] And since the very idea of taking shelter from a massive nuclear attack was ludicrous, Catholic Workers concluded that the essential purpose of the drill was political and psychological: to arouse fear and to spread a war mentality through the government and the populace.

But the primary reason for the Catholic Workers' civil disobedience in 1955 and after was not so much to protest nuclear war in general, or even to resist the civil defense drill as such, but to conduct an "act of repentance" for the American bombing of Hiroshima and Nagasaki in 1945. This feature of the demonstration—as a disciplined act of religious penance for the "sin" of dropping the bomb—is easily overlooked or dismissed, but it is in fact central to understanding the particular character of the Catholic Workers' actions. Dorothy Day stressed this point both in public statements prior to the action and in her subsequent writing about it: "We make this demonstration not only to voice our opposition to war, not only to refuse to participate in psychological warfare, which this air raid drill is, but also as an act of penance for having been the first people in the world to drop the atom bomb, to make the hydrogen bomb. . . .We are engaging only ourselves in this action, not the Church. We are acting as individual Catholics."[25]

Several things are notable about this approach. First, it made clear that the demonstration was more than a political action: it was primarily an expression of religious conviction. Second, it identified the demonstrators with the whole nation's action: it was "we" who had dropped the bomb, and not simply "they" against whom a righteous "we" were protesting. This perspective, in effect, invited all Americans and their government to the side of the demonstration—nonexistent though that prospect was. Finally, conducting the demonstration as an act of penance guaranteed its success. If the purposes were only political—ending nuclear preparation or at least the civil defense drill—then its success or failure could be measured in practical terms. But Dorothy Day refused to accept the narrow political calculus of victory and defeat: the Catholic Workers' campaign was against the "spiritual evils" that had made the bomb and the drill possible in the first place. Their demonstration implied a willingness on their part to assume partial responsibility for that evil, and their "penance" (including fines and jail terms) suggested a method for helping to overcome it.

The Workers' civil disobedience campaign also worked to undermine the mentality that maintained the cold war against the Russians. "We know this drill is to be a military act in a cold war," declared Ammon Hennacy. Again, the Catholic Workers pointed out that by claiming to rely on means of nuclear war for its own defense, Americans were imitating the very things they claimed to oppose. "In the presence of so great a threat as Communism," one Catholic

Worker wrote, "the 'free world' is attempting to save itself by the same means employed by its 'enemies.'" The lesson the Workers hoped to teach was that social good could only be pursued by good methods, not by morally tarnished actions. When told that they should "tell it to the Russians," as they frequently were during their demonstrations, the Catholic Workers replied that they would indeed give Russians the same message they were trying to give Americans: that following the Christian way of reconciliation was the only way to resolve conflicts, rather than the destructive path of confrontation and retaliation.[26]

The late fifties civil disobedience campaign, like draft resistance and other expressions of Catholic Worker personalism, represented an intensely personal form of peacemaking. Perhaps even more dramatically than the draft, the civil defense drill made tangible the state's pervasive but usually abstract and disguised power to wage war by demanding that all individuals act in accord with its policies. In this sense, the Catholic Workers and other pacifists did not seek a direct conflict with the government: it was rather the government itself that instigated the action by coercing individuals, in effect, to support the goals of nuclear war-making policy. This point was extremely difficult to convey to the public, since it appeared to most people that the civil defense drill was actually designed for the benefit of the civilian population—to save lives in case of a Soviet nuclear attack. Even so liberal a soul as Eleanor Roosevelt was swayed by this logic. When Dorothy Day wrote to her asking for support, Roosevelt replied that "the government is taking this action for your benefit, so I don't understand why you object."[27] But the Workers contended that while they supported actions taken for the common good, it was a contradiction to pursue peace by means of war preparation and forced redirection of civilian life. Since the civil defense program was not intended to prevent war, but was in fact defined and presented as part of the system of national military preparation, those who went along with it were condoning its goals. As with draftees, therefore, the Workers' own willingness to take direct action (in this case, simply sitting on city park benches at the wrong time) and to pay the price of arrest and jail sentences showed, more than any verbal statements, the meaning and depth of their position. At the same time, their Gandhian willingness to accept the penalties showed that their protest was not against society or the principle of law *per se*, but against the misuse of the same.

Finally, the Catholic Worker's civil disobedience campaign of 1955 to 1961 represented a notably effective exercising of Gandhian *satyagraha*—perhaps one of the most salient examples of such action outside the civil rights movement. It conformed in almost every respect to the classic Gandhian campaigns described and interpreted by such theorists of nonviolence as Joan Bondurant and Gene Sharp.[28]

The campaign had a clear focus and a defined objective: to resist the compulsory civil defense drills. While the cosmic issues of nuclear war and military preparation were of course continually present throughout this period, the civil defense drills presented an especially inviting target because they represented a direct intrusion of the government's institutional machinery into the lives of these committed Christian pacifists. By focusing their civil disobedience specifically on this point of intersection between their larger concern—the morality of nuclear war—and the demand for a particular action—taking shelter when the air-raid sirens sounded in New York City—Day and the Workers could practice the politics of personalism in a particularly vivid way that could and did gain public and media attention. As with Gandhi's salt campaign, the air-raid civil disobedience campaign combined the traditional moral stance of individual conscientious witness with a more active social challenge to fundamental policies and assumptions of the state.

A closely related principle of Gandhian nonviolence is that the nature and goals of any such action must be clearly and publicly stated, so that those against whom the behavior is directed, as well as the larger observing public, are made fully aware of precisely what is at stake. In each of the annual demonstrations in which they participated, the Catholic Workers made special efforts to notify the police and other authorities, as well as the media, of their intentions and purposes. Throughout the process of arrest and trial, Dorothy Day especially attempted to keep the focus on the stated purposes—penance for the Hiroshima bombing and protest against nuclear war preparation—rather than on the issues presented by the authorities: disruption of public order and disobedience to police authority. When the sirens went off, the demonstrators remained seated and were arrested, but they offered no verbal or physical resistance or hostility to police and prison officials.[29]

The Workers also followed the Gandhian principle of accepting the penalty for their actions, while continuing to deny the legitimacy of the arrests and convictions. The particular question for those arrested in 1955 was whether to plead guilty to the charges of refusing to take shelter. Some of the demonstrators pled not guilty and took their case to trial, but Day and five other Catholics Workers chose to plead "guilty." Their purpose, again, was to keep attention focused on the larger issue raised by their action and not to become bogged down in an extended courtroom process. At the same time they issued a statement to clarify the meaning of their plea: "Our action in pleading guilty comes from the conviction as to the manner in which we should bear Christian testimony in this instance. It does not constitute admission that the July 15 civil defense drill was in the public interest, that the law under which we were charged is good, or that the charge against us is just." They explained further that "we of the Catholic Worker intended our protest to be an act of penance for our guilt as citizens of a country which used the atomic bomb at Hiroshima and Nagasaki, and as *penance* we were prepared to pay the price of civil disobedience."[30]

In 1955 the convicted Catholic Workers were given suspended sentences. But in 1956 they were sentenced to five days in jail, in 1957 to thirty days, and in 1958 to fifteen days. In each case the Workers, like Gandhi, emphasized publicly that their protest was not against the idea of law or justice or the public welfare, and that they "did not wish to act in a spirit of defiance and rebellion."[31]

While they did not accept imprisonment, any more than they accepted moral guilt for their violation of the law, their willingness to defend their principles in court while enduring the punishment without complaint or expensive legal maneuvering enhanced the witness of their civil disobedience as a conscientious moral act rather than a defiant political tactic. As Ammon Hennacy stated, "We felt that we should plead guilty . . . rather than depend upon technicalities which the lawyers would bring up. We felt that we were not morally guilty, but in the sense of a clear cut case of civil disobedience we did not want to becloud the issue with legal terms. We did not plead guilt to obtain mercy, for we were willing to repeat our witness against this coercive law."[32]

Yet, ironically, the political consequences of this kind of morally consistent witness have often proved to be greater in the long run than more calculated and sophisticated forms of overtly political action. It is a paradox, familiar to those who have carefully studied instances of Gandhian *satyagraha*, that the acceptance of suffering and failure in terms of an immediate goal can create a moral climate for transforming the objectionable social policy in ways that more overt political assaults cannot. In the case of the civil defense drills, the Workers' campaign did not succeed in immediately altering the federal government's civil defense policy, much less in overturning preparations for nuclear attack. Yet by arousing the conscience of numbers of people who recognized their moral good will, even if they did not agree with their general perspective, the pacfists drew increasing support for their goals. Public comments and editorials, which except for the Catholic journal *Commonweal* had been almost universally hostile after the first demonstration, grew increasingly favorable as the years passed. Each year more and more people began turning out for the annual event. In 1960, when over a thousand demonstrators appeared, the police pointedly declined to arrest the Catholic Workers, whom they evidently recognized as spearheads of the movement. Soon afterward the drills were dropped—replaced by a program of individual backyard fallout shelters.[33]

This small victory was, of course, a minuscule achievement measured against the great moral and political transformations that the Catholic Workers sought: an end to nuclear weapons, war preparations, and an aggressive cold war politics. Yet even in relation to these large goals, the long-range effects of this small exercise in civil disobedience, undertaken with what Catholic moral theologians have traditionally called "right intention," ought not be underestimated. Some historians of peace activism consider these and other small antinuclear protests of the fifties to be the spark that awoke the American peace movement from its near-demise in the early fifties. Historian Charles DeBenedetti began his history of the anti–Vietnam War movement with the very civil defense drill of 1955 against which the Catholic Workers protested, and Patricia McNeal cited the Catholic Worker's antinuclear activism as the beginning of the morally conscious wave of peace concern that would sweep through the sixties and beyond.[34]

In the early cold war era from 1945 to 1960, only a handful of Americans were seriously engaged in movements for peace. In the following decade the numbers of people involved would multiply into the hundreds of thousands and even millions. Numerous new peace groups and coalitions would far surpass the Catholic Worker in size and in the political visibility and forcefulness of their actions. Yet the mostly quiet courage and integrity of this small band of witnesses to peace in a hostile era remains, in many respects, a more moving testimony than the mass demonstrations and confrontations of subsequent times. For Dorothy Day and the Catholic Workers showed, as few others did, that before peace can be realized in a hostile globe, it must first take a firm hold within the peacemakers' own minds and spirits.

NOTES

1. Randolph Bourne, *War and the Intellectuals* (New York, 1964), 40-41.

2. Quoted in Lawrence Wittner, *Cold War America* (New York, 1974), 14.

3. Charles DeBenedetti, *The Peace Reform in American History* (Bloomington, Ind., 1980), 146.

4. "We Go on Record," *Catholic Worker,* September 1945, 1.

5. John Hugo, "Peace Without Victory," *Catholic Worker,* September 1945, 2.

6. "Stop That Bomb," *Catholic Worker,* February 1946, 2; "Atomic Bomb," *Catholic Worker*, February 1946, 2.

7. "The Satan Bomb," *Catholic Worker,* February 1950, 2.

8. "We are Un-American/We are Catholics," *Catholic Worker,* April 1948, 2.

9. "European Catholic Pacifists Meet," *Catholic Worker,* February 1952, 2.

10. Chrysostom Tarasevitch, "Church in Russia," *Catholic Worker,* May 1949, 1, 5. Tarasevitch, "Church in Russia, *Catholic Worker,* June 1949, 4.

11. Lawrence S. Wittner, *Rebels Against War: The American Peace Movement, 1941-1960,* (New York, 1969) 167-68, 188-90.

12. Ibid., 185-87.

13. "Atom Bomb and Conscription Issues Still to be Faced," *Catholic Worker,* April 1946, 1.

14. "Do Not Register," *Catholic Worker,* September 1948, 3.

15. Michael Harrington, *Fragments of the Century* (New York, 1973), 23.

16. David Garrow, *Bearing the Cross: Martin Luther King, Jr., and the Southern Christian Leadership Conference* (New York, 1986), 21-82, 113-15.

17. Robert Ludlow, "Meeting at Newburgh," *Catholic Worker,* September 1947, 1.

18. Quoted in Wittner, *Rebels Against War,* 154.

19. Robert Ludlow, "Satyagraha: A Christian Way," *Catholic Worker,* May 1949, 3; Ludlow, "Gandhi Revolution," *Catholic Worker,* February 1950, 5.

20. Eileen Fantino, "Satyagraha—A Positive Method," *Catholic Worker,* October 1952, 2, 6.

21. Robert Ludlow, "The Authority of the Church in Relation to Pacifism," *Catholic Worker,* February 1953, 3, 7.

22. Nancy L. Roberts, *Dorothy Day and the "Catholic Worker"* (Albany, N.Y., 1984), 149-54; Patricia McNeal, *Harder Than War: Catholic Peacemaking in Twentieth-Century America* (New Brunswick, N.J., 1992), 86-94.

23. "You are on Test Today," *New York Times*, 15 June 1955, 30.

24. Dorothy Day, "Creation," *Catholic Worker*, June 1956, 2.

25. Dorothy Day, "Where Are the Poor? They Are in Prisons, Too," *Catholic Worker*, July-August 1955, 1, 8.

26. Robert Steed, "The Russian Revolution—*Quadragesimo Anno*," *Catholic Worker*, November 1957, 2.

27. Quoted in Roberts, *Dorothy Day and the "Catholic Worker,"* 153.

28. Joan Bondurant, *Conquest of Violence: The Gandhian Philosophy of Conflict* (Berkeley, Calif., 1958); Gene Sharp, *The Politics of Nonviolent Action*, 3 Vols. (Boston, 1973).

29. Day, "Where are the Poor? They Are in Prisons, Too," 8.

30. "What is Happening? Trial Continued Until Nov. 16," *Catholic Worker*, November 1955, 2.

31. Dorothy Day, *Loaves and Fishes* (New York, 1963), 160.

32. Ammon Hennacy, "Civil Disobedience," *Catholic Worker*, July-August 1955, 3, 7.

33. Ammon Hennacy, "500 Defy Civil Defense Drill in New York City," *Catholic Worker*, June 1960, 1.

34. Charles DeBenedetti, with Charles Chatfield, *An American Order: The Antiwar Movement of the Vietnam Era* (Syracuse, N.Y., 1990), 9, 24; McNeal, *Harder Than War*, 81, 91-92.

7

The Leaven

James W. Douglass

How does one tell a story of transformation? Jesus did it simply in his parable of the leaven:

"To what shall I compare the kingdom of God? It is like leaven which a woman took and hid in three measures of flour, till it was all leavened" (Luke 13:20-21).

To those who first heard Jesus' parable, leaven was a symbol of corruption.[1] It was banned from every household during the holy season of Passover. The parable assumes this knowledge. It also assumes we know that three measures are an immense quantity of flour, enough to make a meal for over 100 people.[2] The parable tells us that a tiny, corrupt substance, hidden in the flour by the woman, accomplished an unseen, massive transformation. Like the kingdom of God.

My parable of transformation is about a series of events that occurred in Rome between 1962 and 1965, at the periphery of the Second Vatican Council, while the bishops of the Catholic Church struggled with the question of nuclear war. The story begins, however, not in Rome but five years earlier in New York and California. It begins with a leaven, Dorothy Day and the Catholic Worker movement, which an English professor hid in the lives of his students.

The introduction of the leaven in my life took place, unknown to Dorothy Day, in a classroom at the University of Santa Clara in 1957. Dorothy had become a leaven for the nation in New York City by remaining in a park with twenty-eight friends, while millions of other New Yorkers took shelter in basements and subways from a hypothetical hydrogen bomb during a compulsory civil defense drill. The twenty-nine people in the park were, as in Jesus' parable, a tiny, corrupt substance in the consciousness of the nation. They also accomplished a massive transformation: the number of resisters grew and within three years stopped the annual civil defense drill. For her particular act of noncooperation with nuclear war, Dorothy Day went to jail. *Commonweal* published an article on why she did so. I read the article at Santa Clara because my English professor, Herbert Burke, passed it out to our class. I recall Dr. Burke leaning back against the blackboard, a question mark of a professor, observing us over his glasses as we finished reading the subversive article.

He soon learned that the leaven had been uniformly rejected. All of his students thought Dorothy Day was crazy. We suspected that our slyly questioning professor thought differently, as he reintroduced the leaven in Socratic fashion.

Looking back now, three decades later, I remember that spring at Santa Clara as one long meditation on Dorothy Day, her friends in the park, and the world's threatened destruction by nuclear war. I began reading Dorothy Day's newspaper, the *Catholic Worker*. There I discovered that resisting preparations for nuclear war was for the Catholic Worker movement all of a piece with feeding the hungry, sheltering the homeless, and resisting every kind of injustice. They aspired to build a new society, the kingdom of God, within the shell of the old. Jesus' vision of God's kingdom is why Dorothy Day had gone to the park and to jail. My thoughts took a new direction: How could one believe in the kingdom of God and not respond to the world's destruction?

But the leaven in my story is not only Dorothy Day. It is also a philosopher of nuclear war, my Santa Clara ethics professor, Father Austin Fagothey. In a sense, Father Fagothey was truer to Jesus' parable of the leaven than Dorothy Day was. By converting me to her vision, Dorothy had become a holy burr in my conscience, prickly but saintly. Father Fagothey's thinking on nuclear war was, on the other hand, a blasphemy. It was alien, unholy, transforming—a true leaven. Nuclear war was my enemy, and Father Fagothey as my ethics professor justified it with a serene logic. By teaching me skillfully an idea I hated (and still do), Father Fagothey provoked me into thinking it through.

Is the kingdom of God my enemy's truth?

Father Fagothey taught courses on the history of philosophy and ethics. He was a small Jesuit priest in his late fifties with the mental ability to abstract the essence of every philosopher in history and set them all down in a series of propositions our class could remember. The history of philosophy was a marvelous march of Father Fagothey's diagrams and propositions across our blackboard. Besides the power of abstraction, Father Fagothey had a knack for comic relief. In the middle of a lecture, he would sometimes pause with intensity and cross his eyes at the class. He also had a photographic memory. He took roll at the start of each class by scanning the rows of students before him and jotting down the names he carried in his head that corresponded to the vacant seats. Father Fagothey's mind seemed to have the world under control.

It was in his ethics course that we came into conflict. The course was based on *Right and Reason*, the ethics textbook Father Fagothey had written that was used widely at Catholic universities. In light of the just-war doctrine formulated by Augustine and Aquinas, Father Fagothey had begun to develop in *Right and Reason* a concept of total war that would justify the massive use of nuclear weapons. It rested on the (I thought, untenable) assumption of an enemy nation so militarizing its society that it would have "therefore lost all right to a distinction between military and non-military objectives."[3] Father Fagothey's language was cautious and clinical, but what it aroused in my mind thanks to Dorothy Day was the vision of a total evil chosen by ourselves: the death and suffering of entire societies, if not the world. Father Fagothey and I were destined to spend years of our lives struggling on opposite sides of his concept of a just total war, an idea he would develop at length as a revision of traditional moral restraints on war.

Pushed on different levels by Dorothy Day and Austin Fagothey, I wrote an article for the *Catholic Worker* and the Santa Clara literary magazine, using the just-war conditions Father Fagothey had helped me understand, to make a case for nuclear pacifism. Father Fagothey responded with a critique of my article, which also appeared in the literary magazine. Perhaps pushed further by my continuing criticisms, he developed his just nuclear war position in a public lecture at Santa Clara. I raised critical questions from the audience. Our extended debate ceased when I graduated from Santa Clara. Thanks to the fellowships Father Fagothey had recommended me for, I moved on to graduate school. We parted as friends in conflict. I had come to respect him deeply but rejected with all my heart and mind his thinking on nuclear war.

After two years of graduate studies, I moved to Rome to study the theology of war and peace at the Gregorian University, one of the oldest Catholic institutions in the world. My family and I arrived in Rome in September 1962 at the same time as 2,300 bishops from all over the world for the opening of the Second Vatican Council, which would eventually take up the same question as my focus of study.

One day between classes at the Gregorian, I was startled to run into Father Fagothey. What, I asked, was he doing there? Father Fagothey explained that he had come to Rome at a late stage in his career to get a doctorate in theology. (He already had one in philosophy.) My friend looked at me with the ever-present gleam in his eye. He would be doing his dissertation, he said, on a topic that would interest me: the justification of total nuclear war in Catholic teaching.

I was stunned. All I could say was, would he share his research with me? Father Fagothey said he would be glad to do that.

What I began to understand through his developing dissertation was that Father Fagothey had a piece of the truth. He had been honest enough to recognize that a limited nuclear war was a contradiction in terms. Yet it was precisely this abstraction of a strictly limited nuclear war that the U.S. Catholic Church's foremost ethicist, Father John Courtney Murray, had used to justify nuclear weapons in the Kennedy era. The argument for limited nuclear war, as made on strategic grounds by Henry Kissinger, was also taken up and developed by Defense Secretary Robert McNamara into a "surgical strike" (first strike) doctrine that every subsequent administration has further refined.

But Father Fagothey looked at Father Murray's "limited nuclear war" and bit the bullet. The idea was a fantasy. And because like Murray he saw no alternative to a communist takeover except nuclear deterrence, Father Fagothey decided in his logical fashion to justify *total* nuclear war.

The case he argued at the Gregorian was made possible by a partial vacuum, the ambiguities of papal statements on modern war. Father Fagothey thought no pope or church council had ever been definitive enough in statements against total war to rule out its admissibility in Catholic teaching. Thus he could introduce total war in its ultimate, nuclear form as a reality he thought implicit in the just-war doctrine. Father Fagothey's dissertation advisor approved this proposal.

What alarmed me most about Father Fagothey's new project in Rome is that he was no longer presenting his case to Santa Clara students. Now his audience was the most prestigious Catholic theological faculty in the world, one that the Vatican drew upon for its teaching. To sacrifice the distinction between combatants and civilians to a total war necessity, as Father Fagothey proposed doing, was to break through the just-war doctrine's (and the church's) strongest ethical barrier to nuclear war. Father Fagothey had the mind and credentials for such a project. Now he also had the situation in Rome where he could effectively change the Catholic Church's teaching on war to the point of sanctioning the destruction of humanity.

I thought my friend had become one of the most dangerous people on earth.

After a year's work at the Gregorian, Father Fagothey returned to Santa Clara to finish writing his dissertation, which he then hoped to have published in the United States—another chilling thought in terms of its possible consequences.

Helped by Austin Fagothey's insights into the contradictions and ambiguities of Catholic thought on war, I committed my life in Rome for the duration of the Council to a project opposite to his: a lobbying effort to encourage the council fathers to make that definitive Catholic condemnation of total war that Father Fagothey had perceived was lacking.

The next two years in Rome (1963-1965) were filled with grace. A series of extraordinary pilgrims created the "peace lobby" at the Vatican Council. Among them were Eileen Egan, Jean and Hildegard Goss-Mayr, Gordon Zahn, Dick Carbray, Thomas Merton (in his correspondence with bishops), Daniel Berrigan, William J. Nagle, Lanza del Vasto, Hermene and Joe Evans, and Dorothy Day herself. Dorothy came twice to Rome, once on a pilgrimage to Pope John XXIII and again in the final session of the council to fast with other women as a personal appeal to the church fathers for a strong statement on war and peace.

The ten-day fast of the twenty women in Rome in October 1965 was, I believe, the most profoundly transforming leaven of the final session of the

Vatican Council, when the bishops concluded their deliberations on war and peace. The women's fast, and Dorothy Day's in particular, went to the heart of the total war question: the hunger of the world's destitute beneath the waste and terror of the arms race. Dorothy wrote: "I had offered my fast in part for the victims of famine all over the world, and it seemed to me that I had very special pains. . . . [They] seemed to reach into my very bones, and I could only feel that I had been given some little intimation of the hunger of the world.[4]

Moved again by Dorothy Day and Austin Fagothey, but now with the unique situation of living in Rome, between 1963 and 1965 I spoke with every bishop who would listen to a young lay theology student obsessed with the idea that the council must condemn total war and support the right of conscientious objection. I circulated a document to that effect, influenced by the counterinsights of an old professor of mine. Several bishops used it as a basis for their speeches at the council urging that the church take a clear stand against total war.[5]

In December 1965, nearing its conclusion, the Second Vatican Council issued the only condemnation of its four sessions on any subject, a definitive condemnation of total war: "Any act of war aimed indiscriminately at the destruction of entire cities or of extensive areas along with their population is a crime against God and humanity itself. It merits unequivocal and unhesitating condemnation." (in the Pastoral Constitution on the Church in the Modern World, *Gaudium et Spes*, promulgated 7 December 1965)

Twenty-two years later, in the fall of 1987, I spent a morning at the archives of the Jesuit Center in Los Gatos, California, reading the letters and papers of Father Fagothey, who had died in 1975. In the span of years between the Vatican Council's declaration and Father Fagothey's death, we had seen each other on only one occasion, at the scene of our old debates, when I was invited back to Santa Clara to give a talk on nonviolence.

We had sat next to each other at dinner, but with the press of conversation from other friends, had little opportunity to talk together. I did ask Father Fagothey what had become of his dissertation. He said only that he had not been able to complete the project.

Reading through his correspondence with his dissertation advisor twelve years after Father Fagothey's death, I could see the frustrations of an extraordinary mind confronted by the changing tide on peace of a church he thought he understood. The advisor finally told Father Fagothey to forget the idea of ever having his dissertation on total war approved for a doctorate in theology at the Gregorian University. He suggested instead using his material for a book and trying to find a publisher in the United States.

Other letters revealed that Father Fagothey's proposal for such a book was seriously considered for several months by a leading U.S. Catholic publisher. The editor finally wrote back a rejection in the fall of 1965, explaining that between the completion of Father Fagothey's research and the present time "there have been some notable shifts in the thinking of the Church on almost every level on the moral implications of total war."[6]

Reading that sentence, I thought first of Pope John's encyclical, *Pacem in Terris*, the most revolutionary source of change, a leaven coming from the papacy itself. I thought, too, of the man who wrote the letter rejecting Father Fagothey's book, Philip Scharper, then editor of Sheed and Ward, soon to be a founder of Orbis Books and instrumental before his death in 1984 in bringing a wave of liberation theology to the United States, another "notable shift in the thinking of the Church." Philip Sharper had also been one of the pilgrims among the "peace lobby" in Rome, helping to create the council's condemnation of total war and support of conscientious objection.

For the rest of that day, and on many days since then, I thought of Austin Fagothey, who had spent many of his days arguing a counter position to those changes . . . and hereby helped create them. Through the "clarification of thought" he brought about in the peace lobby, as Dorothy Day liked to say of illuminating conflicts, Father Fagothey had been a leaven in the leaven.

Gandhi was once confronted by a government official who questioned his belief in the power of truth. Their dialogue is a simple revelation of what I learned also from Father Fagothey:

Official: However honestly a person may strive in the search for truth, that person's notions of truth may be different from the notions of others. Who then is to determine the truth?

Gandhi: The individual would determine that.

Official: Different individuals would have different views as to truth. Would that not lead to confusion?

Gandhi: I do not think so.[7]

The purity of Gandhi's response to the skeptical government official has echoed in my heart for years. However different our paths may be, the truth is one. Each of us has a piece of the truth. Those pieces can and will eventually come together in a deeper unity. The power of truth and love, acting together, will see to that.

Father Fagothey pursued a truth that I believed profoundly to be wrong in the effect it might have upon the world. He thought the truth I was pursuing was equally misguided in its implications for humanity. Thus we struggled. But in spite of our blindness to the redemptive dimensions of the other's truth, God had introduced another factor between us: respect and friendship. As we struggled, the apparently conflicting truths deepened and in a more unified way reached the lives of others.

In the course of writing this story, I have continued to debate internally with Father Fagothey. He is still my teacher, friend, and opponent—still the leaven.

NOTES

1. For background details and interpretation of the parable of the leaven, I am especially grateful to Robert W. Funk, *Jesus a Precursor* (Missoula, Mont., 1975), 51-72; and Bernard Brandon Scott, *Hear Then the Parable: A Commentary on the Parables of Jesus* (Minneapolis, 1989), 321-29.

2. Joachim Jeremias, *The Parables of Jesus* (New York, 1972), 147.

3. Austin Fagothey, S.J., *Right and Reason* (St. Louis, 1953), 531.

4. Robert Ellsberg, ed., *By Little and By Little: The Selected Writings of Dorothy Day* (New York, 1984), 332-33.

5. I have described the Council's debate on war and peace in "Toward a New Perspective on War: The Vision of Vatican II," *The Non-Violent Cross* (New York, 1968), 100-36.

6. Letter from Philip Scharper to Austin Fagothey, S.J., 29 September 1965.

7. M. K. Gandhi, *Satyagraha* (Ahmadabad, India, 1951), 29.

Dorothy Day, features writer for the *New York Call,* with a copy of the antiwar socialist daily, 9 February 1917. Courtesy Marquette University Archives.

Monsignor G. Barry O'Toole of the Catholic University of America joined Dorothy Day and Joseph Zarrella in opposing peacetime conscription on religious grounds. Courtesy The Catholic University of America Department of Archives and Manuscripts.

During World War II, Reverend John A. Hugo's series "The Weapons of the Spirit" was published in the *Catholic Worker*. Courtesy Marquette University Archives.

BAN THE BOMB

We have reached the point beyond which we travel at the peril of human existence ... We must find some effective and immediate measures which will make the H-bomb morally obsolete before it ever becomes an actual instrument of war ... This is the great human decision of our generation ... America, the first and only nation to use the bomb, must now lead the way to its banning.

(THE PILOT, Archdiocesan Paper of Boston, May 26, 1956)

By Personal Protest

One year ago this June, a group of 27 pacifists broke a New York State law which made it a misdemeanor not to take shelter during a compulsory air-raid drill. We were put under $1500 bail each, tried during the course of the summer, and given a suspended sentence. The penalty for breaking this law is one year in prison and a $500 fine. We are repeating our "misdemeanor" on this air-raid drill of July 20, 1956. We are exercising our own God-given reason in making this decision.

Our "disobedience to law" and readiness to take the penalty for it is in protest against deception of the people by leading them to think there is any shelter from a nuclear weapon attack. Atomic warfare is uncontrollable, wipes out the innocent as well as the guilty, and is contrary to all natural law.

The bomb is defended as a weapon against Communism. One objection to Communism is that "atheism is an integral part of Marxism" as Lenin said. Another is that Communists believe in the use of force and violence to change the social order. We of this country, which we dearly love, believe that use of such weapons of "force and violence" against our brother is a denial of God and of the image of God in our brother. God is our Father and all men are brothers. We are willing to die for this belief. We are ready to do penance for the sins of our country which was the first to drop the bomb. Jail is in a little way a dying. But "unless the grain of wheat falls into the ground and dies, it remains alone, but if it dies, it brings forth much fruit."

JOIN US IN PENANCE AND IN PROTEST AGAINST WAR!

DOROTHY DAY   AMMON HENNACY

July 20, 1956

 223 Chrystie Street, New York (2)

Handbill distributed by Catholic Workers opposing mandatory civil defense air-raid drills, 20 July 1956. Courtesy Marquette University Archives.

Thomas Merton, copyright © David Levine. The writings of Thomas Merton, some of which were published under a pseudonym in the *Catholic Worker*, helped to make pacifism a respectable option for Catholics of the 1960s.

Dorothy Day, copyright © David Levine. David Levine depicted Dorothy Day as a militant pacifist saint in the pages of the *New York Review of Books*.

Eileen Egan, a *Catholic Worker* editor and a founder of Pax Christi. Photo copyright © Rick Reinhard/Impact Visuals.

The ANZUS Plowshares. From left to right, Ciaron O'Reilly, Bill Streit, Sue Frankel, and Moana Cole. Courtesy Ciaron O'Reilly.

8

The Correspondence of Dorothy Day and Thomas Merton

Compiled, introduced, and edited by
William H. Shannon

Thomas Merton had a great respect, even a reverential awe, for the extraordinary cofounder of the Catholic Worker movement. "Poverty for Dorothy Day," he wrote on the dust jacket of her book *Loaves and Fishes*, "is more than a sociological problem; it is also a religious mystery." She was very alive for him as a loving person; she was also a symbol of what to him was a most important element of the Catholic Church: concern for the poor, the neglected, the homeless. Three years before his death, on 29 December 1965, he wrote to her: "If there were no *Catholic Worker* and such forms of witness, I would never have joined the Catholic Church." (*The Hidden Ground of Love: Letters on Religious Experience and Social Concerns,* edited by William H. Shannon. New York 1985. Hereafter *HGL*, 151).

The principal purpose of this chapter is to make available for the first time in published form the twenty-two extant letters of Dorothy Day to Thomas Merton. Merton's twenty-nine letters to Dorothy have already been published in the first volume of the Merton letters. In editing Merton's letters to Dorothy Day, I interspersed brief comments from Dorothy's letters, where it helped to clarify what Merton was saying. Here I shall follow the same procedure in reverse—giving Dorothy's letters in full with comments taken from Merton's letters inserted where they prove to be helpful.

From Dorothy's[1] side of this relationship, it might be said that she did not know any Thomas Merton. "Thomas Merton" was the signature that went with the many articles she published in the *Catholic Worker*; but for her the writer of those letters was the priest and monk whom she revered: Father Louis. Their correspondence extended over a period of nine years—from June 1959 to August 1968. Initially Merton signed his letters "Fr. Louis," but—as with the rest of his friends—from at least 1961, his signature was "Tom Merton" or

"Tom." Dorothy steadfastly refused this offer of a greater familiarity and always wrote to "Fr. Louis" (although her letter of 23 August 1962, inadvertently we must believe, carried the salutation: Dear Fr. Merton). That this slip was inadvertent is clear from her letter of 11 November 1965, wherein she apologized to him "for writing your name wrong on the envelope." She had addressed it to "Father Thomas Merton." She had a deep and simple faith that saw an almost atavistic power in the prayers of a priest and a monk.

This is not to say that Dorothy did not at times disagree with Merton, especially in the area of social commitments. She was not happy with his article on shelter ethics, which appeared in the *Catholic Worker* in November 1961: she felt he was too committed to the "just-war doctrine." She took him to task for describing her fellow workers as "beats" (see letter of 4 June 1962). She also disagreed with the reservations he had about young men burning their draft cards and made this quite clear to him (Merton changed his mind on the issue.) She also handled Merton's near hysteria about the tragic death of Roger LaPorte[2] with gentleness and decisiveness in her letter of 11 November 1965.

Dorothy Day's letters are in no way literary achievements (as some of Merton's are). For the most part they are simple reflections of her day-by-day existence, as she talks of the young people at the Worker and the problems they face, the young and the old for whom she cared with such extraordinary love and compassion. All her letters are included here because cumulatively they move and inspire, not because of any literary merit, but because they tell the story of very ordinary events through which the mercy and goodness of God shine in the life of a loving, strong, and devoted woman.

Feast of the Sacred Heart, 1959

Dear Fr. Louis,

What with jail and a sudden attack of arthritis, I neglected to write to thank you both for your letter and for the gifts you sent to the CW crowd. I remember too with gratitude the copies of *Seven Storey Mountain* [Merton's best-selling autobiography published in 1948] you sent some years ago. A number of the editors of the *Daily Worker* got copies then and now the paper is out of existence, and a few of them have left the party. There is still a *Sunday Worker*, however! Will you please pray for Charles Butterworth, one of our staff, who will be sentenced next Wednesday in a Federal court for harboring a deserter here at CW and helping him to escape. We have done this before and giving [*sic*] the men the time to make up their own minds; one returned to the army and the other took his sentence. Charles plead [*sic*] guilty and we don't know what the penalty is. It may be mandatory. Bob Steed may also have to go since he admitted to the FBI that he tore up his draft card as a protest against conscription. He was at Gethsemane [*sic*] for 18 months. So I beg your prayers for both of them.

July 25 I am off to Montreal to make a retreat with those interested in the spiritual family of Charles de Foucauld.[3] I am trying to join either the secular institute or the association. But am not sure they will have me. I would go on with my work at the CW of course.

We are all intensely grateful to you for all your writings and it delights me especially to see them in bus stations and drugstores as I travel about the country. Gratefully in Christ,

                                                                        Dorothy Day

June 20, 1959

Dear Fr. Louis,

I enclose a letter to cheer your heart and to keep you writing. Your books are regarded as treasures around the CW and keep circulating. One of the editors even made a pilgrimage to your old home on Long Island. Do pray for him, as he is in a sad state of indecision about everything, idleness and melancholy which are hard to combat. The sense of futility is the curse of our time among the young. God bless you always in your work which has done so much for all of us.

Did I tell you that N. N. said she spent all the royalties from her own books, buying yours to distribute to others? She needs prayers. Her husband has left her, and she has gotten to the point where she thinks he is possessed and she is reading up on the devil. A dangerous state to be in—getting too close to *him*. Gratefully in Christ,

                                                                        Dorothy Day

[July 9, 1959—Merton to Dorothy]

December 23, 1959

Dear Fr. Louis,

Your beautiful book containing the beautiful news arrived[4] and Bob Steed had a hard time restraining himself until I came in from the beach to open it. We are all grateful and for the inscription too. And a very happy New Year to you and may you be faithful unto death.

My constant prayer is for final perseverance.—to go on as I am trusting always the Lord Himself will take me by the hair of the head like Habbakuk[5] [sic] and set me where he wants me.

Have you a volume of Cassian?[6] I have an extra one if you want it.

In Jesus' love,

Dorothy Day

Christmas, 1959

Happy and holy Christmas! I forgot to mail the enclosed [probably the above letter], written on the ferry-boat to Staten Island. Hope you can decipher it. All send their love. Jim and Jean [Forest] were over to supper last night, both well.

In Jesus' caritas,

Dorothy

January 22, 1960

Dear Fr. Louis,

Your beautiful and profound essay on Pasternak ["The Pasternak Affair in Perspective," *Thought* 34 (Winter, 1959-60): 485-517] kept me awake from midnight until four in the morning, thinking about it. I am using the final paragraph in my "On Pilgrimage" this coming month. It was very exciting, all of it, and I thank you for writing it, and for sending us a copy. I carried it along with me on my trip west (I am visiting the Indians, the Hutterites and the Doukhobors too). I have been taking care of a cancer patient who just died a week before Ammon [Hennacy] was released from Sandstone, so after her very happy death (she was baptized the night before she died) I set out on a three months' trip which I had been postponing eight months. I get time to read while traveling and am reading Ann[e] Fremantle's *Desert Calling* right now. Very good indeed. Did I tell you I am a postulant in the Jesus Caritas Fraternity of the Charles de Foucauld family? Please pray for me and may God bless you always. In His love,

Dorothy

[February 4, 1960—Merton to Dorothy]

June 4, 1960

Dear Fr. Louis,

How grateful we are to you for your poem. Bob Steed, who makes up the CW, and who was at Gethsemani for some time, is a hero-worshiper of yours, even to the extent of visiting Douglaston, L.I., going out there on a hot afternoon to pick up a donation of clothes from a reader—just because you had lived there. Of course we want the "Prometheus."

I read your article on Pasternak in *Thought* and this morning I read the very moving account of his journal in the *Times*. If you wish, I'll send it to you. Did Bob forward the Cassian? Some Presbyterian publishing house in Michigan is bringing out a new edition of the Fathers, Anglican translation.

An attack of arthritis and flu the last few weeks leaves me full of sloth. It is a good time to stay at the beach houses where rain has driven people away. Aside from a disturbed family for whom I beg your prayers, and two ex-seamen puttering around fixing screens, I am alone. To be with eight people is to be alone at the CW. One of the men, Hugh Madden, was five years a brother at Gethsemane. "Disturbed" or a saint, who can tell? Both probably.

The family is most truly disorderly, deserted by the father. The last child by another man. The children already proclaiming loss of faith, bitterness. They are 10 to 16. The last still a baby, so the mother cannot work as she did before, and that is why they are with us. I tell you these things, so you will most specially pray for them. I used to write the old abbot Dunn [Abbot Frederic Dunne] about my problems.

My own son-in-law, tho strong in faith, has many problems mental and physical and Tamar is having her 9th child in late July. I will be with her for a few weeks then.

Did you ever read "The Friend of the Family" by Dostoievsky? We have one such friend on Peter Maurin Farm this last year. Also many an "Honest Thief" in town. Dostoievsky is spiritual reading for me.

Anyway, I am begging your prayers and be assured I pray for you as I hope you do for me. I am often full of fears about my final perseverance. Gratefully in Christ,

Dorothy Day

[August 17, 1960—Merton to Dorothy]

October 10, 1960

Dear Fr. Louis,

It was good to get your book [*Disputed Questions*, published in 1960, with articles on Pasternak and John Climacus], and I thank you for having sent it to me. I had read the Pasternak affair in *Thought* and was much impressed with it, and quoted from it both during a speaking trip and in the paper. And I am fascinated by St. John Climacus.[7] I do not know Bob Steed's name when he was there. John Stanley was there too. One of the things which bothers me mightily is the bitterness and criticism of angry young men. Do pray for them and all such. Sometimes I try to tell myself, finding myself too critical, "they are prophets crying out in this time." But there are too many of them. Around a place like the *Catholic Worker* there are always too many, too much of the rebellious spirit. From the last year we have had with us a youngish woman, brilliant mentally, but destructive in all her criticisms, and almost blind, covered with rashes and sores, crying out constantly, against her fate. This week she has moved into one of our little apartments in town, to be near clinics, etc. To me she epitomizes rebellion. She always has someone devoted to her, bringing her all the latest drugs and also liquor. She tries every remedy she reads about and the more she doses herself the worse she gets. Ammon Hennacy hates all medicine and has never taken any. He says my arthritis is because I am stiff-necked and advocates fasting for every ailment. He is a continual faster, a vegetarian, and doing without all food every Friday all day. One Lent he fasted as the Moslems do, another he fasted completely all Lent, for 46 days. He is truly a prophet in many ways. But he sure makes us all feel guilty and mediocre.

But all this rebellion makes me long for obedience, hunger and thirst for it, as a woman does for a husband whom she can esteem and who will direct her. Women especially cry out against their terrible freedom. But trying to be obedient and also personally responsible, responsive to the calls made upon one, means we are overburdened.

I don't know whether Candido de Leon ever showed up at Spring Street. He might have come when I was away or he might have encountered one of our group not too sympathetic to his ideas. I hope not. However as our dear Fr. Roy used to say, whatever happened, it was providential. God straightens out our mistakes.

Every night we say the rosary and compline [the liturgical night prayer] in our little chapel over the barn, heavy with the smell of the cow downstairs, (one can hear her chewing her cud) and we have a bulletin board there with names of those who ask prayers. Yours is there. There are half a dozen old men, several earnest young ones, an old woman from the Bowery, a former teacher with one eye, a mother of an illegitimate child, and so on. We all say the rosary, only six remain for compline. Do pray for us too. Your writing has reached many, many people and started them on their way. Be assured of that. It is the work God wants of you, no matter how much you want to run away from it. Like the Cure of Ars. God bless you always.

In Jesus Caritas

Dorothy

[Between Dorothy's letter of October 10, 1960 and Merton's letter of July 23, 1961, there appear to be missing letters on both sides. There is at least one missing letter from Dorothy, as Merton, in his letter of July 23, 1961 mentioned "your good note of a month ago and the enclosed letter from a boy in California, and all the news."]

[July 23, 1961—Merton to Dorothy]

August 15, 1961—Feast of the Assumption

Dear Fr. Louis,

I am terribly sorry about that poem ["Chant to be used in Processions around a Site with Furnaces"]. It was snatched from my hands so fast, and before I knew it, it was at the printers, since we were just going to press. All you said in relation to it was: "Here is a gruesome poem for you." And when I read "for you," I thought it was for the paper you meant it. I am indeed sorry for the sake of your friend on the west coast [Lawrence Ferlinghetti].

Our young friend, Jim Forest, is starting out on a bicycle tour in New England, I imagine to think things over about his vocation. He wrote to ask if he could visit St. John's Abbey, and when the abbot heard he was a c.o., he wrote it was better for him not to come. At Spencer [Massachusetts, in the Trappist monastery] there was also no room. Our position is more unpopular than ever, with recurring crises. We certainly need prayers. Also I have bad personal news: my son-in-law has had to go to the state mental hospital. He is [sic] in bad condition for some time and my daughter has endured a great deal. She has nine children and a heavy burden of work on the farm in which they all share.

Just looked at your letter again, and it did not say "for you." [Merton had simply written a P.S. on the side of the letter: "Here is a gruesome poem."] So again the dear Lord has to right our mistakes.

About nuclear warfare: Juliana of Norwich [fourteenth-century English mystic] said the worst has already happened and been repaired. Nothing worse can ever befall us. On a day like this, the feast of the Assumption, Heaven seems very near. Our Lady, body and soul in heaven; our Lord, body and soul in heaven—it makes heaven a reality for us earthbound creatures. Hope I am not being incoherent. We have had a long day, many visitors, many Puerto Rican children here on the farm. One can't think, which is just as well. Just work. Greetings from us all. With love in Christ,

Dorothy

[August 23, 1961—Merton to Dorothy. This letter marks a crucial juncture Merton had arrived at in his life and thinking. He says, in part: "I don't feel that I can in conscience, at a time like this, go on writing just about things like meditation . . . I think I have to face the big issues, the life-and-death issues."]

[September 22, 1961—Merton to Dorothy. This letter follows the position set forth in the letter of a month earlier. Merton sends Dorothy an article for the *Catholic Worker*. The article, entitled "The Root of War is Fear," was actually a chapter from Merton's soon to be published *New Seeds of Contemplation* (a revision of an earlier work), which had just been passed by the censors of the Order. To the article Merton added three long paragraphs (uncensored!) which, in his words, were simply to "situate these thoughts in the present crisis," but which were, in fact, highly inflammatory, placing Merton in a precarious position as a priest and monk speaking out against what he called the "war sickness" of the world and especially of America. This article launched Merton in the crusade against war. It brought joy to the few Catholics who had taken a definite stand against war and bewilderment to many Catholics who felt this monk would be better occupied in living his monastic vocation and not writing incendiary articles on social issues. From this point on the *Catholic Worker* became the principal publisher of Merton's writing on war and peace.]

[December 20, 1961—Merton to Dorothy. In this letter Merton attempts to clarify what he had written about in "Shelter Ethics" (*Catholic Worker*, November 1961), as he had learned that Dorothy did not agree with his approach.]

[March 21, 1962—Merton to Dorothy. This letter of Merton displayed some of his anxiety about his war-peace writings. It includes a number of corrections for a long article that appeared in two installments in the *Catholic Worker*. It was his effort to rewrite an article that had appeared (February 9, 1962) in *Commonweal* and that had been criticized by several people, some highly placed in the church hierarchy.]

[Missing letter—Dorothy to Merton (referred to by him in his letter of April 9, 1962)]

June 4, 1962

Dear Fr. Louis,

I am writing to beg prayers from you and your novices for Deane Mowrer, one of our editors who is undergoing a most serious operation today on her one remaining eye, hoping to save the sight of it. She is blind now, but they hope that if the membrane is removed from the back of the eye, she may have some little sight left. There is one chance in a thousand, the doctor says. He is a great specialist and she is getting the best of care, as the poor do in this city when it comes to medical aid. It is the middle class who have the hardest time for medical services.

And of course I want to thank you from my heart for the articles you have written and which have been so widely reprinted all over the country. You have been the first voice among the theologians since Fr. [John] Hugo [a priest from Pittsburgh and a frequent speaker at the Catholic Worker house] and his companions in the Second World War.

Of course I understand from your "letters" [*The Cold War Letters*] which Elbert Sisson let me see on my recent visit to Washington that you are not a pacifist and that you are speaking in terms of modern war. This may draw the Catholic layman further along the way of peace.

I am sending the letter [of December 20, 1961] you wrote me to Fr. Hugo, since, in a way, it seems to concern the whole controversy concerning nature and grace and I thought that he would be interested. He is a very busy parish priest now, with a large school (he is highly thought of by Bishop [John] Wright [Bishop of Pittsburgh at this time]) but he might have time to clarify for me some of the points you made in your letter.

Your letters charmed me: there was such a variety of interests, such a richness in them, all of which goes to increase our knowledge and love of God. I am going, I hope to Brazil this summer to visit the Grail and the Papal Volunteers with whom they are working. My book *The Long Loneliness* [New York: Harper and Row, 1952] is translated into Portuguese by Aimee Amorosa Lima [of Brazil] and I shall be very happy to meet her and her so famous family. I understand that there was quite a correspondence with Bernanos which is not translated. I must look up his letters to the English and to his American friends.

We have had visits from a dozen Brazilians connected with unions and the Young Christian Workers who came to our place in New York on a number of occasions. I am looking forward to my trip and this week must get my passport with the amended pledge that I will defend the Constitution according to my conscience or as far as my conscience permits. I will not be going until late July, so I do hope to hear from you. I would most appreciate it if you would put me on your mailing list, for any material which I would keep confidential but which I would like to show our other editors for our own information and enlightenment.

I do assure you that we are not "beats." Charles Butterworth is a Harvard Law School graduate and a convert. He formerly practiced law in Philadelphia and is 43. Ed Forand is a former marine, reconverted by Fr. Hugo when he was in a veterans' hospital in Butler, PA. Walter Karrel is a convert, a lover of music and painting. Judy Gregory is a Radcliffe graduate, and her father is the head of the Law Department of the University of Virginia. She is getting her Ph.D. on Simone Weil and Personalism. Anne Marie Stokes works with non-government agencies at the U.N., teaches French to support herself and uses her apartment to take care of some of our worst problems in an emergency. Bob Steed supports himself by a nightwatchman's job and helps edit the paper. Martin Corbin works with the *Liberation* staff and lives with wife and children at the print shop which supports the Glen Gardner community and so on and so on.

I say all this because in your letters you associate us with "beats," of whom there have been, thank God, but a few and they a fly by night crew who despised and ignored the poor around us and scandalized them by their dress and morals. I am afraid I am uncharitable about the intellectual who shoulders his way in to eat before the men on the line who have done the hard work of the world, and who moves in on the few men in one of the apartments and tries to edge them out with their beer parties and women. They can sleep on park benches as far as I am concerned. Unfortunately we are left with the women who are pregnant for whom I beg your prayers. We have two girls with babies, and three expecting, on the farm now. Three colored and two white, and one of the white girls is expecting a colored baby. She was running with a negro beat in the village, and only came to us because she could not find an abortionist. As far as I am concerned, I must look on these things as a woman, and therefore much concerned with the flesh and with what goes to sustain it. Sin is sin and the sentimental make a mystique of it.

Actually I am not just talking about the recent upsurge of beats that plagues the pacifist movement in England as well as in the U.S. I am talking about the war between the worker and the scholar that Peter Maurin said had to be overcome by the workers becoming scholars and the scholars workers. But enough of this. It is boiling hot, the work piles up and I must get at it.

Our typewriters are all giving out, so please excuse.

Gratefully in Christ,

Dorothy Day

[June 16, 1962—Merton to Dorothy. Merton informs Dorothy that he has been forbidden by the Abbot General in France to write on war and peace. He suggests that his superiors were "alerted by zealous individuals in this country."]

[July 12, 1962—Merton to Dorothy]

July 23, 1962

Dear Fr. Louis,

Thank you for your good letter and above all for the prayers, "spiritual direction," and paper about the English mystics. I read the latter aloud to Deane Mowrer this afternoon while we sat on the beach. It was her birthday—and it was so very, very good: it colored the whole day for us. She is completely blind now, so do keep praying for her. She has an unhappy temperament and a rebellious one. I'm praying she will get to writing more—she can type (touch system), has a tape recorder, record player, FM set, talking books, etc, but lives in misery. So do pray.

I'm trying to get a visa to Cuba. If I get it from our State dept., I'll wait till Sept.—it will take that long to get one: the inefficiency of bureaucracy. I want to see the collective farms, the educational system, the condition of religion.

Thank you again for everything, poem, conferences, etc.

With love from us all, In Christ,

Dorothy

[August 11, 1962—Merton to Dorothy]

August 23, 1962

Dear Father Merton,

Do not fear, your material will get to Brazil, because I am surely going in April with Hildegard Goss-Mayr and her husband [Jean],[8] in a way as a team, a peace team to speak of Christian non-violence throughout South America. I am waiting for them, because I have much to learn from them both. Her husband, whom I met for the first time last spring, on their way to South Africa, was a prisoner of war in the Second World War, and then worked with the priest workers and is committed to the peace position. There is much work to be done, so much to hope from people themselves who want work and land and bread.

Another reason I postponed my trip to Brazil is because my application for a visa to Cuba was granted by our State Department and I also received one from Havana, through the Czechoslovakian Embassy in Washington which is handling their affairs. My boat sails on Sept. 5th, the *Guadalupe*, and there is a chapel and a priest on board, and think of it, while I am on the boat I am under Spanish Law and will be confronted with pictures of Franco no doubt! I have met the ambassadors to the United Nations, Dr. Garcia and Dr. Premelles, and their wives and they are going back to Cuba this Friday to get prepared or briefed for the next session of the General Council, or whatever it is, of the United Nations. So I will see them there. Also I have contacts with others.

Will you please pray for me while I am there, that the U.S. planes do not bomb nor saboteurs blow up buildings, set fire to cane fields, etc., etc., as the *New York Times* says they are doing daily. William Worthy, the correspondent for the *Afro American* says I am quite likely to be shot by a counter-revolutionary so that the blame may be laid to the Castro forces. After all the revolution is still going on. So there is danger.

It is very heartening to see the reaction to your articles. They are being reprinted here and there, and as a matter of fact, we ourselves can reprint them too now and again. Nothing in our paper is copyrighted and we are only too delighted to see our stuff picked up and published all over.

As for Pax, I am afraid that the main reason it was formed was to take care of the fearful souls who do not wish to be associated with the Catholic Worker. I do not know what will come of it. N. N. has the push but not the stuff, as Peter Maurin would say. He jumps from this to that; and when he married out of the Church and insisted marriage had to do with two people and the priest was but a witness, not needed in his case, one realized how little down-to-earth knowledge he had of the sacraments, of the life of grace, of the tremendous teaching of the Church. Now the marriage has been solemnized, but the girl has publicly stated she made promises she did not intend to keep, and that she intends to have no more children, etc., etc., and that, in a nutshell, is why I am so cool to Pax. Actually [he] is the only one in it with any drive. He is so young and works so hard, but at the same time he is so undependible [*sic*]. So pray for them both.

Now here is a favor I am begging of you. Bob Steed, one of our editors, is setting out on a walking trip to Rome, with an English pacifist Catholic friend. He has worked the last four months, twelve hours a night, in a parking lot, saved five hundred dollars by rigid economy, paid his own rent and meals, since he worked nights, and after paying his fare, will arrive in London with little left. Will you give him a letter of introduction so that he can beg hospitality at monasteries for himself and friend along the way? They will be peace pilgrims, but there will be no speeches nor demonstrations, just a pilgrimage of penance and an appeal to the Holy Father to speak.

Bob is from Memphis and is going home by bus tonight to see his mother before he leaves. He may or may not drop by, but if you send me the note, I could convey it to him and we both would be most deeply grateful.

Did I tell you I read aloud your "English Mystics" [later published as an essay in Merton's book, *Mystics and Zen Masters* [New York: Farrar Straus and Giroux, 1967] to Deane Mowrer and it made us both happy. Gratefully in Jesus Christ,

Dorothy Day

[Merton to Dorothy—Note August 1962?]

November 12, 1962

Dear Fr. Louis,

This morning one of the two lovely girls who share the women's apartment with 2 old ladies of 78 and a half-mad Jewish convert of 30, and me, 65,—said: "Thank God for Thomas Merton." That was because of the T. Merton Reader which I keep on my desk there and we share. Also I say it for your essay on "Virginity"[9] which I have not yet read and which is going the rounds.

The girls had just been going on a peace march the night before, and there had been singing and a play, and the peace walk up to Central Park and the beauty of the fall night, and they were so happy, so full of joy, of love of all that is beautiful. But I, like a grandmother, fret and pray. The crowd they are with are drug addicts, perverts and so mixed up morally—so promiscuous!—that I am always fearing for their safety. So do pray for them all, hold them fast, all of them, in your prayers, that they wake out of this fascination which leads to torment.

We have had 5 girls this summer on the farm, two from Alabama, colored, with their babies (which they had at the farm) and 3 waiting. They come to us in such agony. The last two would have got rid of the babies by abortion if they could have, and one threatened to kill her child at birth. One girl is French and the other [*sic*] Italian descent. We have placed one child with one of our readers and are trying to place the other, which has a cleft palate. Both girls are 18. But what misery they have gone thru.

And those in this peace crowd, do not hesitate to have abortions.

I keep thinking of the first psalm.

Thank you for your letters, your goodness to us all.

Ammon was so happy to hear from you.

I am just back from Cuba, Mexico, etc. and now much desk work to do. Your prayers hold us up. God bless you.

Dorothy

March 17, 1963

Dear Father Louis,

I had the best of intentions to write to you before Ash Wednesday but at least you will have this letter by Easter Sunday. Thank you for your loving kindness to us. I enjoy all the things you send—when I can hang on to them. Your Selections from the Desert Fathers [*Wisdom of the Desert*, New York, New Directions, 1960] has already disappeared, books being convenient to walk off with, but I do thank you very much for sending them to me and little by little the books themselves will be reviewed. Jim Forest has one for the next issue.

Poor Jean [Forest] came to make a retreat with us for the first Sunday of Lent and excuse my critical attitude but the priest was duller than ditch water and actually put people to sleep. In our small chapel it was quite obvious. Do pray for her. I was touched that she wanted to come. They have a beautiful baby and I am very happy for them.

I want your prayers too for Ellen who is the one who said, "Thank God for Thomas Merton." She has contracted a civil marriage and had a miscarriage last month and is not too well now. She is a beautiful young girl and the daughter of one of our old Catholic Worker families. And since there are, I can think of this moment, five or six others married outside the Church who are the next generation Catholic Workers I do beg your prayers for them. However, Father Joseph Wood referred me to the book of Osee [Hosea] as comfort in such circumstances.

I have a few friends who are always worrying about your leaving the monastery but from the letters of yours that I read I am sure you will hold fast. I myself pray for final perseverance most fervently having seen one holy old priest suddenly elope with a parishioner. I feel that anything can happen to anybody at any time. But it does irritate me to hear these woeful predictions. As for your writing so much, I am very glad you do. I am sure it is a gift of God and you are just as likely to dry up and not be able to write anything later on, so might as well do all you can now.

Father Bede Griffiths[10] is coming to be a speaker at the Catholic Art Association meeting in Santa Fe this summer and will make a tour around the country. Someone asked me to make a list of places for him to visit and I am sure you would be happy to be seeing him there. We all send you our love. Gratefully in Christ,

Dorothy

P.S. I am probably going to Rome April 16 with a group from Women Strike for Peace who are foolishly expecting to get an audience. I told them it will probably be with 500 other people but a pilgrimage is a pilgrimage and if we can call attention to all the things the Pope has been saying about peace, that in itself is good. We can send our message of thanks to him and if you have any suggestions to offer and if you by any chance get this letter at once instead of having to wait until Easter, do write and let me know what you think.

[Dorothy to Merton—Missing Letter(s)?]

[December 4, 1963—Merton to Dorothy]

[December, 1963?]

Dear Fr. Louis,

Thank you for your good letter. After I heard Fr. N. was recovering, I gave up the idea of going down to see him right now. I have done so much traveling this past year that I feel the need of a "quiet" time at home—in the midst of the CW family.

Just now one of the farm family, a drifter, came in to tell me he was reading your latest paperback. You will never know the good you do. I pray the Lord will continue his inspiration—it is truly your vocation.

Greetings and loving gratitude from us all. In Christ,

Dorothy

St. John [Baptist] Day, June 24, 1965

Dear Father Louis,

Yesterday Dr. [Karl] Stern telephoned me from Montreal asking me to ask the Trappists, and my friends the cloistered Maryknoll Sisters for prayers for a great trouble he has. We are having a retreat here right now and reading the prison meditations of Fr. [Alfred] Delp [a Jesuit priest executed by the Nazis in 1945] with your introduction, and I thought of you right away. The call came right while we were at dinner. So first of all, I am asking you to pray most especially, and begging you to ask the community and since there is no time with God and prayer is retroactive accordingly, I am sure that already his weight of sorrow is lifted somewhat, or that he has had an increase of grace to bear it. He is a daily communicant, and a deeply suffering man. I sometimes think that without his writing and his music he would collapse.

I have been intending to write you for some time, just to thank you for your writings. You will never know the people you have reached, the good you have done. You certainly have used the graces and the talents God has given you. I am afraid I lack the discipline to do the work I ought to do, being occupied with many Martha-cares. Right now we are having a retreat for priests, a small affair, ten of them, and Fr. Hugo remains afterward to give a laymen's retreat.

As usual during retreats there are great distractions. One of our family, who had spent a good many years of his life in prison, in Sing Sing and Dannamora [sic], who had broken his parole and was threatened with a life sentence; who had sanctuary with us for the past ten years, died after much suffering with emphysema, if that is how you spell it. There were the details of grave digging, the pleading with the undertaker for a plain pine box instead of the satin lined casket. He told us only Jews used them, and Jewish cemeteries always smelled what with the decay coming up through the ground! Perhaps he really believed it, perhaps he was taught this—a sales pitch. When Peter Maurin was buried in 1949 the undertaker tried to bully us with tales of handles falling off of cheap caskets, and inexperienced pall bearers dropping the coffin and the body being spilled out on the church steps. How horrifying! There should be a committee in each parish to take care of those details of burial so that poor people need not be harassed and exploited at these sorrowful times. It was such a happy release for our poor man that we could only rejoice at his liberation and I did not at all mind fighting with the undertaker. But the expense anyway! It cost $400 to bury the dead at the very cheapest. And this is what they charge welfare also, to bury the destitute.

On top of our other troubles, two young drug addicts tried to take refuge with us the night before. And refuge for them means a harbor in a libertarian atmosphere, where they will not be interfered with. The peace movement seems to be plagued by such. On the Quebec-Guantanomo [sic] march they had to exact a pledge from the marchers not to indulge in drugs, liquor or extra-marital intercourse. "And what's wrong with that?" six young freedom riders asked me when I expelled from our midst two young people, one an ex-seminarian, who were keeping girls with them in our rooms which they shared with men from the Bowery. I could only explain that people were not sending us money to support them, but to support the destitute. That they should get work, and it was available to them, and support themselves in the way they wished to live. Peter Maurin's philosophy of work, an understanding of it and a living by it, would do a great deal to discipline these young lives.

So you see by this, I am having a hard time right now and I am begging your prayers for me, myself. I am sending you also something I have written about our problems in the city. If you know of someone who could help us, do pass it on.

[no signature]

[July 16, 1965—Merton to Dorothy]

August 11, 1965

Dear Father Louis,

Your letter and manuscript came while Karl Stern was staying with us and he was so happy to get your good words about his book. Caroline Gordon Tate liked it very much too. The review in the *Times* was not good.

Our Pax weekend was very good, thanks to Jim Douglass. He has been urging me to go to Rome to try to reach the bishops directly and at that very weekend a friend gave me $500 to go. So I beg your prayers. We will be there by the 15th of Sept. Martin Corbin and I cannot thank you enough for the Maximus article which we will use in Sept. issue. The Aug. issue was all directed to the bishops of the world.

I am right now at the Catholic Art Assoc. yearly meeting and some Benedictines were much impressed with the *Commonweal* article.

Jim Douglass[11] is outstanding—a daily communicant, most disciplined, strong and gentle. The best of all the peace group. Jim Forest gets better all the time. Tom Cornell is in deep trouble over a critically ill wife. The Pax group, Eileen Egan[12] and Howard Everingham [Everngam], grow in numbers among the older, more conservative. All of us count on your prayers and continued work. God bless you always. With love from us all—

Dorothy

[November 11, 1965—Merton to Dorothy—telegram regarding the tragic death of Roger LaPorte.]

November 16, 1965

Dear Father Louis,

Excuse me for writing your name wrong on the envelope [She had addressed it to "Father Thomas Merton"]. We are so full of distractions these days. I am sitting by the hospital bed of our oldest resident, Agnes, widow of a coal barge captain, who herself lived in barges for thirty years. She has been with us for 15. I look upon her with admiration and wonder and hope I have her sweetness and patience at the close of my life.

About your telegram—we are so glad you know about our tragedy,[13] being assured you are praying for us.

I am certainly behind the boys who burned their draft cards—Tom Cornell has been with us for years, and David Miller and Jim Wilson all summer and working all day, every day, with the poor. As for poor Roger [LaPorte], he was only living with us a few days, while he searched for another apartment. He had worked for Columbia two years and was going to school. When I came back from Rome, I met him for the first time. Since he only came in occasionally to serve tables or to attend our Friday night meetings, I had never actually exchanged a word with him. But he seemed to me older and more mature than his twenty-two years. The pictures in the press were high school ones.

If anyone had ever dreamed he contemplated such an action, he would have been watched day and night by the other young ones such as Jim Wilson, David Miller, Kathy, Nicole and the others. They were all in their early -0's [twenties perhaps?]—and very much "in love" with each other and with life. None of us can understand what happened.

I am only hoping that your reaction, as evidenced by your telegram, that is, holding us responsible, is not general, but I am afraid it may be. We have already received two bomb threats and I myself have been threatened at a public meeting at N.Y. Univ.

Of course, as members of one Body we are all responsible for each other.

The November issue of the *C.W.* will have short comments by other members of our group. Do you receive the paper regularly? Did you receive the July-Aug. issue directed to the bishops of the world, with articles by Jim Douglass and others?

Did you see Cardinal Leger's[14] wonderful speech at Toronto Univ. [Conference on the Second Vatican Council] published in the *Montreal Star* last June? Leslie Dewart[15] sent us his copy which must be returned to him after we copy it.

In view of the terrible things that are happening—the accidental bombing of friendly villagers, the spraying with napalm of our own troops yesterday, there is [sic] bound to be increased protests.

I am glad that there are so many now. The Catholic Worker has borne the burden for 33 years—protesting wars, Chinese-Japanese, Ethiopian, Spanish, World War II, Korean, Algerian and now this.

My nephew, David, (my only sister's son), is reading *Seven Storey Mountain* now. He and his wife are agnostic (She would say atheist) and she refuses to read it. Or rather, in her fear of what the book may do to him, she calls it a bore! They have a three-year-

-old who has no legs and only one arm and he suffers terribly. One other child is ill [?]. They are caring for my daughter's youngest who is 5, the same age as their oldest. Will you please pray for him? I think he is close to the Church. We all love you dearly and please keep praying for us.

Dorothy

[November 22, 1965—Merton to Dorothy]

December 2, 1965

Dear Father Louis,

I hasten to write to thank you from my heart for your most reassuring letter and to tell you that I agree with it in many ways. I am in agreement with the draft card burners because they are young men liable to the draft. You are a contemplative priest and your vocation is another one. Our faith does not count for much if we did not believe that your vocation to bring the suffering world and the individuals in it before the Lord in prayer was infinitely more important than anything else. We have always talked about the primacy of the spiritual and during the Second World War, I took a year off in order to spend my time in prayer and study in an old convent down on Long Island. It was on that occasion that [James Francis Aloysius] Cardinal McIntyre,[16] who was then Bishop, called me into the chancery office, asked me where I would be during the coming year and told me that they would hold me responsible for the work then as well as any other time. This I took as a mandate to continue—a very indirect one.

When I saw Father [Daniel] Berrigan a week before the draft card burning, I advised him not to come to these meetings where there was about to be violence of one kind or another and pointed out to him that the lay person had a distinct vocation to work in the Temporal Order, and I was glad to see that he did not come. I think all of his writing and his speaking have done a wonderful amount of good and even now, his silence will cry out in what people consider his exile in South America. However, my feeling is that he is in some ways young and inexperienced—and that being sent off on such a tour is to his advantage. I base my judgment on two things. One is that some of my friends said that in answering objectors in Detroit, he became pretty sarcastic. Perhaps it was his first experience with the man of the streets—the kind of people who read the *Daily News*. So many priests are used to a collegiate atmosphere and never come up close to the kind of people who come in on our bread lines. These are the masses we will have to reach if we are trying to change men's attitudes. This is the distinctive thing about the Catholic Worker—that in all our houses the majority are these men the world calls derelicts and who really are men who have done much of the hard work of the country. We are not just talking to each other as so many in the pacifist movement do.

And my second judgment was that he was too excited, in his actions—emotional, overwrought. Perhaps I am wrong, but such transfers will deepen his experience and knowledge. I will not protest it, tho the others disagree with me.

I just received your book today and thank you from my heart for it. God has given you a great grace to keep writing as you do—an inspiration to us all.

Received also a copy of the speech Jim Douglass made in Pittsburgh—the best yet. We will use it of course—also Cardinal Leger's Toronto speech.

I speak tomorrow in New Haven and Providence. Then in New York—Fordham and Yeshiva. Next week in Philadelphia. I shall take no more engagements for the winter. It will be good to be quiet, to read, study and enjoy the country.

I count on your prayers. Remember the girl I told you of who said: "Thank God for Thomas Merton"? She was going bad, men and marijuana, and these last two years she is fine—has a good husband, a child and has retreated to the countryside. I am sure you are holding us up in your fruitful solitude. God bless you.

Love from us all. In Christ,

Dorothy

[December 20, 1965—Merton to Dorothy. Merton writes, regarding her evaluation of Daniel Berrigan: "I guess you and I are a bit old-fashioned, but I agree with you."]

[December 1965—card from Dorothy to Merton (referred to in Merton's next letter, but missing.)]

[December 29, 1965—Merton to Dorothy]

[Various notes from Dorothy to Merton in 1966 may be missing.]

[September 12, 1966—Merton to Dorothy]

[October 28, 1966—Merton to Dorothy]

January 29, 1967

Dear Father Louis,

Do please forgive my long silence. I do not remember if I ever thanked you for your wonderful article on Camus ["Albert Camus and the Church," *Catholic Worker*, December 1966] which has had wide repercussions, teachers writing for a score or so copies for their classes, and many individual responses. We get so overcome with visits that we are all overworked, and the mail piles up, as you well know. When I thought of it, I thought you would probably rather not hear from one extra person. I am at present enjoying your *Conjectures of a Guilty Bystander*. We all feel that way. I am enclosing the last issue of the *CW* in which I had to write about [Francis Joseph] Cardinal Spellman [archbishop of New York], not only to cry out in grief, but also to point [*sic*] the fact that we are all guilty. We can never do enough praying, fasting, penance and I'm glad and happy as usual that Lent is beginning, and I can start anew and try harder. A rather childish feeling because I know how comfort seeking I am. You know that wonderful prayer of St. Ephraim, part of his story in Helen Wadell's [*sic*] *Desert Fathers*.[17] I read it years ago, took it from its context, Stanley V., our printer and fellow-editor made a prayer card of it, and within a year or so I find it included in an Eastern prayer book, containing many prayers beside the Byzantine liturgy. Our life is incomparably rich in many ways, in our reading, in our liturgy. I even feel guilty about that, feeling that I am spiritually self-indulgent. However there are deserts too to cross. But women always have the good remedy of housework, meals, people to take care of and that pulls us through.

This is a babbling letter. Please excuse it. It is just to thank you from my heart and to beg you to send us any material you have which we always welcome with great joy. In Christ,

Dorothy

[February 9, 1967—Merton to Dorothy]

July or August 1967

Dear Father Louis,

This suffering soul asked me to forward this to you. She is an old friend, by letters, and has lived in community. I am vague as to the details.

We had a very grand Pax mtg. Gordon Zahn,[18] Eileen Egan, Howard Everingham [Everngam] and 100 others. Two or three more big mtgs. during the summer, including Peacemakers and War Resisters League. Truly ecumenical and including many without belief. Pray for us all this summer. Also some very good CPF [Catholic Peace Fellowship] days of recollection. Jersey and L.I. groups very strong.

Karl Stern just spent a week with us and we had good music. He is a beautiful pianist and there was a very good flute player with a silver flute. Much Mozart too.

Do you have Guardini's *Last Things*, Pantheon, '54? Or St. Catherine of Genoa on Purgatory? Could Karl borrow them? He needs them.

Finally have permit from the city to reconstruct our new headquarters in N.Y. Need 20,000 or more!! If you see any benefactors around, nudge them. Or tell St. Joseph to.

Love and gratitude,

Dorothy

[August 18, 1967—Merton to Dorothy]

September 13, 1967

Dear Father Louis,

Please excuse me for my delay in answering your most welcome letter. I read the article you sent on Auschwitz ["Auschwitz: A Family Camp," a review of *Auschwitz* by Bernard Naumann. *Catholic Worker*, November 1967] and it is an overwhelming account. I told Marty Corbin November would be the best month when we are thinking of the dead and meditating on the four last things. The most awful part of it is how the Germans so soon forget and we so soon forget.

I have had the wonderful good fortune to be going to the Lay Congress and I am sailing on the 30th of September. A dear friend who says she owes her conversion to the Catholic Worker is paying my fare both ways and my upkeep in Rome. I would like to hear more about the seven day fast in Geneva. I had not heard anything about it and neither had Marty.

N. N. was visiting us here for three days. He was fine while he was here but New York is not good for him. I understand that he is now back in the Bahamas but I have a strong feeling that he will be our chaplain here eventually and we will be happy indeed to have him. You probably know his weakness and one of the best things I can say for Cardinal Spellman is that he has never hesitated to give faculties in this diocese to priests who are in difficulties. Whereas the Philadelphia Archdiocese, back in the days when we had a farm near Easton, Pennsylvania, informed us that his Eminence was not at all pleased that we had some of these difficult situations with us. Do please pray for Jack.

And there is another situation I am begging your prayers for and I ask the prayers of the community also. A young girl named Barbara, a widow with a child, is in a truly crucial situation. She is living with the husband of a family Jim McMurry brought up here last summer, a man who went berserk up here, smashing furniture, threatening people, etc. She rashly took him in along with a few others we were not able to handle. Now the others have left, she has thrown away her plans for college and we hear he has a "sixty dollar a day habit." She seems to be in a state of delayed shock and the future can only be grim for her unless a miracle intervenes.

God bless you always. Drop me a line if you can about the fast. With love and gratitude.

Dorothy

[September 19, 1967—Merton to Dorothy]

September 28, 1967

Dear Father Louis,

Thank you for your very prompt answer about the fast. I will be home before it begins, I see. I enjoyed your letter very much. The thing I love about the Little Brothers of Jesus is, they really know how to do nothing. They go settle themselves and there is an aura of peace and joy, not to speak of manual labor and prayer, surrounding them.

I visited them in Detroit and between the conflict of a new house which didn't last too long, made up pretty much of a dissipated young crowd and the older CW group who have kept two houses going for the last twenty years, there was quite a struggle going on and Brother Roger in a beautiful state of detachment brought peace to both sides and certainly to me too. What a tremendous amount can be accomplished by just doing nothing. I am sure you know what I mean. Certainly working a full day in a factory and coming home and spending an hour on your knees when you could be falling over with fatigue of both mind and body is not doing nothing.

I am up to my ears in work getting ready to leave tomorrow for New York. I sail Saturday and I can scarcely think. I am deeply grateful that you are offering Mass for me September 30 and deeply grateful too that you are praying for Barbara.

With love in Christ,

Dorothy

[December 20, 1967—Merton to Dorothy]

[July 25, 1968—Merton to Dorothy]

August 19, 1968

Dear Father Louis,

We have just listened to your poems [the "Freedom Songs," originally written for Robert Lawrence Williams], set to music by Alexander Peloquin. There were four of your eight freedom songs and solos. They were sung by Matthew Fraling of St. Gregory's Church, Baltimore, and by Sister Laetitia, R.S.M. Shall I send you the program? The songs were enough to break down the walls of Jericho. People wept with joy. What beautiful music! Magnificent! Martin Luther King's sister was in the choir, or rather one of the two choirs. There was also most extraordinary musical accompaniment by a small orchestra. Miss King says it will be telecast. One priest said he would give me a tape of it. It is one a.m. and I had to write you at once. I have been so entranced by the music and the words. Thank you, thank you. Also your fascinating paper for the Pax group. You have enriched our lives so many times.

Love and gratitude,

Dorothy

This concluding letter in their correspondence was written from Washington, D.C., where Dorothy had attended the National Liturgical Conference meeting. A special service at the Conference honored Martin Luther King, Jr. [who had been assassinated on April 4, 1968]. Two choirs, the Ebenezer Baptist Choir as well as Dr. Peloquin's Choir from Providence, Rhode Island, sang four of Merton's "Freedom Songs," as Dorothy mentioned in her letter. What she failed to mention is that she too had been honored by the Liturgical Conference for her work on behalf of the poor and the homeless.

NOTES

1. In referring to Dorothy Day, in my notes about this correspondence, I have used her given name rather than what scholarly convention would expect: her surname. I do this to clarify their relationship as seen in this correspondence. Merton had too deep a reverence for her ever to call her "Day." One might object that to be consistent, I should refer to Merton as "Father Louis." I admit the inconsistency but justify it by the fact that no one (except his fellow monks and Dorothy Day) would name him in this way. Furthermore, in the sixties Merton scarcely ever signed his letters with his religious name.

2. In November 1965 Roger LaPorte, a young Catholic Worker, immolated himself on the steps of the United Nations building as a protest against the war in Vietnam.

3. Charles Eugene de Foucauld (1868–1916), a French priest, spent much of his life living in solitude in the Sahara. He left a Trappist monastery and set up a hermitage in the Sahara on the Morocco-Algeria frontier. His writings inspired the founding of the "Little Brothers of Jesus" (1933) and the "Little Sisters of Jesus" (1936).

4. A Merton letter, probably sent in December, appears to be missing.

5. Habakkuk was an Old Testament prophet.

6. John Cassian (c. 360–435) studied the monastic tradition of the monks of the Egyptian desert. He founded two monasteries in Marseilles. His *Institutiones* (setting out rules for monastic life) and his *Conferences* (recounting his conversations with the monks of the Christian East) became standard reading in monasteries in the Middle Ages and even later.

7. John Climacus (c. 570–649) was a monk, later abbot, of the Monastery of St. Catherine's at Mt. Sinai. His *Ladder of Paradise* discusses monastic virtues and vices and the climb to the ideal of complete dispassionateness (*apatheia*).

8. Hildegard Mayr (Austrian) and Jean Goss (French) were married in 1958. They were in Rome actively concerned with peace issues at the Second Vatican Council. They have given their lives to teaching and practicing nonviolence in many areas of the world: Eastern Europe, Brazil, Central America, and the Philippines.

9. "Christian Humanism and Virginity in St. Ambrose" was a conference Merton gave at Gethsemani in 1962. It was later published in *Cistercian Studies* 17 (1982).

10. An English Benedictine who founded an ashram in India.

11. James Douglass is a theologian, writer, and teacher, active at the Second Vatican Council, author of *The Non-Violent Cross* (Macmillan, 1968) and other works on peace. He has been especially active in the Ground Zero Center for Non-Violent Action.

12. Eileen Egan has been and continues to be active in Pax Christi and in the New York Catholic Worker.

13. Roger LaPorte immolated himself in front of the United Nations building in a desperate gesture for peace. Merton, believing this was suicide, sent a telegram asking that his name be withdrawn from the list of sponsors of the Catholic Peace Fellowship.

He later softened his position. See Thomas Merton, *The Hidden Ground of Love: Letters on Religious Experience and Social Concerns*, edited by William H. Shannon (New York, 1985) 87.

14. Paul-Emile Cardinal Leger, archbishop of Montreal, was a leading figure actively involved in the Second Vatican Council.

15. Leslie Dewart taught at the University of Toronto. His publications include *The Future of Unbelief* and other works.

16. James Francis Aloysius Cardinal McIntyre was auxiliary bishop of New York at the time of which Dorothy Day speaks. In 1948 he became archbishop of Los Angeles and subsequently a cardinal.

17. Helen Waddell, *The Desert Fathers* (Constable, 1936).

18. Gordon Zahn, well-known sociologist and pacifist, wrote, among other works, *In Solitary Witness*, the story of Franz Jagerstaetter, a conscientious objector to Hitler's war, who was executed after a military trial. Zahn is national director of Pax Christi USA Center on Conscience and War.

9

The Struggle of the Small Vehicle, Pax

Eileen Egan

On a bright, bracing Sunday in late October 1962 in New York City, fear-stricken and confused, people poured into the streets in the largest peace demonstration in the city's history. It was the climactic day of the Cuban Missile Crisis.

That day we launched a Catholic peace group, the American Pax Association. It was to be linked with Pax-England, a longstanding peace group headed by lay Catholics.

As we met in midtown Manhattan in the Shelbourne Hotel, we could hear the shouted slogans of the marching crowds, an undercurrent to the words of the speaker, Joseph Cunneen. "The sad fact," he told the fifty-some listeners, "is that American Catholics give every evidence of suspending moral categories in the whole area of warfare as long as Communism is the enemy. . . . I would like to know what American bishop has not, by tacit consent of silence, blessed in advance the missile bases that ring the Soviet Empire, as well as the basic operating policy of Western defense."

Only on 22 October had President John F. Kennedy announced to the American people that spy planes revealed the presence of nuclear missile sites on Cuban soil. The secretary of defense appeared on television before an enlarged photograph of the Soviet-built missile sites, using a pointer to show millions of Americans the danger at their doorstep.

Heading towards Cuba, at the order of Premier Nikita Khrushchev, were Soviet ships carrying offensive nuclear missiles. They would be placed ninety miles from the shores of the United States. President Kennedy told the American people that a naval blockade was poised to intercept the Soviet vessels. The heart-stopping question was how Khrushchev would respond. The American and Soviet regimes were staring each other down, and we were staring into the abyss.

That Sunday we grasped as never before the reality that the nuclear powers possessed the readiness to light up the planet with death. We felt the helpless horror of humankind held hostage by the nuclear giants. Our own nation, in a policy called deterrence, dissuasion by terror, had amassed death-dealing instruments capable of vaporizing whole cities along with their inhabitants. The United States had already shown the world how it could be done in unleashing the power of the split atom on two Japanese cities.

Our meeting was interrupted for the news that Khrushchev had ordered the Soviet ships facing the naval blockade to turn back with their lethal cargo. The missiles already delivered would be removed. We realized how close we had come to an apocalypse of destruction when we read the statement of Defense Secretary McNamara describing the evening before the climactic Sunday. "On a beautiful fall evening," he recalled in the *New York Times*, "as I left the President's office to return to the Pentagon, I thought I might never live to see another Saturday night."

With a sense that humankind had been given only a reprieve, the American Pax Association began its life in the United States. When the American Pax Association was born, the Catholic concerned with church teaching on peace and war faced a paucity of choice. Even in Catholic schools and seminaries, the concept of peace, a basic, sometimes referred to as a constituent, element of the gospel was generally not taught as such. The duty of the citizen to the nation during war was emphasized. There was a nod in the direction of certain abstract principles known as the just-war criteria. The role of the Catholic in military service was fairly simple, expressed in the assertion, "When your country calls you, you must go." Two Catholic groups focused on the issues of war and peace, the Catholic Worker movement and the Catholic Association for International Peace.

The Catholic Worker claimed a complete pacifism, often referred to as "Sermon on the Mount" pacifism. It embraces a thoroughgoing gospel nonviolence. The other functioning organization was the Catholic Association for International Peace (CAIP), sponsored by the American Catholic hierarchy. Founded in 1927, its office and staff were part of the Social Action Department of what was then called the National Catholic Welfare Conference. It published valuable studies by expert theologians on international relations, including issues of war and peace.

Homer Jack, a longtime peace activist and leader of the World Conference on Religion and Peace, characterized the CAIP as not a peace organization but rather an association dealing with international relations in general. Robert Ludlow, an editor of the *Catholic Worker* during the fifties, gave a harsher appraisal, describing the organization, perhaps unfairly, as "in peacetime for peace; in wartime for war."

In truth, some of us had expected the CAIP to do more than it was designed to do. It was an educational association, presenting faithfully and cogently the age-old just-war tradition as the moral undergirding for the participation of

Christians in warfare. It was not designed to take the lead in a prophetic approach to the crisis of the times.

A balanced assessment of the CAIP came from William A. Au: "The C.A.I.P. accepted the just war theory of Aquinas as its operative theological position from which it sought to oppose both pacifists and isolationists, both of which were seen as being contrary to papal teaching and to the global responsibilities and interests of the United States."[1]

Robert Hovde, a priest who had been a conscientious objector in the Second World War, Mrs. Hermene Evans, a convinced pacifist and activist, and I attended the annual CAIP conferences, generally held in Washington, D.C. We were never invited to address the public, but we held our own private sessions. We wondered how we could include the option of gospel nonviolence somewhere in the general discussion. On one occasion, at a closed business meeting at the end of a CAIP conference, we were asked for a response to the matter of modern warfare. We proceeded to question the just-war theory, in particular the inevitability of the slaughter of noncombatants. A journalist, an interloper at the closed meeting, made headlines from our contribution, an unhappy development for the organizers of the conference.

Some lay Catholics in New York City, seized with the desire to awaken the American Catholic community to a deeper awareness of the moral aspects of modern war in the light of Catholic teaching, learned of an alternative approach. Archbishop Thomas D. Roberts, former Archbishop of Bombay, and John Heidbrink of the Fellowship of Reconciliation suggested that American Catholics might find a useful model in Pax, a peace association founded and conducted by English lay Catholics.

Beginning late in 1961, the original three, Jim Forest, Howard Everngam, and I, met to explore what was needed in a new peace organization. Jim Forest, released from the Navy as a conscientious objector, had become managing editor of the *Catholic Worker*. Howard Everngam, a harpsichord maker, had, with some difficulty and without help from church agencies, achieved the status of conscientious objector in the period of the universal military draft. He had been influenced by Eric Gill, the English artist and sculptor, one of the founders of Pax in 1936. I had been led into the gospel nonviolence of Jesus by my mother, one of whose heroines was Nurse Edith Cavell, an Englishwoman executed by firing squad in World War I. Accused by the German military of spying because at her Belgian hospital Cavell gave medical aid to soldiers of both sides, she made a memorable statement before her execution. "Standing as I do in view of God and Eternity, I realize that patriotism is not enough," Cavell said. "I must have no hatred or bitterness towards anyone." My mother recited this to me by heart.

Dorothy Day intensified my commitment not only by her words, but by her living example of the daily practice of the works of mercy for the forsaken and the ignored. Appalled by the mercilessness of the Second World War, I found a way to participate in works of mercy for refugees and the war-afflicted through a newly founded agency of the church for overseas aid.

My revulsion against war and violence dated from before my immersion in the agony of Polish survivors of Siberian exile and in Europe's night of misery after the Second World War. The displaced persons cowering in their bleak camps, the millions of expelled ethnic Germans crowded obscenely into barracks and hangars, and the horror of the Dachau concentration camp laid a burden on my heart. Hunger and homelessness faced me from Berlin, Hamburg, Frankfurt, and Cologne to Vienna, Taranto, and Palermo—all speaking of what happens when "man becomes a wolf to man."

Across the world in Calcutta, I accompanied a woman who nursed the spark of life in near-corpses left to die on the street—a witness to the inviolable sacredness of every human life. And further east, in Vietnam, I saw how nearly a million refugees from north of the seventeenth parallel fashioned new villages in a lush country with the most ancient of tools, the human hand. These new villages, I was to discover, died young.

Dorothy Day's often repeated advice to those starting new houses, farms, or new groups was "go ahead." This time, the advice dealt with an initiative close to her heart. She blessed our efforts to bring the peace message of Jesus to the wider Catholic community. We had no funds, no meeting place except our flats. Most often we met in the flat and workroom of Howard Everngam, a walk-up in an old building in Manhattan. It was a peaceful place at the back of the house away from the street noise. We always had the company of a harpsichord at some stage of its fashioning, or an instrument under repair.

We entered into a considerable correspondence with the leaders of Pax and received copies of their publication, the *Pax Bulletin*. Then, my visit to England in July 1962 enabled me to meet with English Pax leaders—John J. O'Connor, secretary, Margaret Maison, vice-chairperson, and Charles S. Thompson, *Pax Bulletin* editor. They and their membership enthusiastically supported a U.S. link with Pax. Meanwhile, on this side of the Atlantic we corresponded with peace-minded persons in Philadelphia, Baltimore, Washington, Chicago, and San Francisco. Our New York group grew to include Ed Rice, editor of *Jubilee*, a much-praised Catholic magazine, Janet Burwash, a social worker, Dorothy Dohen, editor of *Integrity* magazine and a sociologist, and Clare Danielsson, who joined the church with Dorothy Day as her godmother. Kieran Dugan and Arthur Sheehan, both former editors of the *Catholic Worker*, were also part of the early group.

Arthur Sheehan reminded us that a branch of Pax had existed briefly in the United States, taking shape shortly after its founding in England. It focused on the right of conscientious objection to military service. In 1940, Dorothy Day and Peter Maurin asked Sheehan to deal with the more than nine hundred queries received at the Catholic Worker from young men concerned with the imminence of the military draft. The Association of Catholic Conscientious Objectors led by Arthur Sheehan was formed at the outbreak of the Second

World War and it absorbed the early Pax. The description of the purpose of Pax as sent to the United States from London seemed to satisfy everyone: "An association of Catholics and others who seek to promote peace and to encourage the practical application of Christian principles to the question of war." In New York City in 1962, the Pax council (now numbering twelve) simply added to this:

> The Gospel has not one law of charity for individuals and another for states and nations.

(Benedict XV)

The Principles of Pax

> The continuous tradition of Catholic moral teaching affirms that the use of force, especially in war, must be governed by rigid conditions if such use is to be morally justifiable. It is therefore the duty of a Christian, before he engages in war or takes any part in supporting war, to satisfy himself in the light of Catholic morality that attention is paid to these conditions, and that the war is just in its cause, its means, and its effects; for he has the right to examine in the light of his own conscience the actions of a civil government. No individual, no society, is free from the duty of an honest examination of conscience.

(Pius XI)

Before all contingencies, including what may be the lawful one of force, the right of the Christian to choose to practice the counsels of perfection must be recognized.

True peace is the fruit of right order and will be attained only by working for it as arduously and creatively as is done for victory in war.

The Objects of Pax

To unite those who accept these principles on grounds of either Christian morality or natural reason.

To give moral support and practical guidance to conscientious objectors and others whose fidelity to these principles involves them in difficulties.

To study, clarify, and make known the implications of the Christian message to the problems of war and peace, the use of force, nationalism, patriotism and the authority of the state.

The statement of Pope Benedict XV, the Peace Pope of the First World War, regarding the practice of the same law of love by individuals and national communities had revolutionary implications for Christian citizens. It served as an emblem for English Pax. When Pope John XXIII repeated this assertion in his encyclical *Pacem in Terris*, it became an emblem for Pax in the United States. "The right of Christians to choose to practice the counsels of perfection," in the parlance of an earlier day, was another way of asserting the right to pacifism or gospel nonviolence.

Around this statement of purpose, we gathered a group of sponsors led by Dorothy Day. They included Thomas Merton, Ed Rice, and Robert Lax, the three companions of Columbia University days described in Merton's *The Seven Storey Mountain*. Others were Archbishop Roberts, Philip Scharper, editor at Sheed and Ward, Franziskus Stratmann, O.P., Gordon Zahn, author of groundbreaking books on the church and war, and Joseph Cunneen, founder and editor of *Cross Currents*, a quarterly devoted to contemporary implications of Christianity.

When officers were chosen, Jim Forest was not among them, for disagreement with Dorothy Day had led to his leaving the Pax group. In 1964, Forest, with Tom Cornell, Martin Corbin, and Philip Berrigan, started the Catholic Peace Fellowship, affiliated with the Fellowship of Reconciliation, the expressly pacifist, ecumenical peace organization. "Thus, by 1964," William A. Au observed, "the Catholic Worker, Pax and the CPF constituted the organizational backbone of the first viable American Catholic peace movement."[2]

Howard Everngam was named the Pax's chairperson; Kieran Dugan, vice-chairperson; Janet Burwash, treasurer, and I, publications editor. Most of us considered ourselves to be personalists, a term used by Peter Maurin, Dorothy Day's mentor. He took it from the work of Emmanuel Mounier. Dorothy, to stress her separation from impersonal bureaucracies and the power of the state, used the term *anarchism*. Though we knew that she meant the anarchism of Peter Kropotkin, the practice of voluntary associations linking with other voluntary associations, personalism remained our term of choice. We found it easier to explain as a basis for personal moral responsibility. Though many of us had been deeply influenced by Dorothy Day, none of us lived at the Catholic Worker. We all had full-time positions in a variety of occupations.

Because we planned to make our headquarters in New York City, whose Catholic diocese was headed by Francis Cardinal Spellman, we wrote to him to inform him of our plans but did not receive a reply. We decided that the formal launching of the American Pax Association, a movement to apply the message of Jesus to the social organization for violence known as war, would take place on the day in the church calendar known as the Feast of Christ the King. It turned out to be 28 October 1962.

From its beginnings, Pax accepted as members those holding the just-war position as well as pacifists. A distinctive path from the undeviating pacifism of the Catholic Worker, this occurred even though many of the founders and leaders of Pax came from the matrix of the Catholic Worker, or had come under its influence. They considered themselves committed to Sermon on the Mount pacifism. Dorothy Day agreed with the Pax approach and saw the role of Pax as one of awakening Catholics to the reality that Christian principles should not be jettisoned when a nation declares war.

Pax did not treat judgmentally those Catholics still bound by just-war thinking. The magazine of Pax, simply called *Peace*, opened its pages to the dilemma of those struggling with the issue of using violence to expunge evil. We hoped that by explaining the rational just-war formulations, and their contemporary inadequacy, we would help Catholics to question—and even reject—war, at least modern war. Our primary purpose consisted of bringing some "clarification of thought," in Peter Maurin's phrase, to the issue of peace and war. As laypersons, we had considered our task as that of reaching other laypeople. Pax-England indicated another route—approaching the Catholic Church itself for further clarification.

The Second Vatican Council had just brought the Catholic bishops of the entire world to Rome at the call of Pope John XXIII. At a Pax-England weekend conference in Spode, England, in November 1962, we met to frame a statement, actually an appeal, to Pope John:

We, a group of the faithful, gathered to study the problem of modern war, find that the manifest preparations for a war of indiscriminate destruction confront Christians with a grave conflict of conscience. At this time, when the Universal Church is in Council, we ask our Holy Father that this unique opportunity be taken for giving guidance on this subject to Christians throughout the world.

There might have been no connection with the Pax appeal, but less than six months later, on 11 April 1963, Pope John XXIII addressed the letter *Pacem in Terris* (Peace on Earth) to all humanity.

Peace on Earth presented a strong, updated base for Catholic peace efforts. It validated civil disobedience ("God has more right to be obeyed than man"). The letter shocked many cold warriors by urging coexistence between differing political systems, pointing clearly to the warlike stance between the communist world and the "free" or capitalist world. It called for the ending of the arms race and the banning of nuclear weapons. "The truly revolutionary feature of the Encyclical," E. M. Borgese wrote, in the *Nation* "was the abandonment of the age-hallowed distinction between just and unjust wars. It is alien to reason to suppose that in the atomic era war could be an instrument of justice. Pope John XXIII did not say 'war waged by atomic weapons,' but *war as such* is ruled out in the atomic era."[3]

One electrifying statement in Pope John XXIII's letter echoed that of Pope Benedict XV. "The same moral law," asserted Pope John, "which governs relations between individual human beings serves also to regulate the relations of political communities." These twenty words appeared in capitals on the back cover of the premier issue of *Peace*, as though etched on a stone column.

Peace magazine was published as a thirdly, beginning in July 1963. Its first issue featured two significant articles, Joseph Cunneen's "The Need to Face the Question" (cited earlier) and "Catholic Social Doctrine and World Peace" by George H. Dunne, S.J. The magazine was designed by our Pax craftsman,

Howard Everngam, and by a volunteer artist, Tom Lyons. Six line drawings marked the first issue, including that of a skeleton holding what looked to be an umbrella—a nuclear cloud. Donations from members and sponsors made it possible to have *Peace* printed in strikingly clear letterpress.

In two years, it was the turn of American Pax to prod the universal church on the issue of peace and war. The setting was the Third Session of the Vatican Council, on 9 and 10 November 1966, where scarcely more than an hour was given to the opening of the discussion "On Making Lasting Peace."

In one of the most impassioned speeches delivered in St. Peter's Basilica during the entire four council sessions, the Patriarch of Antioch and Jerusalem, His Beatitude Maximos IV, spoke at the opening of the debate. He implored the fathers of the council to defend humankind. "A threat of destruction hangs over humanity, nuclear armaments," said the bearded patriarch, using French rather than the Latin of other church fathers. The patriarch urged the radical condemnation by the church "of modern technological, including nuclear, warfare." The bishops of the world, he said, in condemning atomic, bacterio-logical, and chemical weapons, must see themselves as "defenders of the earthly city."[4]

Contrary voices came chiefly from the United States. Bishop Philip M. Hannan of Washington, D.C., rose to defend the use of nuclear weaponry. In his view, nuclear weaponry might indeed be required for legitimate defense. "Although even a low-yield nuclear weapon inflicts great damage, still it cannot be said that its effects are greater than can be imagined. Its effects are well calculated and can be foreseen. Furthermore, it may be permitted to use these arms with their limited effects against military objectives in a just way according to theological principles."[5]

A paper delineating similar views had been circulated among the council fathers by a committee of American Catholics. The paper came from CAIP, produced by the Arms Control Subcommittee of the CAIP International Law and Juridical Institutions Committee. "Should the Council issue such a blanket condemnation of nuclear weapons," said William V. O'Brien, the committee chairperson, "it would place fifty million American Catholics in an awesome dilemma as to whether to listen to the solemn findings of a Vatican Council or to the hitherto accepted assurances of their government that America's nuclear deterrent is the foundation for international stability and the *sine qua non* of the defense of the United States." Such a dilemma would be forced on "all other Catholics who live in freedom because of the American deterrent."[6]

The council fathers could have been pardoned if they had interpreted the recommendations of the Arms Control Subcommittee of the CAIP International Law and Juridical Institutions Committee as representing a significant segment of the American Catholic community. As Gordon Zahn pointed out, "The C.A.I.P. statement took on an aura of official standing . . . handed down by some massive church bureaucracy." The relationship of the CAIP to the National Catholic Welfare Conference would lend credence to such an interpretation. The extremely impressive title actually represented the thinking of a few persons, those forming the Arms Control Subcommittee and O'Brien.

The framers of the paper had every right to express their opinions. Members of the Pax Council believed that any implication that the CAIP might be expressing an official American Catholic viewpoint should be dispelled. But how to reach the bishops more directly with a strand of American Catholic opinion opposed to that of CAIP? This had clearly become Pax's challenge.

We discussed the matter with our mentor, Dorothy Day, and also with the Pax Council, which then included Clare Danielsson, as well as Daniel J. Sullivan and Dorothy Dohen, both professors at Fordham University, in New York City; Ed Rice, a sponsor and council member; and Valerie Delacorte, a peace-minded Catholic of Hungarian origin. Dorothy Day accepted my idea of preparing a special edition of the *Catholic Worker* for the council fathers in which we would clarify our views. We could send it to key bishops in time for the final council session. She asked me to edit the special edition.

It was May 1965; there was the whole summer to edit the July-August issue of the *Catholic Worker* and mail it before the council reconvened in the fall. I went to work to gather contributors. Every person approached for an article or message on peace responded with enthusiasm: James W. Douglass, Gordon Zahn, George H. Dunne, S.J., John McKenzie, Philip Scharper, Howard Everngam, Benjamin Spock, and Dorothy Day herself.

We learned that about 150 bishops and experts were concerned with drafting the peace section. If only, we thought, we could send the paper to all the bishops. Dorothy had always advised us to depend, as she did, on Providence for our needs. Providence made its appearance through the generosity of Valerie Delacorte. With the agreement of her husband George Delacorte, the publisher, she funded the project of airmailing the council issue of the *Catholic Worker* to every bishop in the world. By the end of August, all copies of the *Catholic Worker* had been dispatched to some 2,400 bishops. There was no announcement to the press and the whole action was known only to the participants. It must be confessed that certain members of the American hierarchy with pro-deterrent views were omitted from the mailing list. They would have received a copy, however, if they were regular subscribers to the *Catholic Worker*.

We wondered what the reaction of a bishop in India, for example, would be to the stark first page of the *Catholic Worker*, with "The Council and the Bomb" in heavy black letters. This was the title of James W. Douglass's article. Above it were the words of Pope Paul VI in letters almost an inch high: "We are responsible for our times, for the life of our brothers, and we are responsible before our Christian consciences." As we saw the finished copy, we realized that it resembled nothing less than a broadside, a broadside of eight pages. The entire intervention of Patriarch Maximos IV was printed. The draft of "On Making Lasting Peace," Article 25 from Schema XIII, which the bishops were discussing, was also featured. The response, particularly from bishops in India, was extremely favorable.

Dorothy Day wrote a review of *In Solitary Witness*, Gordon Zahn's account of the young Austrian Catholic beheaded for his refusal to serve in Hitler's war. She devoted her "On Pilgrimage" column to Pope John XXIII's *Journal of a Soul* and to her thoughts on peace. Day wrote:

One of our Catholic pacifists asked me to write a clear, theoretical, logical, pacifist manifesto, and he added so far in these thirty-two years of the *Catholic Worker*, none had appeared from my pen.

I can write no other than this: unless we use the weapons of the spirit, denying ourselves and taking up our cross and following Jesus, dying with Him and rising with Him, men will go on fighting, and often from the highest motives, believing that they are fighting defensive wars for justice and in self-defense against present or future aggression.[7]

James W. Douglass wrote that "in view of the Church's deepening understanding of Scripture and of the nation's deepening involvement in total war, there would be nothing imprudent in the Council's support of a Christian dedication to total peace, especially by a recommendation in the Schema that each Christian explore in conscience the nonviolent love and teaching of Christ."[8]

John McKenzie, whose *Dictionary of the Bible* had just appeared, stated, "If the warfare based on the deterrent is not immoral warfare, then there is no immoral warfare."[9]   George H. Dunne, S.J., of Georgetown University, asserted that "neither the manufacture nor the use of nuclear or other indiscriminate weaponry could be morally justified."[10]   Benjamin Spock of SANE, the Committee for a Sane Nuclear Policy, spoke for many in asking the world's bishops for "a strong statement for the good of all mankind."[11]

Gordon Zahn, in "American Experts and Schema XIII," discussed the CAIP proposals in detail.[12]   Philip Scharper observed in a short incisive article, "The Church and the Nation," that "[i]n our own time and in our own country, we are not far from the contagion of nationalism, an unquestioned hyper-patriotism, an attempt to identify the cause of the State with the cause of Christ."[13]

In "Questions on Modern War," Howard Everngam pointed out that millions of works of social justice were stillborn because of the outlay in that year of fifty billion dollars on weaponry. He asked: "Is not any act or policy of direct or indiscriminate killing of innocent and non-combatant civilian populations to be condemned?"[14]   This query evoked an echo in the council's final document, as did another question Everngam posed: "Does not every individual have the right and the duty in conscience to abstain from any form of war or killing which he judges not to meet the requirements of reason and morality?"[15]

In the editorial "We are all under judgment," I referred to the judgment of love, the love that the follower of Christ owes even to the one called "enemy."

I drew attention to Thomas Merton's heart-stopping assertion that "total nuclear war would be a sin of mankind second only to that of the crucifixion." "It is in order to avoid that great sin," I concluded, "that we beg clear words from the Fathers of the Council."[16]

Dorothy Day and I had come to Rome late in September in time for the debate, Dorothy to fast for peace and I to lobby among the bishops. Dorothy joined nineteen women from twelve countries in a water fast, not against but with the bishops. The women were united in prayer for correspondence with the Holy Spirit on the part of the whole council. The fast had been organized by Lanza del Vasto and his wife Chanterelle, leaders of the Ark, a Catholic community located in the south of France.

Before starting the fast, Dorothy Day, accompanied by Barbara Wall of English Pax and me, attended the liturgy in St. Peter's Basilica along with the council fathers. Barbara Wall's press card made our presence possible. The liturgy was in ancient Syriac, strange and lovely to our ears. Dorothy disappeared into one of the many confessionals in the vast basilica. She wrote, "I was able to go to confession on that last visit I paid to St. Peter's and I felt with joy and love that warm sense of community, the family which is the church." Bishops and cardinals, she noted, were lined up on either side of the confessionals.

From the beginning of the Vatican Council there had been a peace lobby in Rome. James Douglass spent two years in Rome, working closely with Archbishop Roberts and speaking with every bishop who would listen to him on the right of conscientious objection and the need for a condemnation of nuclear war. Several bishops indicated in their peace statements the influence of their meetings with him and of the document he had shared with them. Hildegarde and Jean Goss-Mayr, longtime peace activists affiliated with the International Fellowship of Reconciliation, maintained contact with many members of the hierarchy. Gordon Zahn had found a warm reception for the concepts of conscientious objection and nonviolence among several key English bishops. Richard Carbray spent the four sessions of the council in Rome so that he could further the cause of peace by serving as secretary to Archbishop Roberts. His wife Mary, a librarian, had supported his witness and made his volunteer service in Rome possible. Barbara Wall of English Pax, the only one with the treasured *tessera*, the official press pass allowing entry to the Basilica, helped all the lobbyists.

By the end of September 1965, Barbara Wall, Richard Carbray, and I were the last in the field. Of course, Dorothy Day and the women on the fast were devoting themselves to what might be called a spiritual lobby.

Meanwhile, Barbara Wall, Richard Carbray, and I started on our rounds, hastening first to a room on the top floor of Salvator Mundi Hospital where His Beatitude Patriarch Maximos IV received us. He sat like an ancient of days, his long white beard stark over a voluminous black robe.

After some preliminary conversation, we came to the point. Would he rise again to speak in St. Peter's, to reemphasize to the council fathers his warning of modern war's danger to the human family?

There was silence. Finally he broke it to reply in French, "I have already spoken."

We tried to move him to change his mind by pointing out that Dorothy Day, at sixty-eight years of age, was on a water fast for the fathers of the council.

He gazed beyond us into a distance we could not see, and in a far-off voice said, "L'eau nourrit." "Water nourishes." The words, coming from a patriarch of the Middle East acquainted with parched land and the preciousness of water, left us with no other arguments. We thanked him and took our leave.

One of our chief concerns was the need to change what Barbara Wall called "a weasel clause" in the peace draft. It opened the door to the possession (and therefore use) of nuclear weapons. The clause affirmed that it would not be "illegitimate" to possess "modern arms" for the sole purpose of "deterring an adversary similarly equipped." "Modern arms" or "scientific weapons" were the code words for nuclear weaponry.

Because of the support of some American Catholics, including ecclesiastics, for deterrence, *Peace* magazine featured an editorial, "Will Nationalism Spoil the Schema?" It represented the thinking of the officers, in particular, Pax chairman Howard Everngam. Strongly worded, it pointed to the danger that we termed "nuclear nationalism." We felt we should share this with the bishops and the experts at that moment engaged in working on the peace section of the schema. And so I approached Abbot Christopher Butler, O.S.B., one of the chief drafters of the section and mentioned that Pax had formulated a peace statement in addition to the special issue of the *Catholic Worker*. In his correct English way, he asked what we had in mind. I explained that as Catholic Americans intensely concerned with church teaching on peace, we thought that what we had to say would be of interest to those drafting the peace section. Our views were distinct from those of some American bishops and of some lay Catholics already heard from. It was a means of supplying information that the drafters were not likely to receive from other sources, I explained.

"That seems reasonable," the abbot agreed. "The statement could be distributed."

Then he added, "Of course, it must be in Latin."

Richard Carbray, ebullient at this breakthrough, rushed with me to the library of the North American College on the Janiculum Hill. Richard, gifted Latinist though he was, had to ponder hard when we came to the term *overkill*. He coined the term *superhomicidium*.

When I met Abbot Butler a day later in St. Peter's Square, I told him that the Pax statement had been turned into Latin and that we could supply as many as needed. "We will need at least a hundred and fifty copies for the drafting committees," he informed me. "Could you deliver them to San Anselmo? We could use them now." Two Jesuit priests from Malta were in charge of the

Documents Office for the Council. They were of one mind with us and agreed to make the necessary copies. Early the next morning I was knocking at the door of the Benedictine Monastery of San Anselmo with one hundred fifty copies of the Latin version of "Will Nationalism Spoil the Schema?"

James Douglass had left with Richard Carbray the list of the Roman addresses of the council bishops. We were able to speed around Rome, first talking with cardinals, since we were informed that cardinals could rise to speak at any time, while bishops had to obtain the signature of their confreres to be allowed the floor. Cardinal Leger of Montreal told us that he was in accord with our views. Archbishop George B. Flahiff, later the cardinal of Winnipeg, asked us for coffee and congratulated Pax on our efforts. His intervention would condemn the preparation for, as well as the execution of, total war. Cardinal Joseph Ritter's press secretary showed us the statement of the cardinal calling for an "absolute condemnation of the possession of arms which involved the intention or the grave peril of total war."

On the whole our reception by the cardinals, archbishops, and bishops was cordial, even at times enthusiastic, though from two or three we met a certain skepticism. We reminded them of the points we had made in the special issue of the *Catholic Worker*, and where it seemed useful, presented a copy of "Will Nationalism Spoil the Schema?"

Then came what Barbara Wall termed the *dies mirabilis* for peace, 5 October. It was the day following the address of Pope Paul VI to the United Nations General Assembly in New York City in which he had cried out, "No more war. War never again." Two English bishops rose to give their support to Cardinal Alfrink, president of Pax Christi International, who urged the elimination of the clause legitimizing the nuclear deterrent. Bishop Pierre Boillon announced to the assembled council fathers that women of various nations were spending ten days in prayer and fasting "in order to ask light for the Council Fathers in their deliberations on the banning of war and the safeguarding of world peace." Boillon, in one of the most poignant speeches of the day, reminded his brother bishops that in his diocese of Verdun there had been 1,300,000 casualties in the First World War.[17]

Bishop Alfred Ancel of Lyons, France, pointed out that the good of the human race demanded an unqualified ban on war. "It is objected," he asserted, "that the Council's rejection of war would serve no good purpose because no one would pay any attention to it. The effectiveness of our statement is not expected to come from the strength of arms but from the fact that acting in the Person of Christ we bear witness to truth before the entire world."[18]

Abbot Butler stated that the intention of waging war unjustly (using indiscriminate weaponry) is itself unjust. He supported the right of conscientious objection, and dismissing out of hand the concept of "presumption of justice" in favor of the warring state, he carried forward Bishop Ancel's concept of Christian witness. "We are the mystical body," he said, "and Christ is our Head. He refused to defend himself and his mission by the sword of his disciples, or even by legions of angels, the ministers of God's justice and love. The weapons of the gospel are not nuclear but spiritual; it wins its victories not by war but by suffering."[19]

We watched the fathers of the council streaming out of the basilica to fill St. Peter's Square. Cardinal birds were well named, their plumage no more brilliant than the scarlet robes of cardinals billowing behind them in the breeze. Hardly less striking were hierarchs in darker crimson robes. Among them all were the gray and brown-robed, and an occasional black-robed ecclesiastic who stood out like an austere crow among birds of more spectacular plumage. Would there be in our lifetime a similar scene, people of God from every land under heaven, gathered under the Sign of the Prince of Peace?

We had no contact with the CAIP representatives, nor with the bishops who shared their views on nuclear deterrence. We learned later of their suspicions of Pax in a letter from the CAIP president. "The European pacifist influence in Rome may need to be offset. Here, too, we need to speak out because of Pax. Like all extremists, they have the most persistent, devoted and persuasive adherents." We realized anew that the Pax action in communicating with the world's bishops had been necessary, and that it had been wise to carry it out surreptitiously as far as the American church was concerned.

From the end of October through November, the fathers of the council were engaged in the drafting of "The Church in the Modern World." The final wording of the peace and war section was at stake. On their return to the United States, two ecclesiastics, Francis Cardinal Spellman and Archbishop Philip M. Hannan, led a revolt against the peace section (for whose voting in Rome they had been absent). We obtained a copy of their statement, cosigned by eight bishops from four countries, detailing their objections to "The Avoidance of War," a key section. They disagreed with the assertion that "scientific weapons increase the danger of war." "These affirmations," said their statement, "do not recognize the fact that the possession of 'scientific weapons' has preserved freedom in a great part of the world. The defense of a great part of the world against aggression is not a crime but a service. . . . In the world of today, there is no adequate defense for the more powerful nations without the possession of scientific weapons."

The statement, circulated to the council members on 2 December 1965, proposed that the "errors" be corrected and that other wording be substituted. Failing this, the whole pastoral "The Church in the Modern World" should receive a *non placet*, in other words, be voted down. It should, at a later time, be turned over to a synod of bishops for further study and correction.

But the American attempt to torpedo the peace statement failed. "The Church in the Modern World" became an official document of the Second Vatican Council on 7 December 1965.

The peace section of "The Church in the Modern World," entitled "The Fostering of Peace," brought joy and encouragement to Catholic peacemakers. Pax members involved in the Vatican Council action were grateful that such lay action for peace as theirs was validated by the world's bishops. Though the final document reflected the goals of Pax and other Catholic peace activists, they could take no credit for the decisions made. They could say no more than that they had brought a lay voice to a discussion affecting the survival of humankind.

"The Church in the Modern World" did not reverse *Peace on Earth*. It made explicit the recognition by the universal church of the right of conscientious objection to military service. It included a validation of the witness of gospel nonviolence. The council fathers cut through any and all discussions by so-called experts and realists on "scientific weapons and weapons of mass destruction" by concentrating on their effects on human beings. Pointing to the need for an "evaluation of war with an entirely new attitude," the bishops stated: "Any act of war aimed at the destruction of entire cities or extensive areas along with their population is a crime against God and man himself. It merits unequivocal and unhesitating condemnation." This constituted the first church condemnation of a method of warfare since the banning of the murderous crossbow by the Lateran Council in 1139.

Catholic peacemakers felt they now had a Magna Carta for renewed action for peace. As we had done following *Peace on Earth*, we featured the key peace sections of "The Church in the Modern World" in *Peace* magazine. Pax was not large, never quite reaching two thousand members, though its literature, including *Peace* magazine, reached much larger numbers, through colleges and parishes throughout the country.

Various activities kept it alive and growing, such as the Pax Tivoli Conferences and the annual peace Mass on 9 August for the victims of Hiroshima and Nagasaki and in memory of Franz Jagerstatter, beheaded on 9 August 1943 for his refusal to fight in Hitler's war. Pax was also involved in a campaign for peace in the Middle East. Abie Nathan, the former Israeli pilot who championed peace between Israelis and Palestinians, had anchored his gleaming white peace ship in New York's East River. He spoke several times for Pax and the Catholic Worker and invited Pax to hold its annual meeting aboard ship.

No peace group could evade the unhealed wound of racism. Pax published an issue of *Peace* devoted to the hopeful events in Selma, Alabama, site of the convergence of an unforgettable interreligious witness. "Selma has shown," said the editorial, "that the leverage of moral witness by clergy . . . is immeasurable. The use of moral weapons in the struggle for civil rights cannot be divorced from the use of moral weapons in the international struggle for peace. Perhaps the present nuclear dilemma of the United States, the fact that our nation seems wedded to an unjust deterrent, is related to the fact that the weight of open moral witness has not been brought to bear by the religious part of our society."[20] We also published Martin Luther King's memorable address on love in accepting the St. Francis Peace Medal from the Third Order of St. Francis. Here as in other speeches he made the memorable distinction between eros, philia, and "agape, creative redemptive goodwill for all men."[21]

Pax decided to communicate directly with our bishops and with governmental leaders concerned with the military draft. It published a paperback book with the peace section of "The Church in the Modern World." From Rome, we had gathered nine powerful peace statements by council fathers, including Patriarch Maximos IV of Jerusalem and Antioch; Bishop Christopher Butler, O.S.B., of London; Archbishop Thomas D. Roberts, formerly of Bombay; Archbishop George B. Flahiff of Winnipeg, Canada; Bishop Pierre Boillon of Lyons, France; and Joseph Cardinal Ritter of St. Louis, Missouri. Articles were contributed by Tom Stonier, James W. Douglass, Gordon Zahn, and Eileen Egan.

The title of the paperback was *The War That Is Forbidden*, taken from the lead article by Tom Stonier. It gave the details of nuclear warfare contained in *Nuclear Disaster*, the book shared with some of the bishops at the council. A copy was sent to every member of Congress and to every American bishop. We envisioned, naively perhaps, a looming collision between the United States, with its nuclear policy in place, and church leaders whose flock was called upon to fund and perhaps execute this policy. The book's title *The War That Is Forbidden*, we hoped, would give lawmakers pause and encourage American bishops to energize their flocks.

A more public campaign of 1968 was the Pax Rights of Conscience Campaign. It was launched with a center-spread advertisement in *Commonweal* magazine under the title "End Discrimination in the Draft Law." Only "all-war" objectors were recognized by the draft law administered through some four thousand local draft boards. Too many young men were given prison sentences for refusing to be inducted when their claims for "just war" or "selective" objection were refused.

The trek of men of draft age to Canada had begun. Eventually, as many as fifty thousand had crossed the Canadian border or found refuge in Sweden. Not all of these, of course, were "selective" objectors, but for their own reasons, they felt revulsion to serving in Vietnam. As for Catholics, the greatest increase in those requesting the status of conscientious objection was registered in the Catholic community.

A change in the U.S. Selective Service Law would be of service to all religious groups who shared the just-war tradition. *Peace* magazine carried reports of numerous cases of "selective" objectors whose appeals from draft board decisions were reaching the higher courts in various states. Opinion was so favorable toward the issue of selective objection that Pax organized a public meeting for further promotion. The subject, "The NOW Issue: Selective Conscientious Objection," was such a fiery topic at the height of opposition to the Vietnam War that it filled the Community Church in mid-Manhattan.

Paul O'Dwyer, a senatorial candidate, and James J. Shannon, auxiliary bishop of St. Paul and Minneapolis, shared the platform. O'Dwyer urged that the Selective Service Law recognize the right of the individual conscience whether that conscience was formed in the "just-war" tradition or in a humanistic moral code. He said that he wanted to see every draftee assured of the right of counsel before his draft board and the right to a court review before induction. O'Dwyer further urged the abolishing of the draft in favor of a volunteer army. He also proposed a Department of Peace that might help correct "the present system of inverted priorities which siphon off the resources for war to the neglect of the immense social and human needs of our society."

Suddenly there was a commotion at the back of the church from a group that had just entered. "You are a pig, O'Dwyer," one of them shrieked. "You are not a peace candidate. You are a war lover." The voice was piercing.

O'Dwyer, long an opponent of the Vietnam War, stood with the repose of a statue. In my capacity as chairperson, I asked O'Dwyer if I should deal with the interruption. He turned to me. "I will handle it," he said decisively.

He faced the audience and announced: "You may have five minutes to state your case."

The young man, somewhat abashed, proceeded to unfurl the flag of Vietnam's National Liberation Front (NLF). "This is our flag," he said. "This flag (the flag of South Vietnam) is the one we have brought for O'Dwyer." As he spoke, screaming insults at war-loving capitalists and the pig establishment, a young girl, blond hair streaming over her shoulders, strode up to the sanctuary and placed the South Vietnamese flag against the podium.

Suddenly, three young people, two young men and a young woman, emerged from the group. They padded silently down the main aisle of the church toward the sanctuary. They were completely naked. The young woman waved the NLF flag.

Howard Everngam, our Pax Chairman, interposed himself between the young woman and the sanctuary. By a jujitsu maneuver, he sent her sprawling down the polished surface of the aisle. Things became blurred as the second white body, and then the third, propelled by Everngam, careened along the brown floor. The audience was bemused and silent.

All at once, the group tossed a great shower of yellow leaflets into the air. We found that they announced a meeting of Youth Against War and Fascism. We awaited further activity, but the group, covering the nakedness of their brothers and sister, moved out of the church.

We discovered that they had clambered aboard a waiting van embellished with a sign, "The Crazies." One of them was heard to remark, "What's the matter with these peace people? Why don't they call the police?"

The meeting resumed, concluding with a spirited question and answer period. The Pax caper must have been, to the actors of the Theater of Revolution, one of their most disappointing performances. There had been no melee with police, no press coverage in the tabloids.

Were the protesters emulating Isaiah, who, at the word of the Lord "went naked and barefoot" in Jerusalem, or were they imitating, as was more likely, Michael Abulafia of Greenwich Village, the presidential candidate, who addressed his supporters naked to prove, he explained, that "he had nothing to hide?"

During 1968, outrage against Vietnam began to express itself in attacks on draft boards. In May of that year, the brothers Daniel Berrigan, S.J., and Philip Berrigan, then a priest of the Society of St. Joseph, along with seven companions, set draft files afire. They seized the Selective Service files from the draft board at Catonsville, Maryland, piled them outside, and set them alight with homemade napalm. The photograph of the flaming files and the protesting priests appeared in the United States and overseas press.

The protest of the "Catonsville Nine" aroused an echo in the hearts of groups nationwide. The courage of the draft file burners and their willingness to suffer imprisonment gave rise to imitators in many cities, including "the Milwaukee Fourteen" and "the Harrisburg Seven." Each prophetic act of resistance served to intensify and harden opposition to the Vietnam conflict. The movement, which came to be known as Plowshares, went on to become a continuing prophetic witness against nuclear proliferation.

Some chided Pax for not being more visible and for not leading overt acts of resistance. The temperament of Pax leaders did not lead them to dramatic public acts of resistance, even though such acts occasioned immediate éclat in print and television media. Dorothy Dohen and Gordon Zahn, both sociologists, wrote books opposing war and its causes (*Nationalism and American Catholicism* and *In Solitary Witness,* respectively). The Pax program addressed itself to the "long haul" of changing the outlook of a great lumbering church on the subject of peace and war.

The time came when we of Pax decided to "hit the bricks," to use the words of the antiwar protesters. It occurred on the streets of Washington, D.C., and was designed to express loving disagreement with our church. It was 1968, three years after the world's bishops had called for the "new evaluation of war" and had announced the ban on indiscriminate warfare. In Vietnam, people burning and village burning were continuing in a war whose horror broke into the evening television news. Our hearts were wrenched as we saw a Vietnamese child running naked from a napalmed village, and a young soldier weeping over a dead comrade.

We could not agree to the continued silence of the American hierarchy in the face of the continued agony. The U.S. bishops were to begin their four-day meeting in Washington, D.C., on 11 November 1968. Pax had sent a memorandum to the chairman of the National Council of Catholic Bishops asking if we could expect a peace statement reflecting the "Fostering of Peace" of the Vatican Council. When no reply came, we prepared an open letter requesting clear statements in November 1968. Before releasing the letter, we asked our new chairperson, Gordon Zahn, to telephone the Bishop-Chairman of the National Council of Catholic Bishops on the matter. Zahn had agreed to succeed Howard Everngam, whose six years of quiet leadership included everything from designing the magazine to mailing it out, to planning and taping the Pax Tivoli Conferences and most meetings. Zahn, already achieving his witness through his books and his teaching, assumed the added task of helping to lead Pax. He was an invaluable counselor, wise and moderate.

Diplomatic though he was, Zahn could not elicit a definite reply from the bishop-chairman. The bishop had bridled at the urgency with which Pax viewed the matter and asked Zahn, "Is this an ultimatum?" Failing in our attempts to receive a reply, we decided to release the open letter.

As we read it later, the letter did savor of an ultimatum. It reflected our extreme dismay that in a time of conflict, our bishops were not responding to the moral needs of young men conscripted for the awesome task of killing, nor to the moral stance of a nation inexorably increasing its stockpile of indiscriminate weapons. The two thousand word letter, entitled "Pax Open Letter to the National Council of Catholic Bishops," offered eight recommendations. The first one said: "We strongly recommend that our bishops act to make the Vatican Council statement on conscientious objection a reality for American Catholics." Other recommendations dealt with the necessity for the hierarchy to clarify the role of nonviolence and for the bishops to be as forthright as Pope Paul VI in his declaration: "We must say and reaffirm that violence is not in accord with the Gospel; that it is not Christian."

A question in large type was designed as an eye-catcher and heart-stopper: ARE YOU READY TO COMMIT INSTANT AUSCHWITZ—TO CREMATE ALIVE 6,000,000 INHABITANTS OF A CITY? YOUR GOVERNMENT IS READY TO DO IT IN YOUR NAME."

The text of the Pax open letter appeared in four Catholic newspapers with a combined circulation of approximately 900,000. The *National Catholic Reporter* and *Commonweal* magazine carried it as paid announcements. *Our Sunday Visitor* carried it as part of a news story and the *Catholic Worker* carried the full text in the October 1968 issue.

Early on the morning of 11 November, well before the bishops were to open their conference at 9 o'clock, a dozen Pax members lined the sidewalk in front of the crescent-shaped Washington Hilton Hotel. We were from New York, Boston, Chicago, Minneapolis, as well as Washington, D.C. It was not lost on us that the date commemorated Armistice Day, later renamed Veterans' Day. It was also the day when a fourth-century Roman conscript, Martin, risked death by declaring that "it is not fitting" for a Christian to serve as a soldier. The day before, Thomas Merton's sudden death had been announced on radio and television.

The police surveyed the silent vigil line and informed us that we had to keep moving; simply standing still was not allowed. They inspected our placards as we unfurled them. They asked if we were going to mount them on sticks. "Sticks," they announced, "are not allowed." Fortunately, our Washington Pax members had already advised us of this. A painter friend had lettered our messages in brilliant acrylic colors on heavy canvas. We wore them yoked back and front as though we were part of an advertising campaign.

"WE BEG OUR BISHOPS FOR A PEACE MESSAGE,"
said one placard;
"REFLECTING THE GOSPEL AND VATICAN II,"
said the other.
We repeated part of the open letter:
"ARE YOU READY TO COMMIT INSTANT AUSCHWITZ?,"
said one placard;
"YOUR GOVERNMENT IS READY TO DO IT IN YOUR NAME,"
said the other.
"SHOULD NOT THE CONSCIENCES,"
said one placard;
"OF JUST WAR OBJECTORS BE RESPECTED?"
asked the other.
"IF THESE SHOULD HOLD THEIR PEACE,"
said one placard;
"THE STONES WILL CRY OUT."
said the next.

Several bishops took time out to greet and visit with us. Bishop John J. Dougherty, chairman of the Commission for World Justice and Peace, after gazing with surprise at our placards, reassured us on the peace content of the pastoral letter that even then was being discussed.

During Monday, Tuesday, and Wednesday we walked back and forth, braving the early blasts of winter. Meanwhile, larger groups of dissenters met noisily inside the hotel. When snow came to Washington on Thursday, 14 November, we decided to stay the course. At one point, there were four of us, Gordon Zahn, Margaret Boyle, editor of *The Catholic Woman*, Richard McSorley, S.J., and I. McSorley wrapped his checkered scarf around his head like a pasha. A bishop, seeing us marching in the snow, came out to tell us he was worried about our health. By then, we were soaked to the skin. "Someone has given me a bottle of whiskey," the bishop said. "Go to my room. Get dried off. Take a drink, if you like." He gave us the key to his room at the Washington Hilton. His invitation was accepted.

On 15 November, the American bishops issued the pastoral letter "Human Life in Our Day." It responded to all the Pax requests except that of complete dissociation from the nuclear deterrent. In that matter, our idealism had carried us away. The pastoral letter repeated all the conclusions of "The Church in the Modern World," including the tenable position of nonviolence, the condemnation of the arms race and indiscriminate war, and finally a section on the draft. It reiterated a Catholic position against compulsory military service and asked for a change in the U.S. draft law:

We recommend a modification of the Selective Service making it possible, although not easy, for so-called selective conscientious objectors to refuse—without fear of imprisonment or loss of citizenship—to serve in wars which they consider unjust or in branches of service (e.g. the strategic nuclear forces) which would subject them to the performance of actions contrary to deeply held moral convictions about indiscriminate killing.

The date of 15 November 1968 was nearly three years after the world's bishops had issued the updated peace teaching and validation of conscientious objection for a world increasingly addicted to war and to compulsory military conscription, feeder of the war machine.

We learned from the response of the print and broadcast media that the topics of peace, war, and conscientious objection are considered far less urgent or fascinating than contraception, the other issue treated in "Human Life in Our Day." The media gave enormous attention to the dissent against the strict interpretation of the ban on artificial contraception and almost none to the issue of conscientious objection despite its relevance to the Vietnam conflict.

One who did notice the bishops' statement on the draft was Director of Selective Service, General Lewis B. Hershey. In dismayed incredulity, he asked, "What kind of a religious belief have you got that causes you to reject some wars and not others?" During General Hershey's service under six presidents, he oversaw the drafting of 14,500,000 Americans in three wars. The religious belief of which the general was ignorant was precisely the just-war tradition. He was right to react, since when young men realized they could cite their just-war tradition to claim selective objection, the draft system would never be the same.

The sentiment of U.S. government leaders, wedded to the deterrent, was hardly favorable to any change that would make American citizens less compliant in their support of it. Exactly a week after the appearance of "Human Life in Our Day," the *New York Times* reported a Senate discussion on what would remain after a nuclear exchange between the United States and the Soviet Union. Senator Richard P. Russell faced up to the "instant Auschwitz" treatment for the cities and areas of the world. He summed up his thinking in one apocalyptic sentence: "If we have to start all over again with another Adam and Eve, then I want them to be American and not Russian—and I want them on this continent and not in Europe."

Those of us who viewed the one condemnation of the Vatican Council as a declaration of supreme and crucial relevance soon suffered a tragic awakening. One of the persons who formulated the CAIP assertions to the Vatican Council in support of the nuclear deterrent found a way to justify the deterrent policy of the United States. In articles and books, the CAIP leader pointed out that strict adherence to the principle of noncombatant immunity would, in effect, interfere with the right of the United States to resist aggression. As a nation had the right to self-defense, the principle of noncombatant community, while an ideal, would have to be modified to make way for a credible defense.[22]

Pax's task was how to give the widest currency to the implications of the peace message: in particular, the bishops' proposal for a modification of the draft law. A special issue of *Peace* magazine, "Catholics, Conscience and the Draft," was soon off the presses. It carried the complete text of the peace statement from "Human Life in Our Day." A feature article by Dennis Keegan dealt with the courts and conscience, describing how many young men denied CO classification were taking their appeals to the law courts. The famous case of James Francis McFadden, a just-war objector, was treated at length. His indictment for refusing to be inducted was set aside on the basis that the Selective Service Law gave preference to pacifist over non-pacifist religions. In other words, the "Selective Service Law violated the First Amendment against the establishment of religion."

The issue published the list of draft counseling centers throughout the nation, including those conducted by the War Resisters League, the American Friends Service Committee, and the Catholic Peace Fellowship. So many requests came for this publication that it was kept in print as long as funds allowed. In 1971, a second and enlarged edition was published, providing an updated list of draft counseling centers. But the issue's most telling statement was the "Resolution on Southeast Asia" by the U.S. bishops, which confronted the morality of the Vietnam War and found that it did not meet just-war criteria. Pax reported that by an almost unanimous vote, the bishops had, in effect, declared the Vietnam conflict unjust. "At this point in history," the bishops concluded on 19 November 1971, "it seems clear that whatever good we hope to achieve through continued involvement in this war is now outweighed by the destruction of life and of moral values which it inflicts." The bishops urged the "speedy ending of the war" as "a moral imperative of the highest order."

Pax pointed out for the first time in the history of the United States, and possibly in many centuries of world history, a national hierarchy had denounced as unjust the conduct of a conflict being waged by its own nation. Pax saw the resolution as another indication of the irrelevance of just-war criteria, either to authorities who declare war or to the conduct of members of the church. *Peace* also published the conclusion drawn by Bishop Thomas Gumbleton, auxiliary bishop of Detroit, who said that anyone who reaches the same moral conclusion "may not participate in the war."[23]

The Catholic Worker Farm, ninety rural acres on a bluff overlooking the wide expanse of the Hudson River, had once been the site of a hotel. The main building, still sturdy, was a bit rundown. There was also a half-ruined stone hulk built in 1842 of which the lower floor was still habitable, and a separate building near the entry road used to shelter "the men of the road." It was decided to hold the annual Pax weekend gatherings at the farm. Since the nearest village was Tivoli, they were called the Pax Tivoli Conferences.

The luminous center of the gatherings was Dorothy Day, who relished the marvelous variety of people who came as speakers or just to exchange views. To the Tivoli conferences came theologians, professors, writers, scientists, priests, psychologists, psychiatrists, nuns, peace activists, students, and young peace and justice seekers from as far away as the West Coast. Students hitchhiked in, bringing their bedrolls. The offering for the weekend was minimal.

Dorothy Day's sense of community was so palpable that those who attended remarked on how quickly they felt part of the Catholic Worker family. Dorothy would introduce John Filliger and Hans Tunnesen and other members of the permanent community to all who came. She would remind the visitors that both old seamen had come to the Catholic Worker in 1936, when the CW had fed and given shelter to the dock strikers on the New York waterfront. This work of mercy had been a dramatic episode in labor history. The two seamen had found new skills. John was now Farmer John, growing vegetables on forty acres of scrubby but tillable land; Hans was the chief cook, in charge of the community kitchen.

To the first Pax Tivoli Conference at the end of August 1964 came Archbishop Thomas D. Roberts, formerly of the diocese of Bombay, India, and Dr. Seymour Melman. In a talk on disarmament and the war on poverty, Melman included the astounding assertion, "If we had dropped the Hiroshima bomb every day of every year from the birth of Jesus to the present [the mid-1960s], the sum of these explosions would not equal the power of our present nuclear stockpile."

Melman, as head of the Industrial Engineering Department of Columbia University, presented a cogent plan for converting outmoded shipyards into plants for the fashioning of prefabricated housing and hospital buildings. His prophetic position on the need for conversion to a peace economy that met human needs was set aside as the Vietnam War escalated. Economic conversion also gave way before the arms stockpiling of the cold war, which eventually gutted the strongest economy the world had ever known.

Archbishop Roberts, a quizzical Englishman and Jesuit, had been a friend of Gandhi. He reminded us that Catholics, accustomed to obedience, were only too ready to give a blank check on their consciences to civil authority in times of war. "Such blank checks are not honored in heaven," he said.

From England came Pax leader Walter Stein to deliver at Tivoli the presentation he had made at the Spode House Conference, "Mercy and Revolution." With superb historical background, Stein analyzed the thorny road Christians must travel towards the Kingdom of God in a violent world.

We were stopped short at Trivoli by such simple questions as that posed by James W. Douglass: "Is it really naive for men to ask: If Christ died out of love for the world, what right would his followers have to join in its destruction?" Douglass's remarks were published in a trenchant article, "Peace: Issue for the Council," in *Peace* magazine.

Dorothy Day hoped for the presence at Tivoli of César Chavez, known around the world as the "Gandhi of the Grapes." When we organized the 1969 conference on the centenary of Gandhi's birth, we invited him to be with us.

Pax was ready with a round-trip ticket. César wired that it was not possible for him to come east, but he asked if the airfare could be used for a valued co-worker, Marion Moses. Then a nurse, but later a medical doctor, Moses was a passionate advocate of the rights of the farm workers. She described the threat to their health, and the health of the larger community and of the planet itself, by the unchecked use of noxious pesticides.

The whole group gathered around Dorothy Day one sunlit afternoon as she talked with us about the grapepickers, nonviolence in social change. She quoted the anarchist thinker Peter Kropotkin on the subject of revolution, that it is not despair but hope which brings about a successful revolution. Describing César Chavez as "a person of absolute nonviolence," she saw him as a leader of a revolution of hope for the "stoop laborers," the least-protected members of the American labor force. She praised him for the nonviolence of his way of life.

Many of the talks delivered at Tivoli appeared in *Peace* magazine, along with addresses given at the Pax annual meeting. The contributors included Philip Scharper, Gordon Zahn, Cecil Gill, Archbishop Paul J. Hallinan, John Leo, and Dorothy Dohen, whose talk, "America: Sacred Nation," became the basis for a book. Thomas Merton sent us from his monastery a paper relating to the conference topic, "Peace and Revolution." I had written asking Merton for a message for the 1968 conference. Though he was preparing for his trip to Bangkok to attend a gathering on monasticism East and West, he prepared an article in time for the conference: "Peace and Revolution: A Footnote from Ulysses." Martin J. Corbin, editor of the *Catholic Worker*, read it to the participants at Tivoli. We could not have known that this was Merton's legacy to Pax.

At the end of 1971, we learned that Pax-England had been accepted for affiliation as the English branch of Pax Christi, the International Catholic Movement for Peace with headquarters in Antwerp, Holland. Barbara Wall, John O'Connor, and Charles Thompson urged us to follow suit in requesting like affiliation. We were informed that an executive council meeting of the international movement would take place in Luxembourg in the second week of April 1972.

For Pax it was a decisive moment. We needed to grasp the opportunity to state our case to become the U.S. branch of the International Catholic Peace Movement. We could not do it by correspondence. Pax had to be present in Luxembourg. Taking a week of vacation and putting together the air-fare—fortunately by Air Icelandic, the lowest of any airline to Europe—I took off. My luggage consisted chiefly of a file of *Peace* magazines, copies of *The War That Is Forbidden*, annual reports and newspaper clippings of our campaigns, and the Pax open letter.

The searching questions and the discussion among the delegates of various countries about Pax activities and goals indicated how seriously the International Movement viewed the question of affiliation. Did Pax have clergy and bishops as members? Would Pax, as a branch of the international organization, agree to have a member of the hierarchy as president?   This was the mode of operation of Pax Christi branches.   Were we of Pax acquainted with bishops who might be willing to serve in the capacity of president?

I assured the council that Pax was on friendly terms with many a bishop who would be happy to serve if Pax were affiliated with the international movement.   I pointed out that seven members of the American hierarchy had signed the Pax Rights of Conscience Campaign, allowing their names to be associated with the organization in the public press.

For my part, I needed to know if each branch of International Pax Christi would have freedom to develop its program to correspond with the needs of the affiliating country.   I was informed that Pax Christi had proceeded along this modality—great freedom—as long as the program was in accordance with church teaching.   Examples were given of how Germany's program developed differently from that of France, how Poland's program was distinct from that of the Netherlands.

The council took the matter under advisement.   The next day, 14 April 1972, the council announced that Pax could be the matrix of the American branch of Pax Christi International.   I was empowered to return with the word that the decision could be put into practice.   Dorothy Day, whose sponsorship extended without a break from Pax to Pax Christi USA, remarked, " What makes me especially happy is that Christ is in your name. "

The meaning of Pax, small vehicle in a worldwide church, only emerged when its ten-year struggle was over.   Some points are worth noting.

Pax actions indicated the maturing of the laity in a hierarchical church when it was moved to affirm the moral autonomy of the person against the demands of the warring state.   Pax put in question, before an unusually obedient community, the presumed right of the state to order its citizens to carry out the awesome task of taking human life.   Any differences with the Catholic hierarchy were affirmed with respect and in a spirit of "loving disagreement."

In a period of moral torpor regarding participation in war, when Christian teaching on war was reduced to a set of propositions, Pax asserted a Christ-centered view emerging from the gospels.   While respecting the consciences of adherents to just-war propositions, Pax upheld the witness of nonviolence, the only gospel option before just-war thinking became a graft on Christianity through Ambrose and Augustine.

It was not surprising that Pax, whose leaders counted many laypeople involved in communication, and who were citizens of a media-suffused society, should pioneer communicating with the leaders of the church.   Besides being the first lay group to send a Catholic newspaper to every bishop in the world, it became the first lay group to publish a paperback book expressly for its hierarchy and national leaders.

In the longer term, Pax and sharers in the Pax and Pax Christi vision, were the carriers of the message of gospel nonviolence as expressed in the life and words of Dorothy Day and Thomas Merton. The immense contribution of this laywoman and this monk could never be measured.

Thomas Merton gave a special legacy to Pax, his last article "Peace and Revolution: A Footnote to Ulysses."[24] By the time it was published in *Peace* magazine, he had died. Merton reminded peacemakers of "the breakdown of language and of communication" that is one of the main themes of *Ulysses*. "Nonviolence as Gandhi conceived it," he pointed out, "is in fact a kind of language. Nonviolence is meant to communicate love not in word but in act." He warned peacemakers of the need "to understand the function of nonviolence against the background of the collapse of language." "Nonviolence," he asserted, "is not primarily the language of efficiency but the language of Kairos."

Certainly Pax members found strength in these words since their actions did not speak the language of efficacy at all. Pax had committed itself to the language of unremitting witness, even of prophetic witness, to warmongers ready to commit "a crime against God and man," and to those who found justification for it.

Pax concentrated on the threat of unleashing the death-dealing light created from the heart of the atom—the threat whose terror was so palpable on the day that Pax got its start. Pax was a small insistent voice for that other light brought by Him who said, "I am the light of the world."

Only at the end of ten years of visible and less visible programs and campaigns, and of reaching the eyes of bishops through publications and their ears by lobbying in Rome, of a peace struggle that demanded unremitting prayers and energy, could Pax learn where these activities were leading. They served as the preparation for the entry into American Catholic life of a larger vehicle, Pax Christi-USA.

The first national assembly of Pax Christi-USA was held in Washington, D.C., at George Washington University, in October 1973. The theme was "Gospel Nonviolence: Catholic Imperative."

"We should not think of ourselves as powerless," said Dorothy Day as the keynote speaker for the weekend gathering. "We have sacramental power." Dorothy had recently come from a California jail where she had spent twelve days for picketing with César Chavez and the United Farm Workers. She rejoiced at the agreement being worked out between the United Farm Workers and the Teamsters Union. "The agreement," she pointed out, was "a victory accomplished by spiritual weapons—nonviolence, prayer and fasting."

The national capital was chosen as the locus of the assembly because the Pax leadership had invited a Washingtonian, Edward Guinan, to serve as general secretary of Pax Christi-USA. Then a Paulist priest, Guinan led a Washington group called the Community for Creative Nonviolence. Like the Catholic Worker, the CCNV focused on works of mercy, including a soup line and a house of hospitality for the homeless.

Guinan seemed a fine candidate to help lead Pax Christi-USA. At a meeting held in Oakridge, attended by Dorothy Day, several Pax activists and lay leaders of other groups including the Community for Creative Nonviolence, Father Guinan accepted the invitation.

But Bishop Carroll T. Dozier, Pax joint moderator, began to ask whether Guinan had caught the spirit of Pax Christi. When he attended a meeting on *Pacem in Terris* in Washington, D.C., Bishop Dozier was upset by a tactic of Guinan and fellow members of the CCNV. They interrupted a talk by Henry Kissinger by operating raucous laugh boxes and were ejected from the hall.

Another action gave Bishop Dozier pause. On learning that the new archbishop of Washington, D.C., intended to buy a residence worth half a million dollars, Guinan stationed himself in front of the mansion and declared a "fast unto death." During the long fast, in 1974 (ending when the decision to purchase the mansion was reversed), it was not possible to conduct Pax Christi matters with Guinan.

Then in July 1974, Patrick Jordan of the directing committee and I sat with Father Guinan in the CCNV hospitality house in Washington, D.C., for a preliminary discussion of the national Pax assembly scheduled for October. We learned to our surprise that plans had already been worked out. Jim Douglass, Guinan told us excitedly, had agreed to come to Washington from Canada for the assembly. Douglass, whom we greatly admired for his peace lobbying at the Vatican Council and for his much-praised book, *The Nonviolent Cross*, had poured blood on Air Force records in Hickam Air Force Base in Hawaii. Arrested and convicted, he had broken parole in traveling to Canada. Guinan said that Douglass would again violate parole by coming to Washington. With enthusiasm, he described how press releases would be timed for Jim Douglass's appearance for Pax Christi-USA, and how the FBI would be informed. Washington, D.C. would be the right place for the drama. Perhaps the FBI would arrest him right on the stage, Guinan told us with relish. Jim Douglass's act of resistance would be the way to put Pax Christi in the public eye.

Patrick Jordan and I listened to the scenario in silence. Finally I said, "But this was not authorized." I pointed out that plans for this assembly, like the first national assembly, should have the agreement and the participation of the directing committee. Pat Jordan and I wanted to carry back ideas for further discussion. The plan to have Douglass as a speaker should be shared with them.

Guinan saw no need of this. He seemed to feel that Douglass's qualifications were so well known in the Catholic community that there was no need to check with the committee. We stressed that Pax Christi was an organization, and I reminded Guinan of our primary focus of peace education, rather than activism. For Guinan there could be no more effective education than the witness of a heroic person ready to suffer for his pacifist conscience. The concept of an obligation to Pax Christi as an organization seemed not to reach him.

Without success I tried to explain to Guinan that I had nothing against the witness of Jim Douglass. But the staging of the scenario he described was not for Pax Christi. It could well be conducted under other auspices. (Later, in fact, it was.)

Patrick Jordan and I left Washington with the sad realization that we had reached an impasse. Guinan followed with a communication to the bishop moderator and the co-chairperson indicating that his continuing as general secretary depended on the upholding of the invitation to Douglass. The letter was an ultimatum rather than an opening for discussion and possible consensus.

On a steamy August morning, Guinan telephoned that an open letter to Pax Christi had been sent to the media. He explained that it was of concern to me and was signed by nine leaders of the Catholic peace community. Guinan had made them privy to our discussion regarding Jim Douglass. When I saw the letter I realized that I was its direct focus.

Guinan had shared with Daniel Berrigan, Philip Berrigan, and others, including Jim Forest of the Catholic Peace Fellowship, his perception of our discussion at the CCNV hospitality house. His perception was that the suggestion to dis-invite James Douglass arose solely from my personal disagreement with him. All the other reasons, including the commitment I had made personally to Pax Christi International to conduct the organization in consonance with the advice of moderators, had been brushed aside. I wondered why none of the signers had asked me for my perception of the meeting before going to the media. Only the editors of *Fellowship*, the magazine of the Fellowship of Reconciliation, checked on the open letter and in publishing excerpts from it noted that the extended invitation had not been authorized by Pax Christi. None of the signers inquired as to the commitment of Pax Christi-USA to the international Pax Christi.

When the open letter was printed in full in *Commonweal* magazine and featured in other magazines and newspapers was a time when I appreciated the pain and rejection Dorothy Day had felt when she returned in 1965 from her peace witness at the second Vatican Council. Some of the young people then at the Catholic Worker had been ready to dispense with people over thirty. It seemed that a Pax Christi issue should have been left to Pax Christi rather than aired through the media, but I decided not to have recourse to the media.

Two weeks later, Guinan resigned as general secretary of Pax Christi-USA. In his letter of resignation, he explained, "I function very poorly in organizations and institutions, possibly an instinctual disbelief in the form; I abhor majority and distrust consensus, possibly an exaggerated belief in the individual; I oppose sacrificing the person for the greater Glory of God, which has brought me to the precipice of our present disagreement."

The error had been ours, perhaps mine in particular. It had been unrealistic on our part to expect an ardent spirit like Edward Guinan to order his time and energies within the constraints of an organization. The fall assembly was cancelled, and Pax Christi, if it was to fulfill a role in the American Catholic Church, would have to be born again.

In retrospect, the hiatus in the process that brought Pax Christi into American Catholic life was necessary, even providential. Gratitude is due Edward Guinan for affording the delay. Every step in the rebirth was taken with prayer and deep deliberation.

Bishop Carroll T. Dozier agreed to take the first step by inviting a small group to his home in Memphis, Tennessee. There Gordon Zahn, Gerard Vanderhaar of Christian Brothers College in Memphis, Joseph Fahey of Manhattan College in New York City, and I planned the initial action. Joseph Fahey accepted the task of being host to a public meeting at Manhattan College. To it were invited peace-concerned Catholics from many states. Dorothy Day was one of the first persons to promise to be present at the relaunching of Pax Christi. An executive council of fourteen persons was set up.

The twice-born organization grew steadily and with increasing vigor. The spiritual ballast of three bishops—Carroll T. Dozier; Thomas Gumbleton, of Detroit, Michigan; and Walter Sullivan, of Richmond, Virginia—helped keep it on course. The immensely gifted national coordinators, Mary Evelyn Jegen of the Sisters of Notre Dame and Mary Lou Kownacki of the Order of St. Benedict, found ways to relate the organization to the heart of the Church while keeping the freedom to tread new and creative paths in gospel peacemaking. The organization could even disagree with the bishops on occasion, as it did on the "weasel clause" in the pastoral letter, "The Challenge of Peace." The clause allowed for "'deterrence' based on balance, not as an end in itself but as a step on the way to progressive disarmament," to be judged "morally acceptable."[25]

In the twentieth year of its rebirth, Pax Christi counted over 12,000 members, 105 of them bishops. Around the country 265 local Pax Christi groups were active in peace programs, seminars, retreats, and acts of witness. One of the acts of witness was the public "Way of the Cross," conducted on the streets of New York by Pax Christi Metro New York every Good Friday. It inspired the annual participation of over 1,500 persons.

The growth of Pax Christi could only point to the task yet to be accomplished. Millions of Americans, among them Catholics, believed in the nuclear deterrent, even after its reason for being, the so-called evil empire, had fallen. One articulate Catholic who still, in 1991, saw a possible use for the deterrent was William O'Brien, whose views on war helped energize Pax for its action at the Second Vatican Council.

Would there come a time when American Catholics would follow the world's bishops in viewing as a "crime against God and humanity itself" the use of the death machine in their country's arsenal? Could Pax Christi help lift up those who were mired in the realism of megadeath? Could it be a vehicle to awaken first Catholics and then other human beings to the realization that "we are the first generation since Genesis with the power to virtually destroy God's creation"?[26] Those who worked with Pax Christi were sustained only by hope, a hope burning in their hearts, that there would be an ultimate victory, not achieved by human power, but by the power of Jesus, the Lamb of God.

NOTES

1. William A. Au, "American Catholics and the Dilemma of War 1960-1980," *U.S. Catholic Historian* (1984); 52.
2. Ibid., 67.
3. E. M. Borgese, *Nation*, (11 April 1966).
4. *The War That Is Forbidden* (New York: Pax, 1968), 66.
5. ["Council Debates Role of Nuclear Weapons,"] *Catholic Standard*, Washington, D.C., 13 November 1964.
6. William V. O'Brien, "Nuclear War and the Schema on the Church in the Modern World," International Law and Juridical Institutions Committee, Catholic Association for International Peace.
7. *Catholic Worker*, July-August 1965, 7.
8. Ibid., 1.
9. Ibid., 6.
10. Ibid., 3.
11. Ibid., 7.
12. Ibid., 6.
13. Ibid., 3.
14. Ibid., 3.
15. Ibid., 3.
16. Ibid., 8.
17. *War That Is Forbidden*, 80.
18. Ibid., 82.
19. Ibid., 71.
20. *Peace*, 2 (Spring 1965), 28.
21. *Peace*, 1 (Spring 1964), 13.
22. William O'Brien, *Nuclear War, Deterrence and Morality* (Westminster, Md., 1967), 82 and passim.
23. Ibid., 24.
24. Thomas Merton, "Peace and Revolution: A Footnote to Ulysses," *Peace*, 3 (1969). Also in Patrick Hart, ed., *The Literary Essays of Thomas Merton* (New York, 1981) and *The Nonviolent Alternative*, Introduction by Gordon Zahn (New York, 1980).
25. "The Challenge of Peace: God's Promise and Our Response," *Origins*, 19 May 1983, 17.
26. "The Challenge of Peace," 30.

10

The Catholic Worker and the Vietnam War

Anne Klejment and Nancy L. Roberts

Ten years before a mass antiwar movement began to take shape in response to skyrocketing U.S. military involvement in Vietnam, Dorothy Day was one of a handful of radical pacifists who dared to defy the political and military conventions of the cold war era.[1] During the spring of 1954, while many Americans were otherwise "absorb[ed] by the televised 'McCarthy-Army game,'" Day sat before her typewriter, composing a remarkable article about Indochina.[2] Overall, she would write little on Vietnam, but in this historical piece Day discussed the clash of gospel Christianity and French imperialism in nineteenth-century Indochina and the prospect of U.S. military intervention in the wake of the French decline abroad.

As in so much of Day's writing, she interwove her religious principles with stories about people whose ideals impressed her. Although she occasionally used the terminology of the Left—such as imperialism and class conflict—to describe global events, she valued spiritual insight above any political ideology for its ability to "dig . . . deeper, get . . . more down to the roots, and make . . . the problems more complicated."[3] With that in mind, she tapped the thoughts of an obscure martyred priest, Theophane Venard, a French missionary in Indochina, to present an authoritative critique of the modern Christian West's desire for empire building, to dominate the peoples and resources of other lands. Often Day sought confirmation for her ideas in the lives and writings of others. Relying on the saintly Venard's spiritual authority, Day drew a parallel between the foreign policy of France in the priest's time and that of the modern United States.

Venard had eagerly joined colonizers of Indochina in their "mission civilisatrice," but, according to Day, he quickly discerned that his efforts to evangelize were being hampered by French political and economic ambitions in a region rich in human and natural resources and conveniently situated near the tempting markets of China. According to the indignant missionary, newspapers propagandized the wonders of Christianity in Asia to the point of "pure fiction." He observed "godless and secular" governments following "the rule" of expediency.[4] Venard and Day shared an unshakable faith in Christianity and an understanding that in a Christian society public affairs are shaped by religious principles. But in Venard's time as in Day's, Christians who aimed to rebuild society on Christian teachings faced enormous structural challenges. Too often the church deferred to secular authority, namely, the nation-state and the narrow economic interests of capitalists. When the Christian nations of the West began their empire building, missionaries often accompanied soldiers. The State typically subordinated religion to the primary quest for power and wealth.

Venard's alternative view of Christian society appealed to Day. With his example in mind, she confidently attacked a central premise of the cold war, namely, that the contest between the communist powers and the United States and its European allies was an ideological and religious struggle of such great consequence, that the governments of the Christian West could use any and all means to secure victory. Day, of course, was a former Leftist who had converted to Catholicism. She had experienced political repression during the World War I era and had watched the dissenting press fold under government pressure. Her long experience of government surveillance of alleged subversives and public hysteria over radicalism failed to silence her. As a young secular radical, Day was overwhelmed by the failure of the Left to make a difference. But as a Catholic radical, the many spiritual gifts she received from her rekindled faith encouraged perseverance and boldness in her opposition to war.

"[I]t is not Christianity and freedom we are defending," Day explained about the cold war, "but our possessions."[5] As she saw it, American Christianity failed to examine critically political, social, and economic power. While the postwar era continues to be popularly mythologized as a time of consensus, religious cohesion, and exemplary family life, Day was troubled by Christianity's easy adaptation to the American way of life. If, as Day believed, the United States was poised to fill the power vacuum in Indochina once the French forces retreated, then the nation's reliance on a military solution embodied its loss of faith—its failure to rely on spiritual weapons.[6]

Just how much influence this single article exerted on U.S. Catholics of the fifties is open to question. The circulation of the *Catholic Worker* was up to 58,000 copies in 1954 from a wartime low of 50,500, an amazing sign of recovery and of cracks in the cold war consensus. However, since the *Worker* was not an official publication of the church, the vast majority of Catholic leaders and church publications could safely ignore it. During the early fifties, Dorothy Day's position on Indochina was probably unique within the Catholic community. Catholic opinion supported the dismantling of the Bamboo Curtain.

Even the liberal Catholic *Commonweal* recited the cold war creed while meditating on Southeast Asia. Ho Chi Minh, the communist nationalist leader of North Vietnam, emerged from its pages in 1947 as a "false George Washington." By the fifties, the magazine preferred nuclear "brinkmanship" to a "Communist-dominated Asia."[7] One could hardly expect church leaders like Francis Cardinal Spellman of New York, who had long enjoyed a measure of political influence, and Bishop Fulton J. Sheen, the "philosopher and prophet"[8] of American Catholic anticommunism, to show anything less than enthusiasm for a world view that helped to draw Catholics closer to the mainstream.

The most widely read Catholic author on Indochina during the fifties was Dr. Tom Dooley, a handsome young Notre Dame graduate, who successfully promoted himself as a Catholic hero. Captivated by Dooley's hard-hitting anticommunism, even *Reader's Digest* found the Catholic doctor's life and ideas worthy of condensation. In the jungles of Southeast Asia, where communists were attempting to enlarge their spheres of influence, Dooley set up clinics and begged supplies for the poor. Dooley's medicine fought communism as well as disease. When treating babies, he would remind parents of the origins of his supplies. "Dai La My-Quoc Vien-Tro" translated into "This is American aid."[9]

Mary and Joseph Average were surrounded by cold war iconography in the secular and religious media. Within the Catholic community the standard cold war position held sway well into the sixties. *America*, a Jesuit publication, as late as 1967 defended the war as a measure "to prevent 17 million Vietnamese from being swallowed up by a voracious and aggressive Communism."[10]

Day's article mattered over the long run. It put the Catholic Worker movement on record against a military "solution" in Vietnam more than a decade before U.S. policy became the key political issue. It laid bare the spiritual defects in conventional anticommunism. This and other writings in the *CW* nurtured a new generation of Catholic thinkers, Thomas Merton and Daniel Berrigan, S.J. among them, who would absorb Day's critique of anticommunism and undergo a conversion to her pioneering pacifism. As priests and successful writers, they would extend Day's influence to a new generation of American Catholics, those who came of age spiritually during the Kennedy presidency, the civil rights movement, the Second Vatican Council, and the Vietnam War.

The article was an integral part of the CW movement's recovery of the Christian pacifist tradition for future consideration by their coreligionists. With help from other Workers and followers, Day had developed during the thirties and forties a spirituality of pacifism rooted in scripture, the history of the early church, and the just-war teaching strictly interpreted. Although the nature of the Second World War, with Hitler's irrepressible lust to dominate Europe and Japan's first strike against Pearl Harbor, had led to heated debates about pacifism and dissension within the movement, a larger number of American Catholics than ever before presented themselves before their draft boards and claimed conscientious objector status with critical support from Day and the movement. By the fifties, as the public began to reconsider the nuclear option for a variety of reasons, the Catholic Worker, largely through the efforts of

Day, Ammon Hennacy, and Robert Ludlow, entered into a new phase of pacifist expression: nonviolent direct action.

The pacifist movement in the United States, including the Catholic Worker movement, other religious dissenters, and the Left, was the first critic of U.S. policy in Indochina, and its antiwar activities preceded the mass Vietnam antiwar movement by many years. During this period of cultural and political transition from cold war consensus to widespread public dissatisfaction with a seemingly unwinnable war, Catholic Worker peace activism took several forms. The *Worker* printed articles on church teaching relating to war and peace, reports on Vietnam, and significant events in the peace movement. Catholic Workers built peace groups outside of the CW movement itself. They supported growing numbers of conscientious objectors and resisted the draft. The paper and informal conferences at the movement's farm in Tivoli, New York educated the public and the church about peace issues. Some of the younger members tested new forms of protest. Day and others clarified the movement's understanding of Christian nonviolence and in word and deed used "spiritual weapons" in the quest for a just society and a peaceful world.

Both Pax and the Catholic Peace Fellowship, which emerged in the early sixties, originated in the Catholic Worker. Lobbying for peace and providing much-needed draft counseling respectively, the new organizations reached a larger constituency than the Catholic Worker could have independently. The draft board raid movement which began in 1967 with the Baltimore Four action also traced its roots to the movement. Philip Berrigan, S.S.J., Tom Lewis, Michael Cullen, and Jim Forest were among the earliest raiders with ties to the Catholic Worker movement.[11]

Magnifying the movement's influence during the sixties were the teachings of Pope John XXIII and the Second Vatican Council[12] and the ongoing social transformation of American Catholics during the fifties and sixties. Once a despised and mistrusted religious minority, by the end of World War II Catholics had begun to enter into the middle-class mainstream. Immigration restrictions during World War I and the postwar era enhanced the ratio of native-born American Catholics to immigrants. New Deal social programs, World War II, and the generous benefits offered to veterans likewise advanced the status of Catholics as solid, productive citizens. And ironically, the nation's postwar obsession with cold war politics neatly complemented Catholic anticommunism and reinforced awareness of Catholics as patriotic citizens.[13] Thus, when the Vietnam War heated up, many U.S. Catholics could eventually align themselves against the war without feeling especially vulnerable.

Catholic Workers were among the first Americans to protest U.S. policy in Vietnam during the sixties. During the Kennedy era U.S. military presence in Southeast Asia was hardly comparable to the levels reached after Lyndon Johnson's decision to send in ground troops in 1965. But the repressive policies of the anticommunist South Vietnamese regime of Ngo Dinh Diem inspired in

1963 what is now considered to be the first domestic protest against American policy in Vietnam.

That August, Tom Cornell and Chris Kearns of the Catholic Worker picketed the residence of the Vietnamese observer to the United Nations. Their outrage stemmed from the brutal suppression of dissenting Buddhist monks and students who demanded more freedoms from the American-backed Saigon regime. As an American Catholic, Cornell felt a special calling to protest the persecution of Buddhists by the Catholic president of South Vietnam. He and Kearns paraded back and forth with signs that demanded an end to U.S. support for the anticommunist Diem regime. On the tenth day of the tiny demonstration, the numbers were swelled by about two hundred other peace activists and ABC News broadcast coverage of the event.[14]

Independently of the Catholic Worker, the Kennedy administration had begun to reassess its support of President Diem after the attacks on Buddhists. The president was troubled by the embarrassingly repressive policies of the U.S. ally, which reflected poorly on the U.S. government's claim that an anticommunist government in Vietnam meant freedom for Vietnamese people. When Kennedy's warnings to President Diem to seek reform seemingly went unheeded, the South Vietnamese regime was ousted in a military coup blessed by the United States. But Vietnam's long civil war continued after the untimely and violent deaths of the two leaders. American policy makers pumped more resources into Vietnam during the Johnson presidency, but the unstable government of the South remained vulnerable to communism.

In 1964 as in 1963, well before the public criticized U.S. policy in Southeast Asia, the Catholic Worker grasped the implications of the deteriorating political situation in Saigon and alarm in Washington. When U.S. destroyers off the coast of communist North Vietnam were allegedly attacked, Congress, with a minimum of dissent, passed the Tonkin Gulf Resolution, which granted the president virtually unlimited power to take defensive and offensive action in Southeast Asia. To illustrate the strength of the anticommunist consensus then, Congress's blank check to the president did not become an election issue in the presidential race. While the resolution's passage was not recorded in the *Worker*—only on the rarest occasions did congressional actions receive mention—the paper was troubled by reports, confirmed by the Department of Defense, that the U.S. military was testing chemical and biological weapons in "Our Undeclared War."[15]

Consistently pacifist since 1933, and with a readership much increased since the forties and fifties, the *Catholic Worker* paper, was, among Catholic periodicals, probably the most effective voice of nonviolence during the Vietnam era. But the paper neither attempted full coverage of the peace movement nor exclusive reporting of antiwar protests. Instead, readers found thoughtful discussion of pacifism during the course of the Vatican Council, a selection of writing on Vietnam by *CW* editors and others, and coverage of a wide range of social issues unrelated to the war. Then, as in World War II, the CW movement resisted narrowing its mission exclusively to peace. Day insisted that the work of the movement included performing works of mercy. Thus, the Worker embraced and represented in its paper the causes of civil rights, the farm workers' movement, poverty, and prison reform.[16]

Writing on the Vietnam War comprised a surprisingly small portion of the *Catholic Worker*'s coverage of peace issues. In 1962 when Dorothy Day traveled to Rome to join others in praying and lobbying for the bishops to endorse pacifism as an official teaching in the pronouncements of the Second Vatican Council, the paper assumed responsibility for educating lay Catholics and clerics about peace.

The *Catholic Worker* helped Catholics to educate their consciences in numerous articles devoted to papal and conciliar teaching on peace and the history of the pacifist tradition. Papal teachings of the sixties, although falling short of an explicit statement of pacifism, provided principles that led thoughtful Catholics to pacifist conclusions.[17] James Hanink found in Pope John XXIII's teachings a condemnation of war in the nuclear age.[18] Philip Berrigan, later a leader in the draft board raid movement, noted the revolutionary implications of Pope John's teaching "that nations are bound to the same essential morality as individuals, since nations are composed of individuals and the institutions they create."[19] Perhaps the heart of Pope John's thought was covered in "Beyond Anti-Communism" by Peter J. Riga. John XXIII's letter *Pacem in Terris* presented a complex understanding of morality, according to Riga. For Pope John, peace could not be equated with the absence of war. Total victory, or unconditional surrender, posed moral harm. Without discarding the just-war tradition of the church, John XXIII, in Riga's view, took a position similar to that of Dorothy Day. He could not conceive of true peace without the practice of love, truth, liberty, and social justice.[20] The pronouncements of Pope Paul VI also merited attention from the paper, including his teachings of social justice and the "war in Asia."[21]

Catholic Worker pacifism, as defined by Dorothy Day, was rooted in the four gospels of the New Testament. In a rare public address at a mass antiwar rally—Day preferred writing to making speeches—she explained that "the word of God" said "thou shalt not kill" and "love your enemies." The spirit of these laws required Christians "not to take the lives of men, women, children, young and old, by bombs and napalm and all the other instruments of war."[22] While she consistently adhered to an absolutely nonviolent ethic, in the sixties as during World War II, she opened the pages of the *Catholic Worker* to those who followed just-war principles to reach a pacifist conclusion. In a strict sense, just-war pacifists argued that theorically a particular war could meet all of the criteria. However modern warfare—with the mobilization of industry, the indiscriminate destruction of civilians, and the disproportionate devastation of nuclear arms—made it virtually impossible for any twentieth-century war to fulfill the criteria for just cause *and* proper procedures as required by the teaching.

Philip Berrigan was the most meticulous and persuasive of writers in the *Catholic Worker* to use just-war reasoning to condemn U.S. policy in Southeast Asia. The means of the war constituted "barbarous . . . immoral[ity]," according to Berrigan. Government plans to bomb North Vietnamese dikes, endangering the survival of thousands of civilians, the continuing use of experimental weapons, and support for an illegitimate government in South Vietnam led him to the conclusion that both the gospel and traditional church teaching on war were being violated. Possession of nuclear, bacteriological, and chemical weapons and their use as deterrents threatened innocent civilians with unspeakable horror. In the climate of cold war between the western powers and the communist giants, the regional fighting in Southeast Asia could evolve into a full-scale nuclear conflict. Berrigan noted that this undeclared war did not fulfill the just-war principle that war must be declared by the proper authority.[23] His points were reinforced a few months later by Peter Riga, who concluded that the war must be condemned, since U.S. destruction of the enemy's rice crop amounted to "an indiscriminate act of total war which no Christian theology could possibly justify."[24]

Daniel Berrigan condemned war in general. He pointed out that war compromises the word of God: "It is astonishing to reflect how in time of war, the word of God tends to become complicated and diffuse. Suddenly, His word has a thousand footnotes, refining, clarifying, explaining away." The Jesuit noted, "The message of peace is interpreted in favor of nationalism, of the ideologies of the movement, of the frenzies of human causes . . . One must now approach God through a thousand others who speak for God, who talk another language than His, who issue commands counter to His commands."[25]

Beginning in 1965, when U.S. troops were sent overseas and the death toll rose, increasing numbers of Americans expressed dissatisfaction with the war. By this time, it was clear that religious pacifists like the Catholic Worker movement were a fraction of the massive, amorphous antiwar movement. Historian Charles DeBenedetti observed that "antiwar opposition clearly proliferated . . . prompting perhaps 4 million people (collected in at least 560 organizations) to take different actions at different places at different times toward different ends."[26] The antiwar coalition, comprised of pacifists, students, radicals, liberals, and the like, was not under the influence of any one person, group, or ideology. Antiwar activists were divided over tactics and strategies. Increasingly, the effectiveness of nonviolence was questioned by the more militant and secular activists. Liberals hoped to make the political system responsive to their concerns about the war. Men of draft age agonized over taking conscientious objector status or school deferments versus resistance or exile abroad.

Catholic Workers were not isolated from the outside political and social forces that were pushing and tugging the antiwar movement in various directions. Dorothy Day, who turned seventy in 1967, as well as younger CW volunteers, struggled to respond to the initatives of a minority that seemed to be redefining nonviolence and civil disobedience. Whether or not to oppose the war was not an issue at the Worker during the sixties as it had been in the forties. A 1965 self-immolation and a series of draft board raids in 1968 rocked CW peacemakers. In each case, someone associated with the Worker had made a controversial choice. The delicate task at hand during the Vietnam War required that the movement's spokespersons set moral limits and propose strategy without splintering the fragile antiwar coalition or destroying the infant Catholic peace movement that had been born when the Second Vatican Council (1962-1965) coincided with the intensification of U.S. military efforts in Southeast Asia.

Early in 1965 Dorothy Day and other pacifists signed a now famous complicity statement, which committed signers to refuse cooperation with the U.S. government's efforts in Vietnam. It urged others to refuse to serve in the armed forces or to manufacture or transport military equipment. Headed by a polite, "Will you sign this?" the document was reprinted in the *Catholic Worker*. Age had not diminished Day's militancy. Signers, as the document noted, risked a five-year prison sentence or a $5,000 fine if convicted of violating the draft law.[27] As U.S. involvement overseas deepened, some antiwar activists began to experiment with tactics that rejected polite protest and mainstream political organization, which they regarded as ineffective.

The CW supported both those draft-age men who sought conscientious objector status as well as nonviolent noncooperators who preferred to risk imprisonment rather than conform their consciences to government rules relating to draft status. Chris Kearns and Tom Cornell, the two Catholic Workers who had picketed in 1963, burned their draft cards as a protest against the war. In the case of Kearns, a *Life* magazine photojournalist snapped a picture of him at a rally where men dropped their draft cards (his was borrowed) into a smoldering pot.[28] As soon as the magazine hit the newsstands, angry congressional hawks vilified draft card burners and quickly passed the Rivers Amendment, which stipulated severe punishment for those convicted of destroying their draft cards.[29] The first violator of the act was another Catholic Worker, David Miller, who destroyed his card on 15 October 1965. He later spent twenty-two months in federal custody.

Acts of individual nonviolent resistance satisfied the Catholic Worker pacifist ethic since these acts reflected the choice made by an informed conscience, openly broke an unjust law, and put others at no risk. Outside of the Worker, however, the destruction of draft cards provoked the expected outcry from hawks, but also criticism from respected peacemakers such as Trappist monk Thomas Merton, who, in his writings and sponsorship of peace organizations, had advanced the cause of nonviolence tremendously during the sixties. Merton eventually reconsidered his position after reading Tom Cornell's articles about draft resistance.[30]

Shortly after David Miller's arrest at the Whitehall Street antidraft rally, a quiet, serious Catholic Worker volunteer decided to take the movement's antiwar resistance in a new direction. Without discussing his plans, Roger LaPorte, once a Cistercian seminarian, offered himself in protest to the war. Setting out before dawn on 9 November 1965 with a two-gallon can of fuel, LaPorte headed uptown to the United Nations, doused himself with kerosene, and ignited himself. The next day he died at Bellevue Hospital.

All at the Catholic Worker were stunned by LaPorte's deed. He had socialized with some of his friends only hours before the self-immolation but had not confided his plans to anyone. Nothing had seemed amiss. His was a thoroughly solitary decision. As he lay dying, he managed to blurt out that he was a Catholic Worker and opposed all wars. "I did this as a religious action. I picked this hour so no one could stop me," he added, well aware that Catholic Workers or even bypassers would have intervened.[31]

No one in the Catholic peace movement had ever before attempted self-immolation; there was no direct Catholic precedent for his deed. But self-immolation as protest had already become a part of the Vietnam War. In 1963 a Buddhist monk, with the knowledge of at least one other, sacrificed himself in a fire he set at one of the busiest intersections in Saigon. News of Thich Quang Duc's protest reached the United States and, in time, two U.S. Quakers, Alice Herz, eighty-two years old, and, a week before LaPorte's act, Norman Morrison, a young parent, had protested the Vietnam War in this fashion.

Not only did LaPorte's suicide shock and confuse Catholic Workers. All were frustrated that they had not been able to stop him. Dorothy Day responded with condemnation of the act but generosity toward a troubled spirit. "It has always been the teaching of the Catholic Church that suicide is sin," she wrote, yet "mercy and loving-kindness dictate . . . another judgment that anyone who took his life was temporarily unbalanced, not in full possession of his facilities, even to be judged temporarily insane, and so absolved of guilt."[32] The official statement on LaPorte's act warned others against using this extreme form of self-sacrifice to oppose the war.[33]

Privately, Catholic Workers wrestled with their consciences over the value of the nonviolent peace witness. Weeks earlier, LaPorte and other Catholic Workers had attended an antiwar rally where Tom Cornell had burned his draft card. Counterdemonstrators that day had shouted at the draft resisters, "Burn yourself, not your cards," and that was what LaPorte ultimately chose to do. Cornell worried that perhaps he had unconsciously played a role in LaPorte's decision.[34]

Many of the usual supporters of the Catholic Worker and the peace movement expressed horror and outrage that LaPorte might have been pressured by the Catholic Worker's position of resistance to war. Thomas Merton questioned how such a tragedy could have happened. Threatening to resign from the Catholic peace movement, the monk declared that peacemakers were obligated to provide reasonable guidance to activists.[35] A letter from Dorothy Day eased his qualms. Meanwhile, the liberal *National Catholic Reporter* joined in the criticism of Catholic pacifism, blaming pacifists for disrupting "young and tender consciences."[36]   Former *Catholic Worker* editor Michael Harrington, who avoided placing blame, presented a more nuanced assessment of the self-immolation. Although Harrington no longer considered himself a pacifist or a Catholic, he believed that the "religious suicides" not only "violate[d] their . . . principles of non-violence" and "their affirmation of the sacredness of life," they also alienated potential peacemakers. But Harrington thought he understood why LaPorte killed himself: it was the loneliness of the resister in the midst of a hostile society with support from only "tiny" like-minded groups.[37] Another one of those who did not lash out at the Catholic Worker movement in the LaPorte tragedy was Jesuit Daniel Berrigan.

Day hoped that other peace activists would not repeat LaPorte's act of self-immolation.   The spirit of Catholic Worker personalism had encouraged individual responsibility for social ills and for one's neighbor. The movement required living in voluntary poverty and sharing. Self-destruction had no place in Catholic Worker spirituality. War resisters faced the taunts and curses of war supporters, and maybe even a beating by a hostile crowd. Bearing the brutality of prison life was likewise a cost accepted by the nonviolent resister. But the nonviolent protester did not have authorization to carry out death by one's own hand, even as an outcry against an endless war.

Two years later, Catholic Workers still were affected by the death. Day was situating responsibility for the act on the war itself: "It is as though such men said, 'We will suffer with you, since we have no way of stopping the bombing, the burning, the napalm, the defoliation, the destruction of homes and entire countryside. There is no act of ours extreme enough, no protest strong enough, to deal with this horror.'"[38]

As the war continued, peace activists experimented with new tactics that they hoped might prove to be effective in ending the war. In October 1967, protesters known as the Baltimore Four launched a new form of nonviolent draft resistance: the draft board raid. Two of them had Catholic Worker connections. Philip Berrigan, S.S.J., a priest activist and World War II combat veteran, was a lifelong reader of the *Worker* and had written some of its strongest articles against the Vietnam War. Tom Lewis was a social activist and artist who is still associated with the Worker. Their protest took place in a Selective Service office where they bloodied draft files to impede the war and to suggest religious sacrifice. Several months later, in May 1968, the Catonsville Nine draft board raid received tremendous publicity, thanks to poet Daniel Berrigan's participation. By the end of the year, still more Catholic Workers participated in this new form of protest.

Initially, Dorothy Day gave her blessing to the raiders. In a letter to Daniel Berrigan, she described the raid as a "very strong and imaginative witness" and she concluded that it met the key criteria required of an act of nonviolent resistance.   Soon, however, she began to worry about such issues as the emotional and spiritual maturity of the resisters and the potential for unintended violence. While she knew that a deep spirituality led the Berrigans to take part in the raids, she already had seen that some of the young Catholic Workers who had burned their draft cards and gone to prison managed the experience with great difficulty. The risks to the raiders were even higher. Jim Forest of the Milwaukee Fourteen remembered: "In the end, she didn't agree with what we had done, but she treasured us and supported us, wrote about us, published our things in the newspaper. . . . But she also made it clear that this was not her idea of the best way to bring about the change that we wanted."[39] Ultimately, Day suggested tried and true alternatives to the raids, including picketing.[40] Not all of the younger Workers approved of the raids either. One young pacifist complained to a raider, whom he felt was judgmental, that "We have an action here [at the CW]. We call it the soupline."[41] Even the longevity of the Vietnam War and the escalating militancy of the antiwar movement did not transform the Catholic Worker into a one-issue group.

A sizable number of draft-age men at Catholic Worker houses engaged in draft refusal, a more traditional form of nonviolent war resistance. Bob Gilliam, a former seminarian who became a volunteer at the Chrystie Street house in New York, had not intended to resist the draft. But when his Minnesota draft board denied his application for objector status, he chose noncooperation. Before going to prison, Gilliam and two other Workers, Jack Cook and Dan Kelly, prepared for the 1967 Easter season by praying and fasting for peace at the National Cathedral in Washington, D.C. A typed handbill reminded passersby that their opposition to the war "[was] not only [a] political but [a] religious" conviction.[42]

Tax resistance likewise was an act of faith. Dorothy Day practiced voluntary poverty and elevated it to a precept of the movement. By volunteers typically earning little and by sharing property, the Catholic Worker was in a strong position to resist war with the nonpayment of taxes.[43] Chicago Catholic Worker Karl Meyer observed that by adopting a Catholic Worker lifestyle, one could resist war taxes: "If you have a concern of conscience about paying war taxes, but feel unready to face the possible consequences of the methods of resistance . . . live in reasonable simplicity and voluntary poverty in the spirit of the Catholic Worker movement."[44]

Ammon Hennacy was the quintessential apostle of war tax resistance at the Worker until his unexpected death in 1970. When federal withholding of income tax began in 1943, Hennacy made certain that he managed to earn less than the amount necessary for the automatic deductions to begin. Hennacy thought of U.S. involvement in Vietnam as "senseless slaughter," and he boasted that he had never paid a dime of federal income taxes—threequarters of which he claimed were earmarked for war expenditures. Every year after 1945 Hennacy openly opposed war taxes while picketing and fasting. A war economy, he firmly believed, would impoverish even the richest nation in the world.[45]

One of Hennacy's protégés, Karl Meyer, carried on the tradition of creative war tax resistance at the Worker. Unflappable when confronted by government bureaucrats, Meyer wrote cogently about the reasons for nonpayment of war tax and his experiences with the Internal Revenue Service. With the Vietnam War costing an estimated two billion dollars per month at its peak, the Johnson administration needed to finance burdensome military expenditures without totally destroying Great Society social programming. A federal telephone surcharge was devised to meet these costs. Meyer's call for resistance to the telephone tax noted that the telephone service of resisters would not be cut. By 1971 he claimed that this particular type of war resistance had become a mass tactic, with an estimated 100,000 persons engaged in this "easiest and most common form of *principled* [emphasis added] tax resistance." Taking the call to love one's neighbor in a literal way, Meyer suggested that all citizens could claim a massive W-4E exemption on the grounds that all of the peoples of the world were one's dependents.[46]

By the time the Paris Peace Accord was signed in January 1973, bringing a cease-fire to Vietnam, the mass antiwar movement was exhausted and in disarray. Some of the strongest leaders were in jail. The public, often as critical of the antiwar movement as it was of the war itself, lost interest in the civil war ten thousand miles away. Patrick Jordan spoke for many at the Worker when he declared, "No, we do not find ourselves joyful at the news of 'peace.' The conflict continues in much of Indochina, and it is the poor who suffer, not ourselves."[47] At pacifist Catholic Worker houses throughout the United States, resistance to war continued after the cease-fire and the reunification of Vietnam in 1975.

The Catholic Worker belief that economic imperialism, militarism, arms competition, and nationalism fuels wars was rooted in Dorothy Day's experiences during World War I and her work for the Anti Imperialist League in the late twenties, but it influenced younger Workers. Mike DeGregory rephrased a question that went to the heart of the movement's pacifist spirituality. If we render to Caesar, he noted, we must determine that "it is compatible with the things that are God's."[48] One year after the peace agreement, the United States was sending hundreds of millions of dollars in aid to South Vietnam, some of it destined to bolster the military. During that year, continuing violence resulted in roughly between fifty and one hundred thousand casualties. The Worker was one of the few groups to pay attention to Vietnamese as well as American victims of war. Tax resistance was suggested as one approach.[49] The war had devastated many areas of Indochina, destroying hospitals and maiming civilians who had little prospect of proper medical care under the circumstances. Catholic Workers, showing concern for North and South Vietnamese people alike, tried to raise money to help with the relief and rebuilding efforts. To interest others in the needs of Southeast Asians, Catholic Workers advocated walking for peace, holding vigils, praying, and distributing leaflets. Pacifist liturgies, protesting U.S. bombings in Cambodia, were held outside the White House. As in 1917, when Dorothy Day stood silently with a women's suffrage banner, the Washington protesters were arrested for obstruction.[50]   The movement persisted in following the pacifist path and in educating readers of its paper about nonviolent means, but, during the height of the Vietnam War, the mass media regarded the most militant antiwar activists as the most newsworthy. Ignored in the mainstream media, the quiet nonviolent witness of religious pacifists primarily interested alternative publications.

Twenty years after the end of the Vietnam War, assessment of the Catholic Worker's contribution to the antiwar effort is no simple matter. The values of the Catholic Worker do not harmonize nicely with American society's culture of individualism and success. Therefore the history of the CW movement in the Vietnam era makes little sense if judged solely by the standards of the dominant culture.

Committed to a philosophy of personalism, Catholic Workers are, in Peter Maurin's quaint phraseology "go-givers" not "go-getters." To be a peacemaker, one attempts to do good for others. Measurement of the good done by Christians violated the spirit of Christ's sacrifice. Many times Dorothy Day noted, "What we do is so little we may seem to be constantly failing. But so did He fail. He met with apparent failure on the Cross. But unless the seed fall into the earth and die, there is no harvest."[51]

The history of Catholic Worker pacifism has supported Day's view about looking at long-range development over short-term gains. During the Vietnam War, the foundation of religious pacifism built by Day and first generation Workers remained firm, despite pressure not only from the Right, but the Left as well. Although Day's venerable presence, the vitality of the Catholic Worker witness, and the movement's evolving pacifist tradition could not prevent all excesses, Catholic Worker pacifists responded with commitment and creativity to the moral issues raised by the Vietnam War.

The years spent in developing a spirituality of pacifism helped to convince many post–Vatican II Catholics that their faith required mature judgment on issues of war and peace. During the Vietnam War era one could witness an increase in Catholic antiwar opinion, Catholic conscientious objection, and Catholic war resistance. Having influenced the philosophy of nonviolence of such intellectuals as Thomas Merton, Daniel Berrigan, and James Douglass, ideas derived from the philosophy and practice of Catholic Worker pacifism received a larger hearing inside and outside of the church.[52] By this time, historian Richard Hofstadter's criticism that American Catholicism had failed to add a "distinctive leaven" to national political debates missed one of the key developments of the renewal of American Catholicism that was well underway a generation before the Second Vatican Council.[53]

As a tiny portion of a much larger social movement, the Catholic Worker contributed to the war's end. But as historian Charles Chatfield observed, "The antiwar movement did not end the war: the American people did that by withdrawing passive support for it."[54] At every level of the American Catholic Church, the influence of the Worker could be felt, whether at the Vatican Council, where the movement's ideas were circulated, debated, and adapted, or in homes, schools, and churches, or on the streets. Wherever the works of mercy, spiritual weapons such as prayer, fasting, penance, and picketing are discussed and practiced, it is quite likely that it is through the legacy of Dorothy Day and the Catholic Workers.

NOTES

1. The best account of the cold war peace movement is found in Lawrence S. Wittner, *Rebels Against War: The American Peace Movement, 1941-1969* (New York, 1969), supplemented by Charles DeBenedetti, *The Peace Reform in American History* (Bloomington, Ind., 1980), 138-64; Harriet Hyman Alonso, *Peace as a Woman's Issue* (Syracuse, N.Y., 1993), 157-92 ; Amy Swerdlow, *Women Strike for Peace* (Chicago, 1993), 97-124. For an interesting view of Catholic Worker noncooperation with the Civil Defense drills as a part of American culture, see James Farrell, "Personalist Politics: Routes and Roots of Sixties Protest," paper presented at the 1994 meeting of the Organization of American Historians in Atlanta and *The Spirit of the Sixties: The Making of Postwar Radicalism* (New York, forthcoming 1996).

2. "Theophane Venard and Ho Chi Minh," *Catholic Worker*, May 1954.

3. Ibid.

4. Ibid.

5. Ibid.

6. Ibid.

7. For circulation figures, see Nancy L. Roberts, *Dorothy Day and the "Catholic Worker"* (Albany, N.Y., 1984), 180. *Commonweal*'s positions are discussed in Roger Van Allen, *"The Commonweal" and American Catholicism* (Philadelphia, 1974), 153-54.

8. Donald F. Crosby, S.J., *God, Church and Flag: Senator Joseph McCarthy and the Catholic Church, 1950-1957* (Chapel Hill, N.C., 1978), 15.

9. A recent appraisal of Dooley can be found in James Terence Fisher, *The Catholic Counterculture in America, 1933-1962* (Chapel Hill, N.C., 1989), 131-204. The quote is from Robert Scheer, "Hang Down Your Head Tom Dooley," *Ramparts* (January-February 1965), 26.

10. Quoted in John Deedy, "The Catholic Press and Vietnam," in Thomas Quigley, ed., *American Catholics and Vietnam* (Grand Rapids, Mich., 1968), 130. For a useful discussion on changing Catholic opinion on the Vietnam War, see David J. O'Brien, "Catholic Opposition to the Vietnam War," in Thomas A. Shannon, ed., *War or Peace?: The Search for New Answers* (Maryknoll, N.Y., 1980), 131-36. On the anticommunism of Catholic realists, see William A. Au, *The Cross, the Flag, and the Bomb: American Catholics Debate War and Peace, 1960-1983* (Westport, Conn., 1985), 62 and passim. The complex and changing views of Catholics on communism are illustrated in a case study of Daniel and Philip Berrigan by Anne Klejment, "In the Lions' Den: The Social Catholicism of Daniel and Philip Berrigan, 1955-1965" (unpublished Ph.D. dissertation, State University of New York at Binghamton, 1980), 236-77.

11. For example, see Jim Forest, "The Roots of Catholic Resistance," *Catholic World* (November 1971), 61-65; Michael Cullen with Don Ranly, *A Time to Dance* (Celina, Ohio, 1972), 57-58ff; Charles A. Meconis, *With Clumsy Grace: The American Catholic Left 1961-1975* (New York, 1979), passim; Rosalie Riegle Troester, ed., *Voices from the Catholic Worker* (Philadelphia, 1993), 183-216.

12. Refer to the chapters in this volume by James Douglass and Eileen Egan.

13. Countless church leaders, including Popes Pius XI and XII, Cardinal Spellman, Charles Coughlin, Fulton Sheen, and the lesser-known Louis Gales, founder of the *Catholic Digest* and the Catechetical Guild, tenderly nurtured Catholic anticommunism since the thirties. Surprisingly, there is no adequate study of American Catholic anticommunism. On the social changes that influenced religious fermentation, see Jay P. Dolan, et al., eds., *Transforming the Parish Ministry* (New York, 1989), 222-23, 307-20.

14. Nancy Zaroulis and Gerald Sullivan, *Who Spoke Up? American Protest against the War in Vietnam, 1963-1975* (Garden City, N.Y., 1984), 12-13.

15. "Our Undeclared War," *Catholic Worker*, July-August 1964 was a reprint of a press release of the Federation of American Scientists.

16. The diversity of topics in the *Catholic Worker* can be explored in Anne Klejment and Alice Klejment, *Dorothy Day and "The Catholic Worker": A Bibliography and Index* (New York, 1986), especially 259-97.

17. For two different views of papal and conciliar teachings on peace, see James W. Douglass, *The Non-violent Cross* (New York, 1968), 81-136 for a vigorous defense of the implicit pacifism of the documents; Au, *The Cross*, 165-78 challenges the pacifist reading.

18. James Hanink, "Notes on Permanent Revolution," *Catholic Worker*, November 1968, 2.

19. Philip Berrigan, "Vietnam and America's Conscience," *Catholic Worker*, October 1965, 4.

20. Peter J. Riga, "Beyond Anti-Communism," *Catholic Worker*, January 1966, 2.

21. Paul VI, "'With Piercing Cry and with Tears,'" *Catholic Worker*, September 1966, 1.

22. Quoted in Tom Cornell, "Life & Death on the Streets of New York," *Catholic Worker*, November 1965, 8.

23. Philip Berrigan, "Vietnam and America's Conscience," 2, 6.

24. Peter J. Riga, "Rice Crop Spraying," *Catholic Worker*, January 1966, 2.

25. Daniel Berrigan, "In Peaceable Conflict," *Catholic Worker*, March 1965, 1.

26. DeBenedetti, *Peace Reform*, 172-73.

27. "Declaration of Conscience," *Catholic Worker*, February 1965.

28. *Life* (20 August 1965); 30. Neither Kearns nor the Catholic Worker was identified.

29. Michael Ferber and Staughton Lynd, *The Resistance* (Boston, 1971), 21-22.

30. See William H. Shannon, ed., *The Hidden Ground of Love* (New York, 1985), especially the letter to Dorothy Day, 149; letter to James Douglass, 161; letters to Jim Forest, 286-88, 292; letter to John Heidbrink, 423.

31. Quoted in James H. Forest, "Reflections on the Self-Burning of Roger LaPorte," *Ave Maria* (18 December 1965): 20, 22; also see Cornell, "Life & Death," 1, 8

32. Dorothy Day, "Suicide or Sacrifice?" *Catholic Worker*, November 1965, 1.

33. Cornell, "Life & Death," 8.

34. Ibid.

35. Merton's telegram to Day read: "Just heard tragic death of Roger LaPorte. Deeply shocked and concerned about current developments in the peace movement. Will these do grave harm to cause of peace? Do they represent a right understanding of nonviolence? I think not." Quoted in Mel Piehl, *Breaking Bread: The Catholic Worker*

and the Origin of Catholic Radicalism in America, (Philadelphia, 1982), 232. Later, after a letter from Day, Merton disavowed his "rather ill-considered" telegram. See Shannon, ed., *Hidden Ground*, 149. On the resignation, refer to Interview of Gordon Zahn by Anne Klejment, April 1985, St. Paul, Minn.

36. Quoted in Piehl, *Breaking Bread*, 232.

37. Michael Harrington, "The Death of Roger LaPorte," *New York Herald Tribune,* 14 November 1965.

38. Dorothy Day, "Tribute," *Catholic Worker*, February 1968, 2.

39. Quoted in Troester, ed., *Voices from the Catholic Worker*, 197.

40. For fuller analysis of Day's response, see Anne Klejment, "War Resistance and Property Destruction" in Patrick Coy, ed., *A Revolution of the Heart: Essays on the Catholic Worker* (Philadelphia, 1988), especially 284-300.

41. Confidential interview statement to Anne Klejment.

42. Interview of Robert Gilliam by Anne Klejment, 1985, Brockport, N.Y.; William R. MacKaye, "3 Fast at Shrine to Protest War," *Washington Post*, 21 March 1967; [unsigned], "Fast and Pray," [n.p., n.d.]; Gilliam, "To Stand Where One Must Stand . . ." *Catholic Worker*, July-August 1968.

43. A brief account of war tax resistance at the New York Catholic Worker during the Vietnam War is printed in Robert Ellsberg, ed., *By Little and By Little: The Selected Writings of Dorothy Day* (New York, 1983), 311-17.

44. Karl Meyer, "New Resistance to War Taxes," *Catholic Worker*, January 1971, 3.

45. Ammon Hennacy, "No Taxes for War in Vietnam," *Catholic Worker*, July-August 1964, 3; "No Taxes for War in Vietnam," *Catholic Worker*, July-August 1966, 3; "The One Man Revolution," *Catholic Worker*, October 1968, 2; and "No Taxes for War in Vietnam!" *Catholic Worker*, July-August 1969, 3.

46. For Meyer's philosophy of tax resistance, see "A Fund for Mankind," *Catholic Worker*, October-November 1969, 1; his views on the telephone surcharge are explained in "War Escalates, Tax Refusal Called For," *Catholic Worker*, January 1967, 1, 8; the figures for telephone tax refusal are presented in "New Resistance to War Taxes," *Catholic Worker*, January 1971, 1, 3, 6.

47. "Vietnam: Our Peace Is Christ," *Catholic Worker*, February 1973, 1, 8.

48. DeGregory, "Render to God: The Imperative to Resist," *Catholic Worker*, March-April 1973, 3.

49. "Notes in Brief: U.S. Continues Involvement in Indochina War," *Catholic Worker*, February 1974, 4.

50. Deborah A. Peck, "Pilgrim for Peace," *Catholic Worker*, February 1973, 7 and Shawn Donovan, "Vigils for Peace," *Catholic Worker*, June 1973, 4; Brendan Walsh, "(Prayers and Protesters:) Decry Cambodia Bombing," *Catholic Worker*, July-August 1973, 1.

51. Day, "Aims and Purposes," in Ellsberg, ed., *By Little and By Little*, 92.

52. See Patricia McNeal, *Harder Than War: Catholic Peacemaking in Twentieth-Century America* (New Brunswick, N.J., 1992), 105-258. For survey data on changing Catholic opinion on the war, see John E. Mueller, *War, Presidents and Public Opinion* (New York, 1972), 140-45 and George Gallup, Jr. and Jim Castelli, *The American Catholic People* (Garden City, N.Y., 1987), 77-82. For a brief analysis of how Day's spirituality transformed draft board raiders into the plowshares movement, see Anne

Klejment, "Philip Berrigan," in David DeLeon, *Leaders from the Sixties* (Westport, Conn., 1994), 184-95.

53. Richard Hofstadter, *Anti-intellectualism in American Life* (New York, 1963), 136.

54. Charles Chatfield, *The American Peace Movement: Ideals and Activism* (Boston, 1992), 142-43. Also see Melvin Small, *Johnson, Nixon, and the Doves* (New Brunswick, N.J., 1988), especially 21, 242-43 n. 86.

11

ANZUS Plowshares: A Nonviolent Campaign

Ciaron O'Reilly

Early New Year's Day morning 1991, Moana Cole, a Catholic Worker from New Zealand, Ciaron O'Reilly, a Catholic Worker from Australia, and Susan Frankel and Bill Streit, members of the Dorothy Day Catholic Worker Community in Washington, D.C., calling themselves the ANZUS (Australia, New Zealand and United States) Plowshares, entered the Griffiss Air Force Base in Rome, New York. After cutting through several fences Bill and Sue entered a deadly force area. They hammered and poured blood on a KC-135 (a refuelling plane for B-52s) and then proceeded to hammer and pour blood on a nearby cruise missile-armed B-52 bomber. They presented their action statement and an indictment to base security who encircled them moments later.

Simultaneously, Moana and Ciaron entered the base at the opposite end of the runway and made a sign of the cross with blood on the runway, spraypainted "'Love Your Enemies'—Jesus Christ," "No More Bombing of Children—Hiroshima, Vietnam, Middle East or Anywhere Else!" and "Isaiah Strikes Again!" For approximately one and one-half hours they hammered upon the runway, chipping at two sections, one being five feet in diameter, before they were detained. In their action statement they declared that they joined from three different countries to reclaim the acronym from the ANZUS Treaty and create a "new pact for peace, which is the way of the Lord." They also asserted that they were acting to prevent war in the Persian Gulf and called upon people to nonviolently resist war and oppression. In their indictment they cited the U.S. government for war crimes and violation of international law. All four were indicted on 9 January 1991 on federal charges of conspiracy and property destruction, carrying maximum sentences of fifteen years in prison.

On 16 January the U.S. massacre in the gulf was begun when eight B-52s took off from the U.S. mainland and flew a 14,000-mile roundtrip, unleashing thirty-five air-launched cruise missiles on high priority targets in Iraq. The

ANZUS Plowshares went to trial in Syracuse, New York. On 21 August they were sentenced to a year in jail.

Catholic Workers are radical Christians whose pacifism is based on the sanctity of human life. Our anarchist disposition to government and pacifist rejection of violence have not been grafted onto an otherwise privatized piety and faith. Those principles are implicit in the Gospels and fulfilled in the life, death, and resurrection of Jesus. We view Jesus' public acts of exorcism and healing as prophetic, nonviolent acts of social transformation.

It is within this prophetic tradition that today's Plowshares' actions are located. The term *prophecy* is often confused with crystal ball gazing. However, prophecy remains a powerful interplay between present and future. It is first, to incarnate in the present future hopes of peace, justice, and liberation and second, to point to present trends, articulate their dangerous conclusions, and resist them. For the Plowshares movement this means building community and disarming weaponry.

Since 1980, over forty Plowshares communities in North America, Europe, and Australia have begun the disarmament of a variety of weapon systems. They have broken into factories, bases, and aboard warships to disarm First Strike components, F1-11s, Missile Silos, Tomahawk Cruise Missile Launchers, heli-gunships, and an array of other death machines. The building of each Plowshares community has taken from three to eighteen months of intense retreats and discernment. These are very serious and costly actions. To confront the State's idols in such a manner is to risk life and liberty. Plowshares people have received sentences of one, three, five, eight, and eighteen years, and many guns have been pointed in their direction.

When the ANZUS Plowshares went to Griffiss Air Force Base in New York State on New Year's Day 1991, it was the work of prophesy that we were about. To say that the world is not big enough for children and the B-52, and that it is the B-52 that will have to go! To say that the runway will not end at Griffiss but in the deaths of thousands of children, the destruction of homes, earth, and water. To prophesy that this is the future, unless we initiate a radically different present. Unless we begin to take up the hammer and begin the work now. As Dan Berrigan simply puts it, "For swords into plowshares, the hammer has to fall!"

Our disarmament would be both actual and symbolic. Radical Christians are particularly sensitive to the power of the symbolic battle that occurs for the hearts, minds, wills, and allegiance of people. We enter an action with a certain detachment from its consequences. It is our responsibility to prophesy, to witness, to resist; it is up to the Holy Spirit to convert. This detachment is intended to preserve us from spiritual pride, obsession with technique, or attempts to codify results in terms of capitalist press coverage, applause, or length of prison sentences.

It is in this spirit that we entered Griffiss Air Force Base. Plowshares members do not believe it will be an elite of clever nonviolent commandoes that will save the day. It will be people accepting their complicity, awakening to their responsibility, and embarking on the road of repentance and resistance. It is not "hit and split"! Rather, we stay on site to accept responsibility, call for conversion, and explain the disarmament.

The role of resistance is to break free from the institutions of death and bring home to authenticity—human community. The "Swords into Plowshares" prophecy of Isaiah 2:4 points not only to the converted sword, but to the converted community of peace and justice.

Moana and I took part in a Plowshares process from February of 1990, exploring the prophecy and possibilities of community during retreats every other weekend. Bill and Sue joined us in July and were quickly resolved to act following Bush's massive deployment to the Middle East. On these weekends we explored scripture, the nuclear and interventionary weapon systems arrayed, the history of Plowshares actions, our life journeys that had brought us thus far, self doubts, doubts about each other, and so on. We were unique as a Plowshares community, all being of a Catholic Worker background. We shared the Gospels, Catholic tradition, and experiences with the poor as common terms of reference. This was both a strength and weakness. Other Plowshares communities have involved participants from a variety of faith backgrounds— Catholic, Protestant, Jewish, Buddhist and agnostic—which offers a pluralism of experience and expression. We were an international group and keen to subvert the ANZUS ties that had bound our countries in a pact of death and destruction. We also sprang from a variety of transplanted cultural back-grounds—Irish, Polynesian, Jewish, and German—which made life together interesting and exciting.

Having the Catholic sacraments available during such a long and intense process that included a year of live-in community was deeply sustaining. By the end we had celebrated Moana's baptism, various eucharists by ourselves and with others, and much-needed rites of reconciliation facilitated by a spiritual director. On the night of our action we received the last rites of oils and before the trial witnessed the celebration of Bill and Sue's marriage. The sacraments, in the context of an illegal community of resistance, were powerfully authentic.

Secrecy was an issue with which we continually wrestled to protect both the action and also friends from potential grand jury conspiracy charges. We need to build a mature underground that deals effectively with issues of ego and curiosity when it comes to the need to know the constraints of high-risk actions. Two support people, both veterans of Plowshares actions, accompanied us through the entire process, right up to the drop-off. Other specialists—to assist with legal advice, scoping, and fatality issues—were brought in as needed.

We made several preliminary trips to Syracuse, where we knew our trial would take place. We introduced ourselves to local activists without revealing our specific purpose. One weekend we attended the Griffiss Air Force Base Open Day. On another occasion, I gave a public talk on "The Peace Movement in Australia." We also carried out some initial scoping of the base on these occasions.

After failing to penetrate base security and carry out the action in early December 1990, it was a testament to the depth of our community that we could regroup, reevaluate, develop a fresh approach, and return on New Year's Day 1991. After much reflection, we carefully selected our symbols. We had collected blood from ourselves and friends. We carried this rich symbol in baby bottles covered by photographs of Iraqi children and infants who lived in our communities. The sledge and household hammers were bought or gathered from community and family tool sheds. We engraved them with scriptural and other relevant quotes: "Swords into Plowshares," "No More Bombing of Children . . . Hiroshima, Vietnam, Middle East or Anywhere Else!" "The War Ends Here!" and so on. We prepared, signed, and packed a number of statements, including a ten-page indictment of Bush, Cheney, and Co. for planning war crimes. The preparation of these statements had fostered an essential process of internal community clarification. After the previous infiltration of the base and last-minute scoping to observe the behavior of security patrols, depth of stream, position of fences—there came the step of faith. Faith does not vanquish fear, but enables us to move in spite of our fears.

The action surpassed all our expectations. Bill and Sue made it through three fences into the "ten-minute scramble area" of the nuclear-tipped, Cruise-loaded B-52s, where they poured blood and began the disarmament of a KC-135 Refueler and a loaded, ready-to-go B-52 bomber. Moana and I spent over an hour and a half working on the runway, passed six times by patrols within 200 yards. We were able to pour the blood in a huge cross, write "No More Bombing of Children . . . Hiroshima, Vietnam, Middle East or Anywhere Else!" "Isaiah Strikes Again!" and "Love Your Enemies!" and take up many chunks of runway. The runway that was deploying B-52s, Galaxies, and Starlifters was closed for an hour. The disarmed B-52 bomber was grounded for six weeks, during a period in which other B-52s would drop 30 percent of the total explosives used in the Persian Gulf War massacre.

So moved was the Strategic Air Command by this loss of control that they raised all SAC bases to a higher state of security alert. SAC dispatched an investigatory team from its Omaha headquarters and eventually courtmartialed six officers. We responded to this obsession by pointing out that the action had exposed the double illusion that "the weapons are secure/the weapons secure us."

Our role-playing of the action's most dangerous moments, "discovery" and "interrogation," proved to be helpful. M16s were put to all our heads. We were to learn that one of the guards had killed an unarmed intruder in a similar situation in Panama the year before and had been duly decorated. At the moment of discovery we dropped our hammers, raised our hands, and fell to our knees in prayer. Moana and I went through this routine six times in one and a half hours as the patrol vehicles would pass by. We would then pick up our hammers and get back to work.

The discussion over the next weeks concerned the nature of entry into a "deadly force zone." The decision to address the runway, have two targets for disarmament, two entry points around dawn, with the possibility of the capture of one couple providing a diversion for the other, seemed a good way to maximize the possibility of the community disarming. However, neither couple ended up waiting for dawn. Moments after we were dropped off, a patrol car went by and we were not going to wait the expected forty-five minutes for the next one. When Sue and Bill arrived at their drop-off, the security vehicle that had been there in December was not visible. They said a prayer of abandonment and moved off quickly.

Questions of acting around deadly force zones remain and cannot be treated flippantly. Given that the action took place at a major SAC base fifteen days before a war deadline, the enormous hype of "potential Arab terrorism" and the fact that weeks previously an unarmed trespasser taking a shortcut through Andrews A.F.B. was shot dead without much fuss—the question of where to act on the base relative to deadly force may have been moot. Still, all this remains a serious question for future Plowshares communities.

The following day the four of us were brought to court in Syracuse, the site of our eventual trial. The sympathetic judge conducting the bail hearing recognized us as Catholic Workers who had taken the equivalent of a vow of poverty, and waived cash bail. He also gave us wide scope to make public statements about the issues at hand. We informed him that we could not accept the other bail conditions not to return to Griffiss or break the law, as the nation was speeding toward massacre in the Persian Gulf. We were charged with two felonies, conspiracy and destruction of government property, carrying maximum sentences of fifteen years. Our co-counsel, the city's resident radical lawyer, filed motions for discovery, preservation of evidence, and inspection by an independent expert.

We had brought with us to Syracuse a support group of four who did a very effective job of getting the news out locally, nationally, and internationally. They also contacted and mobilized local activists for a support demonstration outside the court on 2 January. The following week, as we were brought to be indicted by the grand jury, eight local peace activists were arrested returning our indictment to Griffiss.

The decision to remain in jail and refuse bail conditions was sound. It gave us time to sit with the reality of the witness and its consequences. It was a sustained response to the approaching massacre and a catalyst for others to act in solidarity. Our jail cells quickly took on the appearance of peace offices as we continued correspondence and media work. While incarcerated, we heard from people in England, Australia, New Zealand, and North America, including Syracuse, who had been awakened and moved to action by the disarmament.

For their part, the federal marshals were geared to removing us from Syracuse and separating us. Bill and I were moved hundreds of miles downstate into the Catskills, while Sue and Moana were transported to the nearby city of Rochester. After two weeks, our initial support group had to leave Syracuse because of various commitments. The transition to a hardcore group of local support was not accomplished, leaving the burden on one local family.

Our original intention was to remain in jail throughout the trial and sentencing. At the end of the Air War, we reevaluated and decided to come out for three reasons:

1. *To prepare for trial.* Four sympathetic local lawyers had come forward to set up a legal defense team. As we had been removed from Syracuse and separated, trial preparations were proving to be nearly impossible. We realized that we would have to come out and start working with each other and co-counsel to ensure a coherent approach inside the courtroom.

2. *To organize around the trial.* We all felt that the trial would be as important as the action as an opportunity to speak truth to power and reality to the nation's war hysteria. The trial would be a battle of interpretation of the events of January/February 1991 and the B-52's role in it. We began to realize that if our trial was to be a catalyst for continued resistance to Griffiss, B-52s, and the imperial state, we had to come out and do the catalyzing ourselves.

3. *The peace movement needed help.* By March 1991 it was apparent that the peace movement had been decimated by Bush's military victory. Embracing the slogan "No More Vietnams," Bush delivered a low-U.S.-casualty "Hiroshima." The large peace movement that had been mobilized in January/February was feeling left "prophetically wrong," stupid, and disoriented. Many of these folks had been politicized for the first time. We wanted to share with them the experience and hope of disarmament. We also wanted to share a deeper analysis of the roots and magnitude of the massacre that had occurred.

We agreed to leave jail on the basis that we all stay on-site in Syracuse, form a live-in community, and commit ourselves to the work of catalyzing around and preparing for trial. This was unique in the Plowshares experience. Most groups have either remained focused in jail or risked dissipation upon coming out and returning to families, communities, and hometowns, while awaiting trial. Our presence in Syracuse over the next four months was dynamic and invigorating. As the peace movement collapsed around the country, we provided living proof that the war was not over for us, scores of military-resisters, or millions of Iraqis and refugees. Besides the media work and networking with peace groups, we spoke at an array of forums—a religious educators' conference, church services, peace conferences, concerts, campus meetings, and even a "10,000 Maniacs" concert. The Syracuse Peace Council and its widely distributed newsletter, the Pax Christi branch which has offered consistent resistance at Griffiss over the previous decade, the "young guns" of the Nonviolent Action Group, SANE/FREEZE, Vietnam veterans, and a traditional left coalition were all receptive and keen to support our mission.

Catholic Worker and resistance communities throughout the Northeast organized "Celebrations of Hope" that combined music, poetry, politics, and celebration. Over the four months we traveled to Washington D.C., Philadelphia, New York City, and other northeastern destinations, to celebrate the reality of disarmament dawning in these dark times. In Syracuse we began a weekly vigil and distributing leaflets at the Federal Building, which also contained the military recruitment offices and the court where we would eventually go to trial.

We were given a floor of an old warehouse to set up living and office space. We used office equipment from the defunct chapter of Witness for Peace. We were embraced into the daily rhythm of the local Keough family and other people came forward with food, money, and vehicle access. A spiritual director surfaced and helped to keep our community life on an even keel, with weekly meetings to work through rising conflicts and anxieties. The local Jesuits made available their retreat center for time out, which we took individually and collectively.

We started each day with scripture and prayer and a community meeting before setting to work. We would be representing ourselves with four lawyers as advisers. We made it clear from the outset that our priority was not to "get off"; rather, the purpose was to put the weapon and war on trial. This, of course, went against all their professional training and legal instincts. We had ample creative conflict, devil's advocacy, tutoring in legalese, and fun. Our decision to try to engage the court, to explore and make it accountable to its own rhetoric, demanded much work and preparation.

Our pretrial hearing was set in front of Judge McCurn for 20 May 1991. We began to organize a two-hour vigil for peace prisoners and military resisters to precede it. We wanted to make our trial an act of solidarity with others, not our own privatized predicament. Over one hundred local people dressed in black gathered, carrying the names of imprisoned military and civilian resisters, their "crimes" and "sentences." The silent vigil accompanied by a solemn drum beat was extremely powerful.

Inside the courtroom, Bill argued that the charges were unconstitutional, owing to the existence of a State religion of "nuclearism" and accompanying laws that directly conflicted with constitutional guarantees of our freedom of religion. Moana argued that the charges were not valid as the weapon system disarmed was in direct contradiction of international law, thereby having no legal status as "property" under U.S. law. I argued that given the massive support for the war (90 percent at the time) and the accompanying hostility toward antiwar activists in the community, that a "fair trial" would demand an extensive and expanded voir dire (jury selection). I reminded the judge that in better times than these, the "Chicago Eight" convictions had been overturned on the basis of limited voir dire. I suggested individual and extensive interviews of prospective jurors to be conducted by the defendants. These were powerful arguments that explored the rhetoric of the court, its terms of reference, and the politics surrounding the war and the act of disarmament.

Judge McCurn came back and denied all our pretrial motions. He granted some of our requests on discovery, granting access to some of the government's evidence.

Our legal strategy thus became one of exploring the necessity defense, recognized as legitimate under U.S. law, but with few legal precedents. We used these four elements as a framework to delegate the research and work:

1. An imminent threat.
2. No legal alternative.
3. A causal relationship between our action and the removal of the threat.
4. Proportionality between the action and the threat.

Each defendant was allocated a lawyer. (Joe Heath's ponytail and my dreads seemed destined for each other!) We would meet as an entire group weekly to check progress and allocate tasks. It was a unique situation for Plowshares, since between the action and the trial the weapon system had actually been used. In past trials "imminence" (give the court a specific date that nuclear war is to start) has always been ruled as an impediment to a necessity defense.

Our expert witness starting lineup included

1. *Imminent Threat:*

Ramsey Clark, former U.S. attorney general under President Lyndon Johnson.
—had witnessed the effects of aerial bombardment in World War II, Korea, Vietnam, Grenada, Panama, and Iraq.
—had visited Iraq and President Saddam Hussein in November 1990 and many U.S. government officials, trying to remove the looming threat of bombardment.
—had been in Iraq during the U.S. bombing, witnessing the death and destruction of B-52 bombardment.

Admiral Eugene Carroll, a former U.S. military commander in the Middle East theater.
—expert knowledge of U.S. military strategy.
—expert opinion that the decision to unleash aerial bombardment using B-52 bombers had been made before 1 January 1991.

Sister Anne Montgomery, R.S.C.J., had been present in the International Peace Camp in Iraq. On 16 January she had heard the last moments of the B-52 threat (roaring overhead) passing from "imminent" to "actual."

Bill Cross, Vietnam War combat veteran, psychologist, graduate of and former lecturer at West Point.
—expertise in the social and individual psychology of "denial of imminent threat" in combat and when confronted by the mass destruction of modern warfare.

2. *No legal alternative:*

Bill Griffin and Ollie Clubb, political scientists.
—expert witnesses that there were no options offered by the U.S. electoral process, fifteen days before the deadline.

Francis Boyle, an international law expert.
—was willing to testify to the illegality of the B-52. He would argue that the B-52 had no status as "property" under international law.

3. *A causal relationship between our action and the removal of the threat:*

David Lange, who as a lawyer in New Zealand had defended antinuclear activists in the seventies and who had blockaded nuclear warships. As New Zealand's prime minister in the eighties, he signed into law the criminalization of nuclear weapons. He was prepared to testify that such nonviolent actions had initiated a chain of events that had removed the threat of nuclear weapons from New Zealand.

The government witnesses, who were to testify that the bomber had been grounded and the runway closed by the action.

Howard Zinn, bombardier over Dresden, radical historian, and author; expert in nonviolent action bringing about social change in the United States.

4. *Proportionality between action and threat:*

Paul Walker, a former U.S. Intelligence Officer and now a social scientist with an expertise in armaments.
—could offer expert testimony in relation to fuel air explosives, napalm, and cluster bomb units dropped by B-52s in Iraq.
The court had financed Paul, at our request, as an expert to carry out an independent inspection of the disarmament at Griffiss. Paul would testify that the Air Force had grossly inflated the repair costs to the B-52.

We pursued these witnesses and others. Our objective remained to put the war and weapon system on trial. Our approach was to continue to explore the court's rhetoric—the necessity defense—and develop our own terms of reference in our personal testimonies.

As trial day approached, energy and time for the witness inside and outside the courtroom competed. We had been very fortunate to have been embraced, upon our release, by the most high-energy peace group then in town, the Nonviolent Action Committee. They had postponed all other projects and devoted their weekly meetings to catalyze around the trial. We were expecting a large number of people from out of town, and St. Andrew's Church gave us their hall for the length of the trial. It became a center for cooking, sleeping, reflection, and celebration.

A few days before the trial, the defendants moved out of the ware-house/office and into an empty seminary, a quiet space with few distractions. Max "the Fax," a Plowshares media specialist, drove into town with his portable fax machine and linked up with the media and office collectives.

Jury trial was intense and exhausting: a full day in court, post-court meetings with lawyers and defendants to review and plan, media work, then back to the hall for support activities and preparation for the next day. It is important that the defendants hand over the activist catalyst to supporters and focus on the trial. It is important for the supporters to use the trial as an opportunity for their own continued resistance.

On the eve of the trial we had a wonderful coffeehouse celebration with local talent as well as imports from out of state, New Zealand, and Australia. We would kick off each trial day with an hour-long vigil outside the court in solidarity with civilian and military resisters imprisoned, awaiting court martial or trial. Meanwhile, three wise monkeys, complete with blindfolds, gags, and signs reading "SEE NO DEAD CHILDREN," "HEAR NO DEAD CHILDREN," "SPEAK NO DEAD CHILDREN" took up position at the court's entrance as the jury entered each morning.

Picnics were organized at the court for lunch breaks and meals in the evening at the hall where most of the out-of-town folks slept. Throughout the whole event there was great crossover between local activists, many who had been mobilized for the first time by the war, and the experienced Plowshares movement from out of town. One evening Liz McAlister (from the "Harrisburg Conspiracy" and the previous "Griffiss Plowshares") gave us a lecture on the idolatry of law.

We went to trial in an intensely hostile time, wedged between Memorial Day and Independence Day, when media reports were claiming a 90 percent approval rating for the war. At one point ten of the fourteen prospective jurors acknowledged dependence on, or close relatives in, the military. At another point, eight of the fourteen raised their hands to acknowledge displaying yellow ribbons on their homes as President Bush had requested during the war. No jurors were struck for these reasons. Rather, the judge would suggest that none of these factors would prejudice them and the jurors would nod.

As the trial opened, we reminded the jury that they had been called here not as "legal experts" but as the "conscience of the community," and that we, too, were present for reasons of conscience. The next two days the government presented its case. Predictably the military witnesses lied through their teeth, denying statements we had made to them, claiming they had not read banners or what had been painted on the runway and claiming to have seen things that did not exist. Most significantly the judge refused to accept evidence we presented as admissible that was found on the site, gathered and brought to court by the F.B.I.—statements, and baby bottles decorated with children's photos now covered in blood. It proved helpful that we had engraved the hammers and signed our ten-page indictment as the government could not help but introduce them as evidence.

I made quite a few mistakes in losing my temper with the manipulations of the judge, prosecutor, and government witnesses. All my previous court appearances had been in front of sole police magistrates in Queensland,

Australia. A jury trial is different. You have got to remember the people you are concerned to communicate with—to look at—are the jury!

The decision of when to enter into defense in the courtroom is difficult. It has been taken at different stages by various Plowshares communities. Helen Woodson, now serving eighteen years, refused to participate in her trial at all. She clearly stated that the courts are there to legalize the criminality of nuclear weapons. We had decided to pursue a twofold strategy to engage those gathered in the court. First, to explore the court's own rhetoric and how it conflicts with B-52s, Griffiss A.F.B., and the nuclear and conventional weapons of mass destruction. The rhetoric consisted of the U.S. Constitution, international law, U.S. legal recognition of the necessity defense, and the question of the presence of "criminal intent." Second, we hoped to explain our conscience—faith background, scriptural understanding, the threat the weapons and war provided—to the "conscience of the community," the jury.

The judge was quite willing to jettison the Constitution, international law, and even legal procedure to "get the job done." His ruling of irrelevant and nonadmissible evidence collected at the scene was obviously prejudicial. He ruled *in* an ornamental angel left at the first cut fence and ruled *out* baby bottles, photographs, and statements found under the bomber and on the runway. We tried our best to flash the denied evidence at the jury and read the statements over the cries of "objection" and "sustained."

On the Friday of the first week of trial, the government closed its case. We moved "no case to answer," got overruled, and called our first witness. We started with Sister Anne Montgomery (participant in five Plowshares actions and the recent Peace Camp in the war zone). The prosecutor objected on the basis of relevance and called for an "offer of proof." The judge cleared the court of the jury. Sister Montgomery described the nature of the threat of the B-52s as perceived by herself in Iraq. She described the evening of 16 January, when she heard the threat roaring overhead, passing from "imminent" to "actual." The judge took a recess, returned, and ruled Anne's testimony irrelevant. The jury filed back in.

We then put on Ramsey Clark, former U.S. attorney general. In Iraq during the Air War, he had witnessed the results of B-52 bombing raids. The prosecutor objected, calling for an "offer of proof." The judge cleared the courtroom of the jury, and Ramsey gave a powerful afternoon of testimony of his firsthand experience of the effects of aerial bombardment on human populations in World War II Europe, Vietnam, Grenada, and Panama. He then told of how by 1 January 1991 all legal alternatives to stay the threat had been exhausted. He described in moving detail the towns, morgues, hospitals, countryside, and people of Iraq that had recently experienced the effects of B-52 bombardment. The crowded courtroom greeted his testimony with a standing ovation. Without leaving his seat the judge ruled the testimony "very interesting but irrelevant," closed for the day, and announced that he would deliver a ruling on our necessity defense before resuming in five days. He then dismissed the jury for the day. In our first day of defense, the jury had spent less than ten minutes in the court.

Judge McCurn and his assistants spent Wednesday morning studying the briefs and developing a response. In the afternoon supporters and military officials packed the courtroom. Also present were the judge and prosecutor who had sent the previous Griffiss Plowshares away for two and three years in 1984. Judge McCurn came in and ruled our necessity defense inadmissible on some pretty wild reasoning. He claimed, among other deficiencies, that we would have had to disarm every B-52 in the U.S. arsenal to have qualified for one element.

At this stage we were left with Paul Walker, whom the government had recognized (and paid expenses for) as an expert on independent inspection, and our personal testimonies. The latter would be the best opportunity to relate to the jurors as human beings and present our motives. We spoke about the influences that had shaped our moral development and response. We told of our growing awareness of the threat and the necessity to act. We all recounted the early hours of January first and how these life experiences, morality, and awareness had coalesced in the act for which we had been brought to trial. We all succeeded in answering cross-examination while looking at, and talking to, the jury rather than the prosecutor.

Our major weakness was that we had not found the time to role-play cross-examination. We had not prepared to combat the levels to which the prosecutor would stoop. For Sue, he attempted to widen the conspiracy. Who drove you there? Where did you stop for gas? Who was with you? He continued with more such questions. This comes up in every Plowshares trial and we should have been better prepared. The second day of our defense ended dramatically with the judge adjourning to decide whether he would hold Sue in contempt for not answering the questions and imprison her immediately. He came back the next day to rule further questioning on a wider conspiracy irrelevant—a great relief for us and the co-conspirators present in the courtroom. For Bill, the prosecutor tried to make a *National Inquirer* case about his being a Catholic priest who was now married, ultimately a self-defeating strategy for the prosecution. Armed with my Queensland Police Record (thanks, guys!), my Australian Security Intelligence Organization file, and Immigration and Naturalization Services and Interpol reports, he set out to prove my habitual criminality. We objected on the basis of relevancy and called for an offer of proof. The judge removed the jury and I set out to convince him that life behind the "Banana Curtain" (Queensland) under Premier Jon Bjelke Petersen was not protected by the freedoms guaranteed by the U.S. Constitution; therefore these previous convictions were irrelevant in this court.

We introduced Paul Walker as our next witness. An expert witness veteran of over a dozen Plowshares trials, he was an artist at handling cross-examination. He estimated that it would have cost only $477, not the $6,300 quoted by the Air Force, to repair the fuel tank. We then began to ask Paul to describe to the jury the nature and destructive capacity of the napalm, cluster bombs, and fuel-air explosives dropped by the B-52. The prosecutor and judge aggressively suppressed our questions. Fearing undue influence, the judge then called a recess to clear the jury from the court. I quickly stood up and told the jury, "This trial is about the massacre of 55,000 children by B-52s and aerial bombardment. The government rules these children irrelevant because the government has ruled these children expendable!" It was a spontaneous act of noncooperation with the suppression of our defense. After the jury was cleared from the court, Judge McCurn threatened to remove me from the court for the rest of the trial.

Moana was the last to take the stand. She tried to speak about how nuclear testing in the Pacific and the accompanying destruction of her Polynesian kin had influenced her decision to go to Griffiss. The judge and prosecutor clamped down severely. The nod was given and three people progressively stood up in the gallery and addressed the jury as to the government's suppression of evidence. They were evicted from the courtroom by the federal marshals.

In cross-examination, the prosecutor laid out a scenario to Moana: What if she awoke one morning to find four people with hammers taking up the Catholic Worker driveway? What if they started beating on the Catholic Worker soup van? We concluded our defense with one question on redirect: "Moana, describe the destructive payload of the Catholic Worker soup van?" Moana went on to explain that the van does not carry cluster bombs, napalm, and nuclear weapons. It carries soup and water to those who hunger and thirst.

The last trial day was preceded by a large march led by "Prosecutor" and "Judge" in legal gowns. The crowd would chant "TRUTH," the Prosecutor would respond, "OBJECTION," and the Judge, "SUSTAINED"—a very clear, colorful, and appropriate procession.

Closings are stacked against the defendant because the prosecutor gets to speak first and last. Theoretically, he or she is not supposed to raise anything new in response to the defendent's closing. Ours reemphasized the issues, the jury's role not as legal experts but as the conscience of the community, the ability of even one of them to break the consensus of death and hang the jury. The prosecutor rose to rant and rave, threw the sledgehammer on his desk, and invoked Pearl Harbor, World War II, and America's glorious victory over the Nazis. We had no right of reply.

The judge issued the jury a questionnaire with the charges and boxes to record "guilty" or "not guilty." This was a swift maneuver that really outflanked our "If they offer you two alternatives, choose the third!" plea to the jury. The possibility of not reaching a decision had been factored out on the sheet. We did not realize this until it was too late.

The jury retired for three hours. It came back once for a question of clarification, an indication that perhaps some jurors were thinking.

Eventually we were called back. The jury was ushered in and we all stood waiting for the judge who was delayed. Then from the gallery, "We pray for the soldiers who refused to kill!" . . . . "Lord hear our prayer!" "We pray for the children of Iraq!" . . . . "Lord hear our prayer!" and more.

A moment of prophetic transformation took place. A den of untruth and injustice was transformed into a house of prayer. The judge returned to restore "order." The verdict was delivered: guilty on both counts.

That night we celebrated. The next morning we were back at Griffiss. When security foiled our "MAKE PAR NOT WAR!" action planned for the base golf course, we regrouped and marched on the front gate behind a banner that read "NONVIOLENT RESISTANCE CONTINUES!" complete with drums, singing and a huge peace bird. Twelve folks were arrested redelivering the indictment.

With the sentencing seven weeks away, we returned briefly to Syracuse for presentencing interviews with probation. They were confused about our willingness to accept responsibility, but our failure to display remorse.

Four days before sentencing we returned to Syracuse to meet for the last time as a community. We concluded that we wanted to bring a spirit of celebration and resistance to the sentencing. Our last few days in Syracuse were a truly pentecostal experience. At a time when Pax Americana posed triumphant, the large peace movement lay scattered, scores of military resisters were imprisoned, and thousands of Iraqi children were still dying from U.S. bombing, over two hundred people from a variety of backgrounds gathered with us to declare another history and claim another future. The Plowshares witness, universal and true, understood by Christian, Jew, Rasta, Deadhead, churched, unchurched, young, old, German, Pakistani, veteran, neophyte, artist, pragmatist, friend, family, stranger . . . it spoke clearly and deeply and all these people stood with it.

Local people took responsibility for the final three events. On Sunday sixty of us, mostly local folks, came together in a day of reflection and to share eucharist. We shared our understanding of the war and the meaning of the prophecy and where it was taking us. Over the next twenty-four hours, many friends rolled into town from throughout the Northeast. On Monday night it was time to celebrate resistance, hope, and community. Friends catered wonderfully for one hundred fifty friends, Catholic Workers, and Plowshares folks who gathered at St. Andrew's church.

On sentencing morning, we gathered for a last liturgy and then headed to the armory where the local Nonviolent Action Committee was hosting a march on the Federal Building. The Canadian Catholic Worker unfurled a gigantic "You Can Jail the Resister, But Not the Resistance!" banner, folks had collected bunches of wild flowers from the side of the highway, there were many drums, and two hundred people had gathered. It was wild, something like a cross between a New Orleans funeral and one of the more bizarre scenes from *Oliver*. Things got increasingly surreal as we passed a woman in Armory Square who was performing with an electric guitar and amplifier. She broke into that classic 1960s, Buffalo Springfield hit-the-streets "Stop, children" number.

When we hit the Federal Building, the N.A.C. members quickly occupied the large cubist sculpture in the courtyard, while a bunch of us swung into the Federal Building that houses the military recruitment offices on the ground floor. It was a confined area and there were many of us—we sat in, spoke out, and delivered copies of the *Harvard Medical Report* on the U.S. massacre in the Middle East. Two friends dressed as cholera and typhoid made quite a visual impact.

We moved through the corridors and emerged from the building as the N.A.C. members were beginning their street theater. They had transformed the sculpture into prison cells and read from Mohandas Gandhi, Emma Goldman, Phil Berrigan, Eugene Debs, Anne Montgomery, and many other prisoners of conscience. Following the theater, interrupted occasionally by edgy federal marshals, there was more dancing, hollering, and finally the blessing before we moved into court.

The judge performed some preliminaries and then Moana stood up holding a tennis ball. She said that this was the size of a cluster bomblet, that each one contained more than 600 razor-sharp metal shards. A cluster bomb unit contains over 200 bomblets. It was the second most often used munition of the Gulf Massacre. A B-52 can carry 40 cluster bomb units of 8,080 bomblets and can destroy every living thing in an area of 176 million square yards. The B-52 was the largest contributor to the Gulf Massacre, dropping 30 percent of all explosives. Moana said, "I go to jail in solidarity with my friends who refused to be deployed in the Persian Gulf, those sitting in military brigs because they obeyed the commands of Christ and conscience *not* to kill—Yolanda Huet Vaughn, Darwin Arola, Doug DeBoer, and many others."

Sue was next to address Judge McCurn. "I must tell you, you missed an incredible celebration last night. I have come to court eagerly. Not eager to go to jail—there's a lot of other things I'd rather be doing—but eager for the Kingdom. And I know the Kingdom is present here, and whenever someone enfleshes the words of Isaiah, to beat swords into plowshares."

Bill spoke to the moral incongruities of the courts when it comes to serial killing in uniform: "A country that is horrified by a serial killer (Jeffrey Dahmer in Milwaukee) who chops up people, but is *not* horrified when hundreds of thousands are chopped up and maimed is a country that is totally blinded. Dropping bombs from an airplane is serial murder. People are being killed and as long as laws legitimize that killing, we won't obey them." Bill concluded by inviting the judge to come down and join us.

I told the judge that we had not had a jury of our peers as guaranteed by the U.S. Constitution. Although I did not expect to see dreadlocks on the jury, the process of choosing it was superficial and insufficient in a time of mass war hysteria and deep antagonism against we who stood against: "the popular victorious war effort." It should have been the jury deciding if our defense fulfilled the requirements of necessity. Our witnesses, evidence, and defense had been censored by him. I do not have faith in the U.S. Constitution, but apparently he did, so he should stick to its requirements in his courtroom. I then turned to the gallery and said, "Don't seek justice in this court or peace in the military, but in community and continued resistance!"

As Judge McCurn began to sentence, we moved into the middle of the courtroom and said we could not accept his sentence as it criminalized peacemaking and legalized massacre. We dropped to our knees, circled, and began the Lord's Prayer. We were joined by folks in the gallery, who then continued the witness with statements until the court was cleared. We remained on the floor as Judge McCurn sentenced us all to a year and departed.

We were taken downstairs, shackled, and driven into a van to the Oneida County Jail. Rain was falling, we were all joyous and tired, and it was kind of cozy as we entered the third stage of the witness.

We had had January/February to taste and experiment with the prison witness as the Persian Gulf War raged and we refused bail conditions. We all concurred on the power of the prison witness of others in our own lives and conversion. As Phil Berrigan says, "Brothers and sisters in prison speak to our consciences, which is how God speaks to us!" We go along with the old I.W.W. maxim, "We're in here for you! You're out there for us!"

The old prison maxim, "You do your own time" is true. You have to organize your time to serve your purpose, rather than you serving the time. In such a total institution that is designed to dehumanize and disorient, you have to develop your own self-activating routine of prayer, study, exercise, correspondence, social life, and "visiting the prisoner." Prison is the setting where we can enter into the deepest solidarity with the poor. To me, the bedrock of survival in prison is one's sense of spirituality and sense of solidarity with brothers and sisters who continue the struggle for peace and justice.

As I write, I am halfway through my sentence in the Texas outback, thousands of miles from my codefendants. I am in a cage with twenty-four men who do not speak English. It is an interesting time, not at all what I expected or planned. The act of disarmament has been a beautiful gift. I have sensed the ripples as close as my own family and as far as Australia, Europe, North America, New Zealand, Iraq, and the Philippines. Like the loaves and fishes, we offer the little we can muster and it seems to be mystically multiplied.

12

The Catholic Worker and Peace: Resources in the Marquette University Archives

Phillip M. Runkel

Most students of the Catholic Worker movement, many Workers themselves, and more than a few other folks with at least a passing interest in the CW phenomenon know that the movement's main archives are located in Memorial Library of Marquette University in Milwaukee, Wisconsin, owing to Dorothy Day's decision in the late fifties to commit her personal papers and the records of the New York Catholic Worker to Marquette. It is not as well known—but nevertheless true and worthy of note—that the Dorothy Day–Catholic Worker Collection (CW Archives) contains a substantial body of information concerning the peace advocacy of Catholic Workers and their communities, as well as the relationship of the CW to the broader peace movement. The papers of Dorothy Day, for example, include many letters from such noted peace activists as Thomas Cornell, Eileen Egan, James Forest, Ammon Hennacy, and Karl Meyer. Related records of the New York Catholic Worker, including correspondence, newspaper clippings, and publications, document its leading role in the campaign against civil defense drills in the fifties and resistance to the growing U.S. involvement in the Vietnam War in the mid-sixties, and its support of conscientious objectors during the Second World War and the early postwar period. The Catholic Worker's opposition to the nuclear weapons buildup and concurrent military intervention in Central America during the Reagan administration is documented in the papers of John Baranski and Frank Cordaro, the records of Casa Maria Catholic Worker Community (Milwaukee), and the backfiles of many CW periodicals in addition to the *Catholic Worker*—notably *At the Door* (Chicago), the *Catholic Agitator* (Los Angeles), *Round Table* (St. Louis), and *Via Pacis* (Des Moines). The sizeable number of letters from Catholic Workers in jails and prisons for Plowshares actions, line crossings, and other acts of civil resistance testifies to the high cost many paid for their discipleship, a burden most Workers bore with considerable courage and grace.

Besides textual records, the Catholic Worker Archives include an expanding collection of television programs and talks on videotape, and more than eight hundred audiocassette recordings of oral history interviews, talks, and discussions. Speakers on peace themes include Meg Brodhead, Frank Cordaro, Tom Cornell, Dorothy Day, Eileen Egan, Jim Forest, Ammon Hennacy, Karl Meyer, and Marcia Timmel. Most tapes may be borrowed or purchased at cost from the Marquette University Archives.

Although access to the private correspondence and journals of Dorothy Day and several other Catholic Workers has been restricted at the donors' request to protect the privacy of correspondents and others mentioned in the records, a large portion of the collection is open to research use, which has increased markedly in the last ten years. The archivists welcome inquiries, requests, and "tours of inspection" by scholars, activists, and the general public. For further information, please write or telephone:

The Department of Special Collections and University Archives
Memorial Library
Marquette University
P.O. Box 3141
Milwaukee, WI 53201-3141
Telephone: (414) 288-7256
FAX: (414) 288-3123
Internet: 970 FRUNKELP@VMS.CSD.MU.EDU

Index

All-America Anti-Imperialist League (AIL), and Day, 5, 23, 164

America, 155

American Catholic hierarchy: and *Catholic Worker*, 58-59; and Chicago Catholic Worker, 70; and conscientious objection, 40, 41, 55, 58; and Day, 39-40, 58, 81; and nuclear warfare, 42; and obliteration bombing, 41, 55; and Vietnam War, 144; and World War II, 67, 70. *See also* National Catholic Welfare Conference; National Conference of Catholic Bishops; National Council of Catholic Bishops; individual names of members

American Catholic pacifism, 1, 83-84; and Catholic Worker movement, 7, 12, 35, 51, 65, 81-82, 157; and Day, 1, 2, 6, 8, 12, 18, 24, 25, 26, 27, 33, 34, 39; in early Christianity, 33; influence of lyrical left on, 25. *See also* Gospel pacifism, Just-war tradition, Pacifism

American Friends Service Committee (AFSC), 4, 6, 8, 10, 12

Ancel, Alfred, 135

Anti-Conscription League. *See* Catholic Association for International Peace

ANZUS (Australia, New Zealand and United States) Plowshares, 12, 171-72, 173; Griffiss action, 173-74, 175; Griffiss court case, 177-84; pretrial activity, 175-77; sentencing in Griffiss case, 184-86

Association of Catholic Conscientious Objectors (ACCO), 40, 126-27. *See also* Pax

Atomic bomb. *See* Nuclear warfare

Baird, Peggy, 21, 22

Baltimore Four, 11, 156, 162

Baranski, John, 187

Batterham, Forster, 23

Becker, Maurice, 20

Benedict XV, Pope, 127

Berrigan, Daniel, S.J.: and Day, 11, 115, 155; draft board raid, 11, 140, 162; and Plowshares movement, 172; on war, 159

Berrigan, Philip, S.S.J., 128, 158, 186; and Day, 11; draft board raid, 11, 140, 156, 162; and Vietnam, 159

Boillon, Pierre, 135

About the Editors and Contributors

THE EDITORS

ANNE KLEJMENT teaches U.S. history and is an adjunct professor of church history at the School of Divinity, University of St. Thomas. Her books include *The Berrigans: A Bibliography* and, with Alice Klejment, *Dorothy Day and "The Catholic Worker": A Bibliography and Index*. She is researching the history of the *Catholic Digest*.

NANCY L. ROBERTS teaches journalism history at the University of Minnesota. Among her publications are *Dorothy Day and the "Catholic Worker"* and *American Peace Writers, Editors, and Periodicals: A Dictionary*.

THE CONTRIBUTORS

CHARLES CHATFIELD is a professor of history at Wittenberg College in Springfield, Ohio. Coeditor of *The Garland Library of War and Peace*, he is author of many books and articles on the history of pacifism. His recent works include *The American Peace Movement: Ideals and Activism*; (co-author) *An American Ordeal* (recipient of the Warren Kuehl prize); and (co-editor) *Peace/Mir: An Anthology of Alternatives to War*.

PATRICK G. COY is assistant professor of Political Science at Kent State University, with primary teaching duties in the Center for Applied Conflict Management. Formerly a fellow of The Albert Einstein Institution, he is the editor of *A Revolution of the Heart: Essays on the Catholic Worker*. His most recent publications focus on the nonviolent protective accompaniment work of Peace Brigades International, and on U.S. peace movement opposition to the

Gulf War. He was a member of the St. Louis Catholic Worker community for seven years.

JAMES W. DOUGLASS has written four books on the theology of nonviolence, including *The Non-violent Cross*. He lives in Birmingham, Alabama.

EILEEN EGAN, a recipient of the John XXIII Peace Award, has a long association with Catholic Relief Services. She is a contributing editor of the *Catholic Worker* and a founder of Pax Christi-USA. Among her publications are *Such a Vision of the Street*, a biography of Mother Teresa and most recently, *For Whom There is No Room: Scenes from the Refugee World*.

PATRICIA McNEAL is an associate professor and director of Women's Studies at Indiana University, South Bend. She has written many articles on Catholic peacemaking and Dorothy Day. Her major work is *Harder Than War: Catholic Peacemaking in Twentieth-Century America*.

CIARON O'REILLY is a founding member of the Catholic Worker community in Australia. He is the author of the book on the ANZUS Plowshares witness, *Bomber Grounded: Runway Closed*.

MEL PIEHL teaches history and humanities in Christ College at Valparaiso University. He is the author of *Breaking Bread: The Catholic Worker and the Origin of Catholic Radicalism in America* and writes on American Catholicism and twentieth-century intellectual history.

PHILLIP M. RUNKEL is the Catholic Worker movement archivist at Marquette University in Milwaukee, Wisconsin. A "weekend resister," he has participated in several memorable peace initiatives, including the Missouri Peace Planting (1988) and the Walk for a Peaceful Future in the Middle East (1992).

WILLIAM H. SHANNON, a Catholic priest of the diocese of Rochester, New York and professor emeritus at Nazareth College of Rochester, is general editor of the five published volumes of the Thomas Merton Letters. Founding president of the International Thomas Merton Society, he has written extensively on Merton (e.g., his highly acclaimed biography, *Silent Lamp: The Thomas Merton Story*) and on spirituality (e.g., *Silence on Fire: The Prayer of Awareness*). Recently he edited *Passion for Peace: The Social Essays/Thomas Merton*.

FRANCIS J. SICIUS, author of *The Word Made Flesh: The Chicago Catholic Worker and the Emergence of Lay Activism in the Church*, teaches history at St. Thomas University in Miami, Florida. His current project deals with Catholic social thought and the environment.